D0903416

Published by Rowman & Littlefield
An imprint of The Rowman & Littlefield Publishing Group, Inc.
4501 Forbes Boulevard, Suite 200, Lanham, Maryland 20706
www.rowman.com

86-90 Paul Street, London EC2A 4NE

Distributed by NATIONAL BOOK NETWORK

British Library Cataloguing in Publication Information Available

Library of Congress Cataloging-in-Publication Data
Names: Boxer Wachler, Brian S., author.
Title: Influenced : the impact of social media on our perception / Brian Boxer Wachler, MD.
Description: Lanham, Maryland : Rowman & Littlefield Publishing Group, [2022] | Includes bibliographical references and index.
Identifiers: LCCN 2022008605 (print) | LCCN 2022008606 (ebook) | ISBN 9781538164198 (cloth) | ISBN 9781538164204 (epub)
Subjects: LCSH: Perception. | Consciousness. | Social media. | Internet personalities.
Classification: LCC BF311 .B6453 2022 (print) | LCC BF311 (ebook) | DDC 153—dc23/eng/20220413
LC record available at https://lccn.loc.gov/2022008605
LC ebook record available at https://lccn.loc.gov/2022008606

∞™ The paper used in this publication meets the minimum requirements of American National Standard for Information Sciences—Permanence of Paper for Printed Library Materials, ANSI/NISO Z39.48-1992.

Praise for *Influenced*

"An incredibly insightful book that dives into the effects of social media on our minds, written by one of the most impactful leaders in the creator economy. Highly recommend!" —**Josh Otusanya**, comedian

"Brilliantly written book highlighting how social media can be used for positive influence in the world, which also gives a very honest look at some of the harmful effects of social media. Great read by someone I truly admire and respect. Enjoy!" —**Grant Collins, DDS**

"With social media being embedded in everything we do in today's world, this is a MUST-READ! From the beginner to the seasoned content creator, or to the parent of a teen who has a phone, this book will provide incredible insight and value!" —**Tommy Martin, MD**

"A fascinating book with multiple unique perspectives on how social media affects our lives. Dr. Brian is able to weave in his own experiences and the experience of others to tell a compelling story of how we are all 'influenced'—no cap." —**Muneeb Shah, DO, aka DermDoctor**

"Dr. Brian shares his great insight into the science of influence in today's world of social media, and he backs it up with latest research and real-world examples. This book is essential to understanding social media and learning how to live with it, whether you're an influencer or not." —**Siyamak Saleh, MD**

"Dr. Brian delves into the nitty gritty of how social media hacks our brains to leave us in an endless scroll hole. In this detailed book, he investigates how social media and its 'influencers' have shaped our modern-day society—for better and for worse. An addictive read." —**Karan Rajan, MRCS, MBBS**

"An insider's detailed and honest perspective on what it means to be an influencer in today's world. Dr. Brian provides a candid look at the true effects of social media." —**Jess Andrade, DO**

"This was a great book about what goes on behind the scenes—the good, the bad, and everything in between." —**Dana Brems, DPM, aka FootDocDana**

"Dr. Brian impeccably lifts the veil to deliver powerful insight that's life changing. Beautifully written, his book leaves you with sensible knowledge on social media, including how to manage it and understand it. A must-read for anyone and everyone." —**Azadeh Shirazi, MD**

"This book is a must-read if you are curious about insights into what we all go through using social media for fun or for business. You will begin to realize that no matter how big or small your account, we all have a grave responsibility to ourselves and our followers in order to preserve mental health." —**Ricky J. Brown, MD, FACS**

"Through his own experiences and anecdotes of other influencers, and utilizing the science of psychology, Dr. Brian powerfully and thoughtfully reveals how social media has become simultaneously a constructive and destructive force. *Influenced* is more than a 'must-read'; it is a 'must-live'!" —**William Dorfman, FAACD**, *New York Times* best-selling author and philanthropist

"*Influenced* is one of the first books that I have come across that really dives into the world of an influencer, not just from a consumer's perspective but also the creators themselves, shedding light on both the positives and the negatives of this emerging market." —**Fayez Ajib, DO, aka LifeofaDoctor**

"*Influenced* is such an impactful piece of literature! Everyone who gets their hands on this book is going to be so attached—it's absolutely brilliant!" —**Krysten Mayers**, cofounder of Krysmay L.P.

"I think there is a fairy tale ideology around social media that's just not true. Whether you are a creator, consumer, or aspiring creator, everything online is carefully constructed, just like movies, TV shows, and commercials. As social media becomes more and more intertwined in our lives, it's important to educate ourselves on how to handle it properly to live the best lives we can live, and I wish *Influenced* was around when I started my own career in social media five years ago." —**Caleb Simpson**, influencer

"*Influenced* is truly revolutionary, as it really gives an insider perspective on what an influencer is and the responsibilities involved." —**Jermaine Hogstrom, DO, and Jeremy Hogstrom, DO, aka Twin.Doctors.J**

"*Influenced* is a must-read for anyone living in the age of social media. I read it for a deeper understanding of the world our kids are growing up in but found it just as relevant and informative for adults. If you want to navigate the landscape of a world with social media, then this book is the North Star you need to move through it in an informed, thoughtful way." —**Matt Bomer**, actor

Influenced

The Impact of Social Media on Our Perception

BRIAN BOXER WACHLER, MD

ROWMAN & LITTLEFIELD
Lanham • Boulder • New York • London

To my twin daughters, Jordanna and Micaela—a.k.a. Micaela and Jordanna (I hope no one feels slighted now). This book wouldn't exist if it hadn't been for your suggestion that I dive into the TikTok pool during the COVID-19 pandemic when my practice and life slowed down. You guided me as I found my voice, style, and wigs on the platform.

Influenced is also dedicated to Professor Tom Miller, my UCLA Speech and Debate Team coach, who taught me the importance of critical thinking and weighing both sides in the search for the truth.

Influence may be the highest level of human skills.

—*Unknown*[1]

Often we don't realize that our attitude toward something has been influenced by the number of times we have been exposed to it in the past.

—*Robert B. Cialdini, PhD, author of* Influence[2]

I'm not trying to influence anyone else.

—*Kim Kardashian*[3]

Contents

Foreword

I'm a social media influencer with millions of followers across TikTok, Instagram, and YouTube, and I'm a board-certified plastic surgeon. I first met Brian because, well, I really didn't have a choice in the matter. If that piqued your curiosity, then you can appreciate how Brian got *my* attention.

On TikTok there was a viral doctor "Bruh chain" video series (that's where someone bops their head to a song and turns to the camera and lip-synchs "Bruh" on cue). It was a fun trend. This is how it worked: after someone did a reaction video, the next doctor in line performed a reaction video, and so on, like dominos. I remember that day. I was busy in my office seeing patients, and my followers started notifying (tagging) me since I was next in line to do a video response. My phone kept blowing up from people repeatedly tagging me to "fulfill my duty" because I was in the batter's box. I wondered, *How'd this whole "doctor Bruh chain" thing start?* I looked back in the video sequences to see who had made the first video and tagged all the doctors to be in the chain: it was Brian. And, of course, I had fun playing my part.

Since then, I've observed Brian's meteoric rise on TikTok, a feat I've seen few other people do in mere months. I witnessed how he creatively adopted his own style of addressing health-related videos on the platform as either true or false, known as *cap* in Gen-Zese. Whereas everyone was using the word *cap* and the blue emoji of a cap in videos to call out false information, Brian took it to the next level. He bought an actual royal blue cap (same color as the emoji cap) and taped a piece of white rectangular paper on the front and emblazoned it with a Sharpie: CAP. That was how he started what would become iconic for him across social media platforms. Brian and that blue cap! It was fun and catchy, but, more important, he used it to address a pandemic on social media: false information.

The social media apps don't have a "fact police" before a video gets cleared for viral takeoff. Brian threw himself into the role of being a doctor who researches any topic in a video and responds with the power of not saying a single word—only putting on his blue CAP hat at the video's end (denoting its false information). Over time, people trusted him as a credible source; now viewers eagerly watch his videos not knowing his response until the end, like the townsfolk anxiously wringing their hands around the groundhog hole to see whether Punxsutawney Phil will come out (signifying that spring will soon arrive). Brian understands the power of social media and also that his video technique can save thousands—perhaps millions—of people from trying or buying something that, at best, won't have any health benefits or, at worst, could cause them harm. Alternatively, if he says something is "not cap," you can be confident that video information is true.

As you probably can sense, Brian has a rare combination of curiosity, creativity, analytical skills, work ethic, caring, experience, and devotion to public service. These are the reasons that Brian is the perfect person to write *Influenced*—the most comprehensive "nothing held back" book on social media.

Have you ever found yourself scrolling and scrolling, watching one video after another only to suddenly realize that one or two hours have flown by? Are you constantly interrupting what you're doing to check your phone because of the "ding," "buzz," or vibration alerts? Do you check your social media first thing when you wake up, and is it the last thing you look at before you go to bed? Do you start to feel anxious if you haven't checked your social media feeds in a bit? These aren't coincidences—this result is by design, as *Influenced* unearths.

Social media provides endless amounts of information and entertainment for us to consume; it's a powerful outlet for creative expression, and it connects us with others. Yet there is a dark side of social media. Whether you're (1) a concerned parent wanting to know whether your child has a healthy relationship with social media, (2) a researcher who wants to understand how social media affects our perceptions and brains, or (3) someone who aspires to become an influencer, *Influenced* covers it all, including interviews with many other influencers who, for the first time ever, share their experiences—the good and the bad.

Influenced will help you understand how social media affects the ways our brains perceive and process information, how the apps determine what information we see, how to know whether an influencer is being paid for a post, how influencers affect children and teens differently than adults, how to determine whether you're addicted to social media and what to do about it, how social media positively or negatively affects our mental and physical health, whether we can make independent decisions without social media influence, what the role of sex workers on social media is, what effect shaming has on children and adults, how you can become an influencer, and what the future of social media looks like. This book "pulls the curtain back" on these topics and so much more.

Influenced is a gripping reveal about the positives of social media as well as its underbelly. In these pages, Brian has impressively and beautifully curated insider information from influencers, including himself, and from other sources that no one else could do. The inner-sanctum insights in this book can't be found elsewhere in any one place. After reading *Influenced*, you will come away feeling refreshed and confident with life-changing, powerful knowledge about social media and how to successfully manage life with it, since the social media air is only going to get thicker.

I chose to write this foreword because *Influenced* is an important book that we all need to read. This book is a *game changer* for everyone with any interest in this topic. I predict it will be referenced for years to come. *Influenced* is THE BOOK on social media, and you are about to take the ride of your life with it. Just like Brian's videos, you won't be able to turn away from *Influenced* until you've finished. And then you'll start reading it again. It's *that* type of book. Enjoy!

—Tony Youn, MD

Acknowledgments

To my cherished reader: you took a chance by picking up this book, which covers a topic that touches virtually everyone's life. I know you had many purchasing options, so I offer my appreciation for having selected *Influenced*.

I'll let you in on a little secret about authors: largely, we write for you—not for ourselves. To move you. To inspire you. To entertain you. My hope is that, within these pages, you'll discover many insights that will have you shouting aloud, "Wow! I didn't know that!" "That's amazing!" "I'm going to use this pearl!" or some other similar comment.

There are many caring and talented people who help shape and shepherd a professional book, which starts out as just a rough idea. My agent, Gordon Warnock at Fuse Literary, is the key person who has been with me from the start of my career as an author.

Gordon—you saw something in me that I didn't know I possessed. You have offered more than your time and skills as an agent; you've invested so much of yourself to help this book realize its full potential. I know that took countless additional hours of your time and focus that could have been spent on your other responsibilities. I am eternally grateful for your limitless talent, astute guidance, loyal advocacy, and genuine care for this project. I am honored that you remain an important part of my life. I cannot express all the gratitude I have for you as my gifted agent and dear friend.

Thank you, Suzanne Staszak-Silva at Rowman & Littlefield—my publisher. I am deeply appreciative that you championed this book from Gordon's first pitch. I am grateful for all the time you invested, along with Patricia Stevenson and Deni Remsberg, reading and editing the manuscript to tighten it up and using 300-grit sandpaper to provide polish. I am honored that your skilled creative team helped deliver this book to the world. I appreciate you, April Austin, for making sure I didn't leave any undotted *i*'s or bare *t*'s lying about.

To Gary M. Krebs, my writing consultant. Gary, you were instrumental in helping mold my vision for this book into what it now is. You were never afraid to get too close to the smoldering kiln—at risk of burning your hands—to ensure that this book took proper shape. Thank you for your hard work and diligence working with me as I exploded out of the starting gate; settled in with perfect pacing after what seemed like countless laps; and, finally, sprinted in the last one hundred meters to cross the finish line—tank emptied. Thank you again for being an incredibly valuable member of the team and for being a friend.

To my friends, my fellow influencers, you were all so generous with your precious time as I interviewed you for this book: thank you. You added a profound layer of depth, insight, understanding, and nuance through your unfiltered, firsthand experiences in the influencer universe. I recognize that you placed a high level of trust in me by sharing your vast experiences, private stories, and epiphanic insights. I value this trust and promise to never take it for granted. In some ways, I think of this book as being like Anthony Bourdain's *Kitchen Confidential* (but on social media, not food, of course) because of how brave and open you were.

Below, in alphabetical order, according to their last names, are my social media interviewees with their handles:

Natalie Aguilar: TikTok @nnatalieaguilar, Instagram @nnatalieagui-lar, YouTube @Natalie & the Aguilars

Fayez Ajib, DO: TikTok @lifeofadoctor, Instagram @doctorfayez, YouTube @lifeofadoctor

Jess Andrade, DO: TikTok @doctorjesss, Instagram @doctorjesss, YouTube @Doctorjesss

Spencer Barbosa: TikTok @spencer.barbosa, Instagram @spencer.barbosa, YouTube @spencer barbosa

Dana Brems, DPM: TikTok @footdocdana, Instagram @footdoc-dana, YouTube @FootDocDana

Ricky Brown, MD: TikTok @therealtiktokdoc, Instagram @drrich-ardjbrown, YouTube @Doctor Ricky

Tommy Martin, MD: TikTok @dr.tommymartin, Instagram @dr.tommymartin, YouTube @Dr. Tommy Martin

Krysten Mayers: TikTok @krysmay, Instagram @krysmay_official, YouTube @Krysmay Official

Josh Otusanya: TikTok @joshotusanya, Instagram @josh.otusanya, YouTube @Josh Otusanya

Magnolia Printz, MD: TikTok @balancedanesthesia, Instagram @magnoliaprintzmd

Karan Rajan, MRCS, MBBS, BSc: TikTok @dr.karanr, Instagram @drkaranrajan, YouTube @Dr Karan

Sarah Rav, MD: TikTok @sarahrav, Instagram @sarahrav

Siyamak Saleh, MD: TikTok @doctor.siya, Instagram @doctor.siya, YouTube @Siyamak Saleh MD

Muneeb Shah, DO: TikTok @dermdoctor, Instagram @doctorly, YouTube @Doctorly

Tony Youn, MD: TikTok @tonyyounmd, Instagram @tonyyounmd, YouTube @Youn Plastic Surgery

Andy Pattison: I truly appreciate the insights you provided for this book. I am also thankful for the opportunity to be a member of the World Health Organization's Fides group of influencers and help support your mission of countering the misinformation pandemic on social media.

I also interviewed a prominent social media talent manager, who chose to remain anonymous. Thank you for your invaluable behind-the-scenes input!

Daniel Liebeskind: your contributions about the metaverse were invaluable. See you in the future!

Last and most important: I would like to express my sincere gratitude to my wife, Selina. Your support of me through this long process (publishing a book is a marathon, not a sprint) never wavered. You gave me plenty of leash and miles of patience as I pursued this passion. I can't imagine my world without you and your unconditional love. You continually inspire me to be a better version of myself. I love you, Selina, so *everythingly*! F and A!

Prologue

Confessions of an Influencer

We mock the things we are to be.

—Mel Brooks[1]

I have a confession to make. Actually, I have *three* confessions to make.

First, I admit that I was not a full-fledged influencer when I began this project. I had a respectable platform consisting of many social media friends, followers, and fans and had a great deal of media exposure, but I was not any closer to the level of a "true" influencer.

Second, in February 2020, when I made a deliberate attempt to engage with people on TikTok, I didn't have a clue what I was doing.

Third, once I started gaining some traction as an influencer with my posts going viral, I unknowingly ended up succumbing to many of the same pitfalls I had been researching while writing this book.

Now that I've just hung out my dirty laundry, I'll backtrack and explain my journey to becoming an *influencer* and how I became *influenced* by what started out as an innocent curiosity.

During the COVID shutdowns, my medical practice—like that of most doctors—dramatically slowed down, giving me a lot of unaccustomed downtime. One day, my twin daughters approached me and urged, "Dad, there are some really good doctors on TikTok. You should be one."

To my surprise, I found that the notion intrigued me. In addition to being open to finding something to do that would fill my newfound spare time, I came up with three reasons for testing my chops on Tik-Tok: it might be a good way to dispel misinformation being spread on TikTok (there is plenty of good information too); I could gain a more comprehensive perspective as part of my research for this book; and, as I will explain in full in the subsequent chapters, I thought it showed some promise of providing me with fun and a pleasurable dopamine rush. (As we'll discuss in the introduction and chapter 3 in detail, this is the same neurochemical release that occurs when one gambles, eats chocolate, takes drugs, etc.) Also, I suppose, there was a part of me that wanted to prove that I was a "cool dad" to my daughters.

I donned my scientist's hat and approached the effort with the tenacity and meticulousness of initiating a research project. I set a goal of one thousand followers on TikTok and told my daughters that, once we hit it, I'd buy myself a new iPad. I set about recording and posting different types of videos and immersed myself in TikTok's data. I analyzed the results to determine which topics had higher ratios—video likes divided by video views—and which ones led to the most shares. I created my own metric, which I dubbed "the follower efficiency ratio": the number of total video likes for my account divided by the number of new followers for a given time period (e.g., six hours or a day). At first, it took more than one hundred video likes to acquire one follower, a ratio of 100:1. So, I reasoned, if my channel were to receive ten thousand total likes across all my videos, I would gain one hundred new followers. I tweaked and tinkered with my profile information and biography wording to optimize the best ratio and boiled it down to a ratio of 26:1; by my calculations, the ten thousand likes would yield about 384 new followers, a dramatic increase in efficiency.

I posted videos nearly every day and frequently engaged with my followers, either in response to comments or when they tagged me in other videos. TikTok Live is another feature that I experimented with to directly engage with followers in Q&A. This process mushroomed lowers—especially as my popularity began to surpass many household-name celebrities and well-established influencers.

It reached a breaking point when my daughters attempted to talk to me about their day. I was too busy responding to TikTok comments to pay attention to what they were saying. My wife and daughters felt that they had no other option than to conduct a TikTok intervention.

It backfired. I felt betrayed because I interpreted my daughters' actions as meaning they were no longer supportive of my goals. Part of me felt that they were jealous and resentful of losing my attention, which, at the time, I didn't think was fair. I struck back by continuing as if the intervention had never happened and refusing to discuss TikTok with them.

There is always that moment when karma catches up with an addict (and yes, I fell into that category). My payback hit me when a new video was once again accused of a community guidelines violation.

The feeling of having a suppressed account was agonizing. How could TikTok not promote my viral videos? How could I be so neglectful and not take care of my virtual children?

I was forced to take a step back and experienced a psychological state known as learned helplessness; no matter how hard I tried, I could not get any videos to go viral. This time, during the separation from TikTok, reality set in and my epiphany occurred. I had been guilty of ignoring my real-life children in favor of my virtual ones. I realized that I was the influencer—and also the one being influenced as if a spell had been coursing through my neuro-machinery. I had become severely detached from my family, and the unleashed guilt was staggering. I solemnly walked to my bedroom, closed the door, and cried.

I profusely apologized to my family, begging their forgiveness. Thankfully, they accepted. Once the viral videos resumed, I approached being an influencer from an entirely different perspective, one that was grounded and healthy. I had to control my dopamine balance and always put my family first. They are far more important to me than my millions of followers.

So, there you have it: my confession. I am a recovered "TikToka-holic."

Being an influencer has the potential to be addictive and destructive. Mine is a cautionary tale—but at least I can say I safely made it to the other side with my sanity and family intact.

Another consolation is that I am not alone with my predicament. As you'll soon discover, virtually every influencer I interviewed while researching this book admitted that, at some point, they went through a similar phase in which their social media lives spiraled out of control, sometimes like a roller coaster careening off the tracks. It's fascinating to me that what I experienced seems to be the norm, rather than the exception—and yet there does not (at least as of yet) exist a manual for influencers, followers, and users on how to prevent this phenomenon or how to cope with the problem before it gets out of hand. Filling that void became another reason for writing *Influenced*.

The poet T. S. Eliot once wrote, "People exercise an unconscious selection in being influenced."[2] I believe his logic goes both ways—whether you are an influencer or the one being influenced. View, like, comment, share, and post until you're as satiated as taking down a Las Vegas buffet—but do so with both eyes wide open to be sure it's worth your time and energy; be discriminating about what information you believe as truth; and always choose to spend time with your flesh-and-blood loved ones above the ones flashing on your screen.

That is precisely what *Influenced* is all about.

Introduction

We Are All under the Influence

In a bygone era, when the television was first mass produced, there were warnings to the public about the dangers of overexposure to TV. Some medical authorities believed that the radioactivity emanating from screens would cause mass incidents of brain cancer. Social scientists put forth the hypothesis that the programs on the air would "dumb people down" and rot the minds of children. A whole new generation would become mindless automatons, the experts said.

These predictions never quite came to pass—the boomer generation seemed to get through the TV revolution well enough—but today we have a whole new multitentacled octopus to contend with: social media. Whether we are aware of it or not, its influence is all around us—and its potentially positive or detrimental impact on the human brain and behavior is genuine and cause for evaluation.

Is our brain chemistry and behavior impacted by what we read, see, hear, and experience on social media? Do certain types of posts in a Facebook news feed impact what we do immediately afterward? Of course not, right? Think again. In a research experiment conducted on Facebook, positive or negative posts were significantly correlated with the tone of those from friends and other users. They found that, if a user post had positive words, it increased the likelihood that the friends would post with similar words, and the effect persisted for up to three days after the first post. Conversely, when negative words were used in a post, friends tended to have the same tenor, and this effect lasted for three days as well. Emotional words in posts can be contagious, as they can influence emotions of other users' posts.[1]

Consider: The aforementioned study was just a snapshot of unconscious influence at work involving circles of Facebook friends. What happens to our brains and our behaviors when outside forces—influencers, media, advertisers, politicians, and celebrities—overrun our social media feeds? How and why are they manipulating us? Is there anything we can we do to address it? If discriminating, mature adults can be manipulated by social media, what does this mean for teenagers and children who can be far more hooked on TikTok, YouTube, Instagram, and Twitter than we are? Teenagers have skyrocketing rates of depression and suicide because of the seemingly paradoxical isolation effect of social media. Excessive time on smartphones increases risk of high blood pressure, obesity, low HDL cholesterol (the good one), diabetes, impaired ability to regulate stress, poor bone density, and vision problems.

We are all bombarded by influence 24/7. Nearly 70 percent of the approximately 340 million social media users log on each day for one purpose: to interact with—or perceive a connection with—influencers. How is the marketing world responding? According to the *Influencer Marketing Benchmark Report 2022*, whose survey included two thousand brands (companies), marketing agencies, and PR firms, influencer marketing is expected to grow to over $16 billion per year.[2]

Being an influencer in today's world—where an adolescent girl from Tokyo (Coco) is in the vicinity of six hundred thousand global Instagram followers[3]—can equate to serious bank, and outside of those running the platforms, there is little monitoring or regulating feeds with any kind of understanding or authority. Meanwhile, presidential elections have been influenced by Twitter feeds and Russian bots. For these and many other reasons that will become clear, it is imperative that we understand the pervasiveness and power of social media influence and its influencers: how we are affected by it and what steps can we take to protect ourselves and future generations.

DOPED UP

In one respect, it's not our fault. We are largely oblivious to the mental evolution that is already underway. Science is proving that our reliance on the world of social media and its universe of influencers is having a demonstrable impact on how our brains function, how we think, feel, and perceive everything around us—and even how we react to stimuli.

Dopamine, the neurotransmitter in our brains affiliated with stimulating our pleasure centers, can be released in response to every tweet, Instagram photograph, TikTok video, and Facebook share. According to Harvard researchers, the waves of dopamine generated by social media and its influencers on our brains can be as powerful as drugs and gambling and just as addictive.[4]

Humans are hardwired for getting our dopamine release. One way or another, we often pursue the path of least resistance to get it. When we don't get enough of a dopamine hit from one source, we seek it out from more readily available alternative to satisfy our dopamine behavior balance (DBB), a term I coined. I define this as the balance of dopamine stimulation manifested in individuals seeking out activities that satisfy dopamine release and its pleasure effects. DBB can be too high (e.g., drug addiction) or too low (e.g., depression).

One might think that a "like" is nothing more than a split-second tap on a device. As children and teens utilize social media, more than just likes are occurring; brain changes are being observed, as we will discover in chapter 3.

In one study, adolescents underwent functional magnetic resonance imaging (fMRI) evaluation while viewing various Instagram photographs. They were more prone to click "Like" on the photos that had more "likes" compared to those that had fewer. On the fMRI, the people who clicked "Like" showed great activity in the visual cortex that connected to the precuneus and the cerebellum. When "risky" images were viewed, the fMRI revealed different brain activation areas: left front cortex, precentral gyrus, middle frontal gyrus, and inferior frontal gyrus.[5] These and other studies are proving that total gray area volume correlates with social media usage.

While some may dismiss these findings as trivial, the science indicates otherwise. "Likes" and other symbols that indicate heightened reputation boost an individual's feeling of self-worth, amplify desire for more dopamine hits, and compel the user to thirst for more. In the reverse, negative social comments—manifesting as cyberbullying when it comes to kids—can reduce self-esteem and cause withdrawals from engagement, loneliness, and depression. We light up with every buzz, ding, and alert in anticipation of how our network is responding to us, often inducing solitary confinement from the people physically around us. As we rush to our devices to identify the source of the sound, we are anxiously seeking the approval of others—often people we barely know or don't know at all. Are we becoming like Pavlov's dogs, who salivated after associating receiving food with a certain sound?

I remember an experiment I performed on mice while I was a student at UCLA. An electrode was inserted into the pleasure centers of the mice's brains. When the mice hit a bar with their hands, a gentle current stimulated their brains. Once they learned how to do it, they remained parked at the bar and incessantly pressed it. The mice became so engrossed in the activity, they never paused to eat or drink. Had I not turned off the current, the mice would inevitably have died from dehydration and malnutrition.

As we sit for hour after hour craning our necks over our devices ("text neck," as it is now called, is a real condition) to anxiously review the next tweet, Facebook post, Instagram photo, or TikTok video of influencers or to constantly check the success of our own social media posts, the question arises: Is social media turning us all into these dopamine-addicted mice?

YOUR PI AND INFLUENCE

In my prior book, *Perceptual Intelligence*, I explored how the brain can help see past illusion, misperception, and self-deception. Perceptual Intelligence (PI) is our mind's way of separating reality from fantasy. High PI embraces both critical thinking and, on the other end of the spectrum, intuition or gut feeling. Either may be required depending on the circumstance, whether it's about distinguishing if the outline of a face burned into a grilled cheese sandwich is Virgin Mary (low PI) or powerful instincts convince you not to board an airplane that might crash—and then it does without you on it (high PI).

It's so easy for us to reflexively blink at the effects of influencers. When it comes to separating fact from falsities (a.k.a. cap) in our social media feeds, we require augmentation of our critical thinking spectrum to help us remain sober amid the intoxicating effect of internet celebrity, the ingrained authenticity associated with it. Our insecurities can set us up for believing almost anything that seems to provide a solution for a perceived problem. I see this situation all the time. For example, yearnings to achieve a chiseled jawline in just seven days can be so intense that people will adopt unproven (using your fingers to magically rub away the fat layer) or potentially harmful mouth exercises (repeatedly biting on a firm rubber ball, which risks damage to the temporomandibular joint, or TMJ) recommended by viral TikTok videos.

Your honed critical thinking–based PI tells you: *Don't blink. Think.*

I have helped many of my TikTok and Instagram followers recognize that you cannot be a nodding rubbernecker and believe everything you see on social media. They constantly tag (notify) me on a wide range of videos to verify whether the information in those videos is cap or fact. I will research the topic and often reply with a comment or video indicating whether it's *cap* or *not cap*. Over time, I have become one of the go-to people in the TikTok and Instagram communities for determining whether videos contain true or false health information. The value of this position cannot be underestimated, since anyone can make a video about virtually anything that goes viral and encourages people to believe and/or do some pretty strange—if not harmful—things, examples of which will be discussed in this book.

As we receive and process information, advice, reportage, and recommendations from influencers, it's essential that we shelve our intuition, which is otherwise invaluable to our creative drives and, occasionally, to our survival. Failure to flip on the critical thinking switch in our minds can cause us to accept misinformation at face value and react against our best interests, such as by purchasing something we don't need, emulating a behavior that proves harmful, or practicing a bogus health trend that will fail to yield expected results.

At the same time, critical thinking and high PI can also identify credible and invaluable information from social media influencers that has beneficial, if not life-changing, consequences. If you wish to reverse your hair loss, you might wisely choose to follow the advice of a popular viral video that recommends spraying rosemary water on your scalp to grow more hair. Since we're on the topic of follicles, another viral video about applying minoxidil on the face to stimulate beard hair was backed by medical research.[6]

I know you're probably thinking: *How do I know what to believe and what not to believe?* Read on, my friend, but please recognize that our minds have not been trained to recognize each and every time an influencer suggestion might be a subtle marketing pitch for whatever they are selling and whether it is factual or false. Or it might be a promotion solely to gain more followers—a vital currency for influencers and aspiring influencers. As social media followers, our subconscious has already been programmed to positively favor association with the influencer. We implicitly trust our influencer, who has won us over with proven authenticity that helped forge a faux relationship. We become ripe for our PI to be hijacked and make a decision we might regret.

Stay tuned: we'll cover this topic in much greater depth in chapter 2, "Following the Herd."

IT'S ALL IN THE MIND

My goal is not to cast aspersions on the world of influencers. I have enormous respect for those who provide valuable services—whether it's facts, instruction, entertainment, or a combination therein—to their communities and stay true to themselves on their respective platforms. In fact, rather than rely solely on my own research and observations in writing this book, I personally interviewed a number of well-regarded female and male influencers of diverse ages, backgrounds, interests, and expertise, who are identified in the acknowledgments. The one thing they all have in common is that they have experienced groundbreaking social media success with followers numbering in the millions.

I am also well aware that many people make a living as influencers and/or rely upon influencer marketing to sell their products or services. If you think passing judgment is my intention, ask yourself this question: *As an influencer myself, why would I bite the hand the feeds me?*

My true objective in writing this book is to explore what happens to our minds and our behaviors each time we view; click "Like"; follow an influencer; share or reshare a video or article; post or repost a photograph; report social media abuse; upload a video or photo; experience social media abuse; write a comment; or just scroll away the hours consuming content.

I also seek to challenge our thinking in terms of what is and isn't dangerous or threatening about the universe of social media influence. At present, since the subject is still so young, we have no conclusive idea of what prolonged social media exposure over a period of twenty-five years or more can do to our brains and behaviors. However, we do have shorter-term data that is surprising and even shocking at times. While I don't own tarot cards, I will share what I think the future will look like in the conclusion.

These are just some of the questions I will be addressing:

- Will we become incapable of determining independent emotions and responses without social media influence?

- Will we forget the essential norms of verbal one-on-one and group communication?
- Will our devices determine everything we believe?
- What characteristics define a true influencer?
- What is the distinction between the types of influencers: content creators and lifecasters?
- How do influencers infiltrate our psyches to monetize their platforms?
- What happens to our brains and behaviors when we are under the influence of content posted by social media influencers?
- How does social media influence impact children and teenagers versus adults?
- How does influence inform—if not direct—our personal preferences and decision-making?
- When should one be concerned that one has become too dependent on or addicted to social media influence?
- What unseen impact does social media shaming have on kids and adults?
- To what extent is social media influence responsible for our physical and mental health—good and bad?
- How do we identify when influencers are being paid to show support for a product or service?
- What is the impact of some sex workers having become top influencers?
- How do we know whether we have high enough Perceptual Intelligence (PI) to distinguish what is false (cap) versus what is fact (not cap) on influencer feeds and viral videos?
- How do we separate influencers from con artists and predators?
- How might social media evolve in the future?

In my mind, one of the most wonderful things about social media influence is that virtually anyone and everyone has a chance to make their mark and stand out. One viral video can turn a person from a passing Walter Mitty to a waltergoodboy—a French bulldog with over one hundred thousand Instagram followers.[7] While there are downsides to social media, there are also myriad opportunities for someone with a talent, expertise, creativity, perspective, or look to become a sensation. Being different may equate to uniqueness and originality, which is something to celebrate because, in this case, fame leads to immediate acceptance where it may otherwise have been lacking in that person's life. Often there is nothing wrong with that.

As we embark on this journey together, keep in mind the following quote from best-selling author Dan Schawbel: "What makes you weird, makes you unique and therefore makes you stand out."[8]

Let's all cheerfully click "Like" on this sentiment and share it.

1

Hooked on Clicks

What Is a Social Media Influencer?

I want to perceive and understand the hidden powers and laws of things, in order to have it in my power.

—*Salvador Dali, artist*[1]

You've heard the term; after all, you're reading this book. But what, exactly, is an *influencer*? This is how I define an influencer:

> Anyone with a strong presence on social media who produces content; has an online community; engages with a multitude of followers; and posts ideas and recommendations with the intent of eliciting emotional responses and behaviors from viewers.

Does social media have the power to fan the flames of a budding influencer with one post that goes viral with a stratospheric number of views, likes, comments, and shares? Yes. Is a certain age, talent, or expertise required? No. Is strong writing ability a factor? Usually not. Anyone with a smartphone may win the lottery with the right post at the right time. What does this mean? Anyone can become famous (or start the trek to be famous) without any credentials.

By the very nature of the word *influence*, an influencer wields enormous power—largely without any checks and balances except the number of likes and unflattering comments and the platform guidelines—to be a Pied Piper of thoughts and behaviors. An influencer can lead others into thinking a product or service is trash or worth purchasing, a video or photograph is cool, a bogus health trend is legit, a news story is true (or not), a politician deserves your vote, and so forth.

There are two different categories of influencers:

1. Content creators: bloggers, vloggers, experts, and even animals/inanimate objects/babies/toddlers/memes
2. Lifecasters: those with a special talent, entrepreneurs, models, actors, celebrities, athletes, and politicians

Popular actors we see on a TV show or in a film may not necessarily be influencers, even if they have amassed a large social media following. Think of influencers as *digital-first* celebrities or internet personalities. A notable example would be makeup artist James Charles, who received his "big break" in the social media space from competitive influencer Tati Westbrook, culminating in an explosive feud that played out like a soap opera in front of tens of millions on YouTube.[2] Make no mistake: both Charles and Westbrook each have followings that eclipse those of many mainstream A-list celebrities.

There is a salient difference between influencers and traditional celebrities: *authenticity*. Influencers are perceived by their followers as honest and authentic content creators, whereas conventional celebrities are often actors who became famous for playing roles.

WHY DO PEOPLE WANT TO BECOME INFLUENCERS?

Fact: There are some people who shoot right out of the gate with the purpose of trying to create an influencer platform that will make money. They hear the eye-popping stories about dog influencers and kid influencers who rake in bank from a combination of paid posts and advertising. ("If they can do it, why can't I? It seems so easy!") In some instances, the platforms will offer what they refer to as "creator funds" as a financial incentive to ensure that popular influencers remain faithful to them and keep posting. One needs to be approved to qualify for this fund based on specific criteria, which usually involves a minimum number of followers (e.g., ten thousand) and page views (e.g., one hundred thousand). Unless one is at the Kardashian, Charli D'Amelio, Addison Rae, or ACE family level, it usually doesn't add up to beaucoup bucks, but it does provide a token of appreciation and gratitude to these influencers. A number of full-time influencers generate enough income to fully support themselves and then some. There is risk to the platforms, as influencers are "at-will posters," meaning that generally they do not sign any kind of noncompete contract preventing them from mining engagement opportunities elsewhere on other social media platforms, which they commonly do.

OREO INFLUENCERS GET LICKED

Influencers are allowed to be paid for recommending a product or service in a post. However, there can be major backlash if the influencer fails to reveal that they received marketing/advertising money for it.

One such incident occurred in 2014 when British YouTubers Dan Howell and Phil Lester conducted an "Oreo lick race" that involved a number of other top influencers.[1] This all sounds like good clean fun, except the duo did not disclose that they had an agreement with Mondelez, Oreo's parent company, and were compensated for conducting the contest. A BBC journalist reported them to the UK Advertising Standards Authority and the video was banned, resulting in shame and embarrassment all around. That's how the cookie can crumble when influencers are inauthentic.

NOTE

1. Mark Sweeney, "YouTubers Ads for Oreo Banned for Not Making Clear Purpose of Videos," *Guardian*, November 2014, https://www.theguardian.com/media/2014/nov/26/youtube-ad-oreo-banned-advertising-lick-race.

Is it solely the money that keeps influencers going, or are there other reasons?

There are many reasons depending upon the influencer, but I'll start with myself as the case study—which I explored in my prologue. The flood of dopamine in my brain is intensely powerful when I find my groove posting, analyzing my metrics, and reading and responding to comments. And yes, influencers do read comments on their posts—often with tremendous excitement. We may or may not have the time or inclination to address every single one, but we do receive a buzz from seeing such attention. On the opposite end, zero comments can feel deflating and negative remarks can cause extreme emotions, such as anger and resentment. It often requires a great deal of fortitude for an influencer to ignore insulting and offensive comments. Dana Brems, DPM, a podiatrist and influencer based in Los Angeles, pointed out to me that some people fail to realize that influencers are "real human beings," which is why they feel free to write whatever strikes their fancy at that moment. "People don't understand that influencers *read* their comments."

As I mentioned in the prologue, my head rush to reach various viral benchmark goals became so intoxicated with dopamine that I neglected my own family; for a brief period, I was admittedly a "digital deadbeat dad." For me and many other influencers, social media is not in any way about monetization. It's about satisfying our DBB, which I will cover at greater length as this book progresses. Personally, I rarely accept any advertising money, although I am regularly offered it. (I only do sponsored posts for brands whose products are legitimate, can help people, or that I've personally tried.)

I liken the urgent sensation an influencer feels to a poker player who wins pot after pot, keeps raising bets, and takes increasingly bigger risks. Certainly, gamblers want to clean up and get rich, but what is really egging them on to keep going—even though at a certain point perhaps they should quit while ahead—they can't because the dopamine feels too good and convinces the gambler that they can't lose.

The dopamine crush is most certainly not my only motivation. My underlying purpose on social media (TikTok is my largest platform) is to investigate popular and curious health information circulated as "fact." If you're not already familiar, TikTok is a Chinese-based app, where it is known as Douyin and owned by a company called Byte-Dance.[3] The app enables users to create brief videos that may be used for education, instruction, and/or entertainment. In my account, I create videos—often a duet with someone else's preexisting video—to prove or disprove (known as *cap*, a polite way of calling out BS) a point. Whether the subject concerns coffee and lemon for weight loss, applying toothpaste on pimples, or penis enlargement from drinking aloe vera juice (all of which are cap, by the way), my goal is to dive straight into the medical sources and separate the zirconia from the diamonds. There is quite a lot of misinformation out there, and, in my way, I feel as if I am providing something of a public service, nipping a lot of these viral fallacies in the bud and also confirming information that is valid.

Influencer Krysten Mayers, a New Jersey–based medical student, is motivated by a similar purpose: to "debunk certain things that people think are true but they're not true—creating space for anybody to talk about things that might be happening to them or things that they want to know about themselves and their bodies." Her aim is to sustain what she calls a "safe" teaching space in which she can "spread knowledge and keep educating people every day and help them learn something new."

Tommy Martin, MD, an influencer who specializes in internal medicine and pediatrics at the University of Arkansas for Medical Sciences, frames his purpose so eloquently that it could be emblazoned on the walls of every medical school: "To educate, motivate, and inspire as many people as I can while spreading love and positivity."

Dr. Martin brought to my attention another possible motivational factor for becoming an influencer: charity and philanthropy. When the Pediatric Hematology Oncology Program's biggest fundraiser at Arkansas Children's Hospital was canceled due to COVID, he utilized social media to raise over $16,000 in just two weeks.

Such noble intentions aside, another potential reason why children and adults alike are drawn to becoming influencers is to seek fame. For kids and teenagers, in particular, being an influencer may compensate for social discomfort and lack of popularity in school. If fifteen-year-old girls or boys can grab the attention of one hundred thousand people from a post, it can boost their self-esteem and earn some gravitas and "street cred" among their peers. Success as influencers may mean they can hold their heads up even higher when strolling through the school hallways. It's one thing to be famous in a local school; it's quite another level to be "TikTok famous." For a child or teen, the idea of becoming popular without having to take the risk of showing up somewhere in person and doing something noteworthy (such as at a party, extra-curricular activity, or sports) and potentially being humiliated by the school bully can be quite alluring (although internet bullying is quite real), as is the idea of going from being a "nobody" to a "somebody."

In the case of adults, social media can also provide desired fame for a variety of reasons. Perhaps there are those who never let go of the longing for notoriety, which may stem from a childhood dream that never came to fruition. Maybe there were wannabe actors, musicians, singers, or dancers who never got their big break and had to venture down the path of a nine-to-five day job. It might be a venue to let one's creative juices run wild. It could merely be wanting to sun their buns in the limelight—figuratively and literally. By way of explanation, there was a viral video on TikTok that espoused the health virtues of sunning one's perineum—anatomically speaking, the "taint," the area between the anus and the vagina or penis. There's no benefit to it—it's *cap*—but that didn't stop that video getting six million views and some unfortunate sunburns.

Being an influencer provides a sense of an audience being somewhere out there. While one doesn't receive traditional applause or curtain calls, there is the thrill of seeing an explosion in the number of views and likes and reading all the gushy comments. Influencers have the advantage of not having to perform "live" on a stage in front of people in seats, which can be terrifying. (Public speaking is ranked the number one fear by about 75 percent of the population, above fear of dying.)[4] They can post at their leisure and get the benefit of real-time interaction and results without all the pressure to have to perform live and fret about making mistakes or forgetting lines. For all the botched video takes, there is always the final one that comes out "just right" (or close enough).

Another motivation behind why some people become influencers: they love being granted the opportunity to make a large group of people happy. Natalie Aguilar—a model and influencer on TikTok and Instagram—shares entertaining videos of her family just being themselves.[5] In one particularly amusing series of videos, Natalie's mother purchases a kayak because she is angry at her father. The punch line comes when her father sees the brand-new kayak and observes that his wife hadn't considered buying a paddle to use with it.

These funny "slices of life" from a regular family are relatable to people in a way that can't be scripted, which provides entertainment for people who aren't interested in the excesses of TV reality stars. As Natalie described to me, "I enjoy getting to share funny moments of my family."

Natalie's videos also provide glimpses into warm family situations that some viewers can't experience due to a range of family issues in their own personal situations. The result is that viewers feel uplifted, and their emotional gaps become filled simply by being welcomed into intimate family scenes. "Many of my followers tell me that their parents are no longer together, or they aren't close with them," Natalie explained to me. "Seeing my videos and my family's dynamic makes them happy."

There are also those influencers who genuinely do aspire to someday have careers in front of TV and film cameras. The dream is to springboard their fame from one medium to the other. A talent manager I interviewed for this book recruits talent on platforms such as YouTube (at least a million followers) and Instagram (at least a half million followers) that can become TV personalities (or writers). He tends to avoid working with TikTok influencers at this time because, "in general, I don't think those talents translate to television—at least I haven't seen many that could."

MAKING THE NUMBERS

What number constitutes being a full-fledged influencer? Having one video go viral does not automatically qualify a person as an influencer. It's kind of like a "one-hit wonder" in music, such as Dexy's Midnight Runners with their 1980s hit "Come On Eileen." "One rose does not a bouquet make," just as a single viral video does not an influencer make.

The gold level for an influencer is reaching the million mark of social media followers, friends, or subscribers. However, one may be considered a full-fledged influencer by reaching one hundred thousand, which is enough to command attention and, potentially, advertising dollars. At the lower end of the pecking order, one with ten thousand followers may be referred to as a *micro-influencer.*

The key for everyone in these groupings is to continuously build up a base of active followers. The success is sustained and repeated like Drake, Ariana Grande, the Beatles, Michael Jackson, or Madonna, with one hit single following another over a continuous period of time. A true influencer has some provable staying power via metrics—the algorithm assessing the number of views, likes, comments, and shares.

Sometimes what may seem to be a niche topic from an unknown can mushroom into a substantial, ardent following in the blink of an eye. Consider Muneeb Shah, DO, an influencer who started out with zero platform. Only one year later, he amassed millions of followers across platforms. Dr. Shah shared with me an interesting observation: "On social media you could live anywhere, post a video, and find a community of people who have similar interests, cultures, backgrounds, and ideals to you. If you are really into skating, for example, some people may think you're weird, but that's just the people around you. But when you are online, you can find this large group of people who also have a similar interest or quirk."

Identifying a focus and creating the community are only half the battle, however. Influencers can never ease their foot off the pedal at the risk of losing followers and perceived ranking. By the same token, a dozen or so forgettable dud posts after a viral hit can cause an influencer's impact to sink. Even too much of a lull between posts can reduce an influencer's standing because posting consistency is key. There are no hard and fast rules behind the timing of posts, and each platform is different: YouTube is about one week or twice a day for videos under one minute; Instagram roughly two per week; and TikTok is roughly every day or at least three times a week, but sometimes more than one a day.

Suffice it to say, this much output adds up to a lot of work. However, to the follower or casual observer, being an influencer seems effortless. Toronto-based full-time influencer Spencer Barbosa informs me that her friends cannot comprehend how much effort she puts into her posts. They say things to her along the lines of "'What do you mean you work hard? All you do is film videos all day. That's not a job.' Or people will tell me that I'm not working. I'm working *really hard* and no one else sees it."

I have experienced this reaction as well. Some people assume that being an influencer is easy—just tap Record on your phone and start talking. I'm not looking for sympathy when I say a lot happens behind the scenes that people don't see. For me and many other serious influencers, a great deal of energy and preparation goes into each of our posts: my time may include reviewing medical-related queries from followers who tag me, researching relevant studies, and preparing, recording, and editing the actual videos.

People ask my staff, "Who helps Dr. Brian with his social media?"

They answer, "No one, it's all him."

Usually at that point, eyes begin to glaze.

To keep those numbers heading north, I place a great deal of pressure on myself to ensure that my content is always fresh and/or relevant; it contains an original angle; it has a wide appeal to a strong percentage of followers; it's factually correct; and it will ideally stand the test of time. Good influencers know they've hit the bull's-eye when people respond to posts saying something along the lines of "Wow, I didn't know that!" and "Thank you, that's helpful!" or, if it's a funny post, the comments section becomes a yellow sea of laughing emojis extending to the bottom of the section. I've also tested out ways to make posts "sticky" by dividing them into two segments (e.g., "Body Hacks Part 1" and "Body Hacks Part 2").

When themed videos do well, it can inspire a series of future videos. One series of mine involves me donning a long blond wig (now don't get too excited) and portraying an annoying parent. I then switch to another wig, transforming into the parent's daughter or son.

This series stemmed from the first popular video I did of a mother chastising her son with the phrase "Being on the phone in the dark is gonna ruin your eyes!"

He retorts, "Mom, Dr. Brian on TikTok said that's a myth."

"If it's on TikTok, it's not true!" she snarls; then her face lights like fantasizing about a lover: "But if it was on *Facebook*—"

The numbers have the potential to multiply when a viral post garners mainstream attention, such as on a major TV, internet, or radio network. My "hair growth hack" post—which authenticates spraying rice water on the scalp as an effective treatment to grow a longer, thicker mane (in people, not horses)—was picked up by Yahoo!Money. Another one, "Tips on Growing Taller," was featured on LADBible.com. Such exposure has a cumulative positive effect on an influencer's reach and overall popularity.

THE INFLUENCER SUPPORT POSSE

Some successful influencers, like celebrities, have assistants, makeup people, agents, managers, publicists, technical experts, and attorneys working behind the scenes.

Unbeknownst to many members of an influencer's tribe, the seemingly authentic presentation may be highly curated for effect with organically appearing product or service placement. Product listings on these feeds can be paid for by advertisers, which often include national corporations. Photographs and videos may be doctored. Posts might be written by assistants, publicists, or even professional writers without any substantive reviews by the actual influencer. As soon as one of these natural-looking posts appears on an influencer's feed, however, it bears that personality's official stamp of approval for the followers to receive and process—no matter which hired hand was the actual creator of the content.

A COLLECTIVE COMMUNITY

Of course, the influencer effect is not merely a 1:1 relationship between influencer and follower; it goes way beyond that. Whether the influencer is communicating and engaging with five hundred or five million people, the response group can become a collective community, developing a unique psychology and personality all its own. This group of fans and followers assimilates a mission that, for better or for worse, has the power to spread the influencer's messaging far and wide. In essence, the group becomes the contemporary version of a stampeding wildebeest herd (which we'll cover in greater detail in chapter 2)—sometimes blindly accepting and passing along affirmational cues from the influencer and their peers, even though it may mean becoming the main course for predatorial lions, tigers, and cheetahs.

For example, in 2014 Colgate initiated a product launch of its Slim-Soft Charcoal toothbrush.[6] Instead of starting with traditional ads, it paid two hundred social media influencers who had about twenty-four million combined followers. The influencers incorporated the Colgate toothbrushes in their posts. Using the hashtag #WhatTheBlack, the posts appeared organic, not at all like advertisements. The campaign was highly effective at creating a buzz right out of the gate.

WHAT IS INFLUENCER MARKETING?

Influencer marketing has already become a legitimate business for companies of all varieties. It is a type of social media marketing that involves soliciting and/or actually buying endorsements and/or product mentions from influencers. Many such campaigns are funded in the hope of bolstering sales by tapping into the influencers' outreach and the trust they have earned from their followers.

In his book *Winfluence: Reframing Influencer Marketing to Ignite Your Brand*, Jason Falls tweaks the concept a bit to draw attention to the "influence" part of the word *influencer*—removing the *r* at the end—thereby focusing on the action of influencing someone, rather than on the entity. It's much less about "Hey, we have $1 million in our marketing budget, let's drop it all on a post from Kim Kardashian!" than the strategy behind *what* and *how* you utilize influence to achieve your intended goal and provide real perceived value to your customers.[7]

Some marketing consulting companies have shifted gears to include influencer marketing, whereas other firms have made this their sole domain. Businesses are continuously hunting for the ideal Trojan horse that breaks through all the social media noise and brings national or global attention to their products and services. They may pay for an influencer marketing company and team of content creators that can successfully drive brand awareness, increase website traffic, and throttle up sales. The knowledge and insights behind what's working and what isn't are constantly shifting, so influencer marketers need to keep their eyes glued upon metrics and upcoming trends. It is now becoming easier for brands to bypass influencer marketing companies and go straight to the influencer. For example, TikTok offers the "Creator Marketplace," in which approved influencers and companies may approach each other directly. On Instagram, brands can directly DM influencers.

Now that you know what an influencer is and does, it's time to start investigating what is being perceived on the other side of the screen. What do *you* see and believe when you are surfing social media sites?

2

Following the Herd

How Is Our Perceptual Intelligence (PI) Being Hijacked by Social Media Influence?

Ignorance more frequently begets confidence than does knowledge.

—*Charles Darwin, introduction,* The Descent of Man *(1871)*[1]

Whether you realize it or not, you have "followed the herd" at some point in your life—meaning that you've gone along with the thinking of a mass of people rather than break away based on your own individual thought process. This may be wonderful or tragic, depending on the circumstances. If, for example, you were in a movie theater where someone screamed, "Fire!" and people burst out of their seats toward the emergency exits, you would probably drop your tub of popcorn and join them, right? In this instance, following the herd is a commonsense thing to do without much risk involved, except for missing the movie and losing your snack. Your survival instincts and critical thinking kick in and tell you, *Hey, it's worth the sacrifice—I'd rather be alive than get charred along with my popcorn.*

In his revelatory work *Influence: The Psychology of Persuasion*, Robert Cialdini introduced the cultlike effect of "the herd" when it comes to advertising.[2] If you were choosing between one Chinese restaurant filled with diners and one across the street that is empty, which one would you choose? The full one, of course.

The herd mentality also translates to posts from influencers: the greater number of views and likes, the more inclined you will be to soak up the information that could lead you to change your perspective on a topic or perhaps even sway you into making a purchase. The reverse can also be true; if an influencer trashes a person or product, the herd mentality can kick in as followers commune to ruin someone's reputation or a company's sales. A prominent example of the latter: Peloton was flayed by social media herds who deemed the company's 2019 commercial for exercise equipment "sexist" and "dystopian."[3] Such labels may be subjective and reflect the moving target of society norms, but, when it comes to social media reactions, the top influencers can drive the herd into accepting them as fact and then spreading the message.

One can have high or low Perceptual Intelligence (PI) with regard to the herd mentality, depending on the circumstances. It's not to imply that anyone is more or less intelligent. Rather, it signifies that a person's ability to know when to follow the actions of a large group versus head off on their own is indicative of strong critical thinking (high PI). The individuals who blindly follow the majority without processing and interpreting the available facts and trusting their gut may be well-educated, intelligent people but, at that moment in time, seem to be demonstrating weak levels of critical independent thinking (low PI) with regard to their decision-making.

The same principles apply to the world of social media influence. Sometimes following the herd may be beneficial, whereas there are other occasions when it may be harmful to oneself and/or others to do so. Let's first take a look at the latter.

FOLLOWING THE PIED PIPER

An influencer who is a genuine authority on a specific subject area may be worth their weight in followers. Deploy your critical thinking to determine whether the influencer's suppositions are credible, if their advice is worth following, and whether biases exist (such as a paid, sponsored post). The number of favorable views, likes, and comments

on an influencer's post may or may not be indicative of a recommendation's validity. The potential dangers of the latter are obvious: a viewer
of the post becomes inclined to believe the content at face value, simply
because such a large volume of people enthusiastically rallied behind
it with a splash of emotions wanting it to be true. I often observe no
correlation between factual health information and viral videos on
social media. False information might be driven by the influencer's
self-motivated agenda—including fictitious political propaganda, wishful thinking (what I refer to as *hopeium*), information pandering, or
product marketing—or it could be a simple case of incorrect data on
which a supposition has been made. We live in a world where digital
information is easy to manipulate and cheap to produce, which means
misinformation from a Pied Piper influencer can instantaneously create a massively expanding herd of believers inebriated with hopeium.
The larger the herd becomes, the lower their PI because they often are
susceptible to trusting the pack without utilizing their critical thinking
skills to dig deeper and distinguish fact from fiction.

Take the example of gua sha, an ancient Chinese stone usually made
of quartz or jade. Some influencers have created fifteen-to-thirty-
second videos—which have gone "multiplatinum" viral—of people using a gua sha to rub their mandible and transform it into a cut jawline.[4]
Sounds wonderful, right? The before and after pictures can involve different lighting and camera angles to convince viewers that the treatment
works. What people are possibly seeing in the video is the temporary
effect of moving tissue fluid, which can be accomplished with a number
of objects, including one's own hand. Of course, this story has misled
millions of viewers to believe gua sha contains miraculous properties for
trimming the jawline, which sets unrealistic expectations. People with
strong critical thinking skills realized that no amount of stone rubbing,
jaw massaging, or hopeium will miraculously bestow a chiseled jaw on
anyone.

By contrast, in one medically sound post, dermatologist Dr. Muneeb
Shah describes the effective benefits of skin creams containing salicylic

acid and retinol, which is quite a contrast to another influencer who touted that it is possible to clear up acne by drinking raisin-marinated water (which is *cap* or false).

When it comes to any kind of medical recommendations—including skin care treatments—your rational, questioning mind needs to be on alert, as there exists a great deal of deception out there. Dr. Shah points out how easy it is to fool a viewer into thinking a certain treatment is effective, simply by utilizing visual smoke and mirrors via video trickery. For example, as Dr. Shah explains, "They [influencers or creators] might do a no-filter shoot for a video and claim it's a 'before' photo. Then they throw on a filter to create an 'after' photo. To me, that's pretty much fraud."

Be careful of the Pied Pipers who lead followers to impending disappointment or worse, touting magical products and remedies without the medical facts and studies to back up their claims. At the least, it's irresponsible and causes consumers to waste their money; at worst, it can lead to far worse medical issues than the original problem (such as an allergic response to a product). In our online world in which any image and video can be manipulated, seeing is not necessarily believing.

WAS THERE A REAL PIED PIPER?

In all likelihood, *yes*, the Pied Piper was once a real person, just as Robin Hood (Robin of Loxley) probably once existed in some form. The legend of the Pied Piper appeared in ancient folklore and literature, including poetry by Goethe ("Der Rattenfänger") and a Grimm brothers' story ("The Children of Hamelin"). In the nineteenth century, Robert Browning wrote a famous poem called "The Pied Piper of Hamelin."[1]

In the tale, which originated from some germ of truth, the Pied Piper—whose real name has since been lost to history—was a medieval figure who came to rescue the town of Hamelin (Lower Saxony, Germany) in 1284 from a siege of rats (clearly predating the advent of Raid rat traps). Using his magic flute, the Piper successfully led the rats away from the town and was proclaimed a hero. For whatever reason, the town failed to financially compensate the Piper for his services, so he took revenge by using his magic flute to lure away 130 children, who were never seen again. Hence the origination of the phrase "pay the Piper," meaning one must settle a debt or else suffer an impending serious consequence.

The Pied Piper continues to pop up in modern culture—from different villains (Batman comics and various TV shows, as well as the 2010 animated film *Shrek Forever After*) to various TV series with the name *The Pied Piper*. On the *Silicon Valley* TV show (2014–2019), programmer Richard Hendricks (played by Thomas Middleditch) creates an app that can shrink data down to its smallest possible size. The app and company name are fittingly dubbed "Pied Piper," a not-too-subtle reference to the misfortune awaiting partners, employees, investors, and users who support and follow it.

NOTE

1. Raphael Kadushin, "The Grim Truth behind the Pied Piper," BBC Travel, September 3, 2020, https://www.bbc.com/travel/article/20200902-the-grim-truth-behind-the-pied-piper.

Shame, Shame

Whether we are aware of it or not, each and every one of us has a great deal of power at our fingertips when we post something on social media. We are entitled to express our opinions on any matter under the sun within the boundaries of what our social media platform of choice allows—which is quite a lot of freedom—whether we are qualified and knowledgeable on the subject or need to hit Wikipedia to have a clue. Our influence can raise someone up to deity-like proportions or publicly humiliate and take that person down with a few simple keystrokes. Whether the post is fact, fiction, speculative gossip, or gray area doesn't matter; once a statement is sent out to the online world, it can have long-term ripples, like tossing a pebble in a pond, and will probably hover out there forever in the digital universe with the potential to resurface at any time. The Pew Research Center recently reported that 55 percent of people receive their news from social media, which means that, along with a lot of accurate reports, there is also a ton of false information being accepted as fact without supportive evidence—especially when it comes to behaviors that might in some way be considered scandalous.[5] Human beings, it seems, have a tendency to assume and believe the worst in others, and there seems to be a currency in gossip that likely dates back to the early days of human communication.

Online public shaming of adults is a relatively new concept. In the past, before social media, behind-the-scenes gossip was the main vehicle for spreading rumors, accusations, and judgments. Now all it takes is a simple Facebook post to get the entire community up in arms, especially in parent groups as in the following (somewhat exaggerated) examples:

I can't believe Gillian is allowing her eight-year-old son Mikey to ride a bicycle without a helmet! I saw him yesterday on the corner of McDougal and Vine and took this picture of him on my phone! How irresponsible!

Moira sent her daughter Kendra to preschool with a runny nose this morning! What is the matter with her?!

Sherry is still breastfeeding her son Nick—he's eight years old! I heard him ask for "mommy's milk" at the fundraiser the other day. Gross!

When I was at Trader Joe's, Kaitlyn left her two-year-old daughter in the shopping cart alone for thirty-two and a half seconds while she stepped into the pasta aisle. I have proof in this video—look at the length of time for yourself!

I caught Li on the street allowing her son Jinhai to throw a plastic water bottle in the regular garbage. Terrible. She should be teaching him to recycle!

Ouch—those posts from the parent police sting!

When it comes to sensitive issues related to parenting, herd social media influence has now become an acceptable method of passing judgment in the court of public opinion. In a recent study of 475 mothers conducted by researchers at University of Michigan's C. S. Mott Children's Hospital, 61 percent admitted to having been criticized by their peers on topics ranging from diet and nutrition to breastfeeding to child care decisions.[6]

Here's what often happens: A mom tosses out an innocent question in a chat about the potential risks of childhood vaccines. Another mother assaults her for being ignorant about the subject. Others react to the emotional bomb and join in the fray—each one more seething than the next—assaulting the woman for daring to question the necessity of vaccines. Overnight, this escalates into an all-out stampede against the mom who asked a genuine question. In this way, a mom chat group can devolve into a swarm of bullies, wielding enough power to instantaneously trample this woman's reputation and, ultimately, brand her a "bad mother."

Magnolia Printz, MD, an anesthesiologist and influencer from Milwaukee, Wisconsin, who has a full house of four kids, is especially sensitive to this issue: "As moms, we get called out on that so easily. Like, if you're at the park with your kids and you're trying to multitask and write a quick email. Someone snaps a quick photo of you . . . it gets posted and then everyone piles on to shame you."

We all make minor and major mistakes and have done embarrassing things at various times in our lives. (I certainly have committed my share—especially during my childhood—and I'm glad there were no camera-encrusted smartphones around back then!) However, we are rarely prepared to see our mortifying actions captured and publicly broadcast, as frequently happens on social media. As if the original post isn't embarrassing enough, the other parents in the community—perhaps some outside as well—begin adding their comments expressing equal (if not greater) disdain. Suddenly, everyone becomes the behavioral police, judge, jury, and newscaster. Let the takedown begin! Comments start popping up. It takes only one to trigger a powerful tsunami of responses descending below it. Before long, dozens—perhaps even *hundreds or thousands*—of people follow the herd to shame a friend, neighbor, or someone they don't even know, seriously damaging feelings and reputations.

In March 2020, at the onset of the COVID crisis, a veteran air force tech sergeant named Matt Colvin and his brother, Noah, seized on an opportunity.[7] Anticipating a run on bottles of hand sanitizers, Noah ventured out to every drugstore he could in Tennessee and Kentucky to deplete their stocks of germ killer. On Noah's return, Matt posted approximately 17,700 hoarded bottles of hand sanitizer on Amazon.com at inflated prices. As bottle after bottle sold, the shortage of hand sanitizers became a national crisis for the American people. Upon exposure by the *New York Times*, the Colvins received a cease-and-desist letter from Amazon and a not-so-friendly warning from the state's attorney general, essentially stating that it's against the law to commit price gouging during a national disaster. While the brothers managed to evade a fine and being arrested, they did donate a substantial amount of sanitizer for free.

Did the Colvins commit a questionable business practice? Were they callous and socially irresponsible? While not everyone is capable of offering the Colvins the slightest ounce of forgiveness or sympathy for trying to support their families during hard times (and fewer admire their cunning interpretation of American capitalism), what happened next to the pair—as revealed on the Monica Lewinsky–hosted HBO Max program *15 Minutes of Shame*—should, by all accounts, be considered excessive.[8] Not only did they receive thousands of hate emails and texts, but they were also lambasted in social media feeds to such an extent that they had to shut down their accounts. When their home addresses were exposed—a practice known as *doxxing*—they were subjected to pizza order pranks and death threats. Their families' lives became so threatened that they had to install security cameras, which ended up being a smart move because they caught an intruder at their home bashing on the front door. Fearful for their lives, the families relocated. Someday, perhaps, we can reach a point in cases such as this when we say, "All right, enough is enough already," and social media influencers and account holders can stop pretending to be self-appointed judges and jury members.

Why do people feel emboldened to cast their views into the digital universe with greater ease than a fly-fishing pro? It's not what social media is, but rather what it isn't. What's lacking is the face-to-face interaction. It takes courage—a great deal of it, in fact—to say something critical to a person's face. When was the last time you gave unsolicited corrective feedback to someone in person? Probably a long time ago, right? Most people can't or won't do it. But the uncomfortable in-person barriers no longer exist on social media, and it's easy for even the most timid people to hurl attacks while in their fortresses of solitude clicking away on a phone or computer.

Mean Girls—and Boys

Social media shaming cuts even deeper when it comes to kids and teens. Public humiliation and various forms of bullying have always existed in schools and playgrounds, but now one child can boldly lash out at another with a post in just a few seconds and coax others in the group to jump in with even more shame. For attacked and ostracized preteens and teens, such treatment can have traumatic, lasting impact and can leave behind painful scars. Friendships can become severed as kids are pressured into choosing a side. This has led to escalating numbers of kids with social anxiety and depression and an increased suicide rate.[9]

Kids and teens are unfortunately ripe pickings for social media shaming. The school's influencers (the equivalent of the former "popular kids") can cast judgment on anyone anytime they like and utilize some pretty sly techniques for getting away with controversial posts (e.g., contemporary slang, euphemisms, and emojis that sail over parents' heads). *Fat shaming* is a common theme among adolescents, as is *skin shaming* (with regard to taunts against kids who have a lot of pimples or cases of severe acne) and *slut shaming* (accusing others, usually girls, of promiscuity).

For the most part, the digital shaming and abuse isn't occurring on Facebook, where parents tend to hang out. TikTok, Instagram, and Snapchat are the preferred social media arenas of Gen Zers (born between 1997 and 2012), where their behaviors stand a better chance of flying under the radar of authority figures who might otherwise reprimand them (although social media community guidelines have tightened up). This generation—the most digitally native of all age groups—is particularly hypersensitive to behaviors and language, which means the shaming takes on even greater significance. As one *Forbes* journalist recently put it, "They came of age during recessions, financial crises, war, terror threats, school shootings and under the constant glare of technology and social media. The broad result is a scared generation, cautious and hardened by economic and social turbulence."[10] Add to that the COVID pandemic and the January 6, 2021, attack on the United States Capitol by its own people, and you can understand why some Gen Zers could be just a wee bit apprehensive and cynical of the outside world.

THE HERD AS A COMMUNAL SUPPORT GROUP

We've discussed quite a bit of the "bad" and the "ugly," so now it's time to tackle the "good" when it comes to herd influence in social media. Although positive herd behaviors don't always get the attention they deserve, there exists a great deal of it in social media influence. This is especially true when it comes to giving a voice to unity, which sometimes bridges into humor.

In May 2021, model Dakota Fink posted a video that successfully pranked millions of boys and men. As she peeled off "skin" from her face—which was really a face mask—the video conveyed the message: "Throwback to when men didn't know we had to peel off layers of our skin after our period."[11] Many women went along with the inside joke, commenting lines such as "Thank you so much for normalizing this! Women don't need to be insecure about it!" "Literally did they not have a health class?" and my favorite, "I still remember how scared I was when I [had] to peel for the first time."

Fink brilliantly united millions of women across the globe in one of social media's biggest pranks. Her video received more than twenty-one million views, four million likes, and two hundred thousand comments—most of which were made by women. Believe or not, I later needed to duet her video to explain it was cap (false), as many people became convinced that women really do need to peel off their skin after a menstrual cycle, like a snake molting. It was entertaining to see some see guys trying to save face with replies along the lines of "Let's be honest, we all knew it was cap when we first saw it."

Through technology and communication, we have the capability to send out SOS word-of-mouth cries—not to Superman, but rather to the social media community as a collective superhero for help and/or counsel from a wide swath of people. The immediacy and simplicity of social media outreach enables an influencer, a micro-influencer, or working parents to fundraise for a worthy cause through crowdsourcing and start counting monetary donations within seconds of a post. Or an individual can request that friends send their collective prayers when her father goes into the hospital for emergency surgery.

One community story involving friends of mine, the Moores, comes to mind. The family had just moved from Los Angeles to Park City, Utah, in April 2021; Zeus, their beloved 180-pound dog, disappeared—presumably stolen. The Moores posted Zeus's photograph on Facebook and issued a desperate plea for everyone to help track him down. The herd spread the word. The following morning, a man named Nick

Kennedy in Salt Lake City heard howling in the rain near his workplace and brought the lost dog inside. Employees at the company spread word of the found dog through Facebook. Eventually, the two Facebook threads intersected, and Zeus was safely returned to the comforts and love of the Moores.[12]

I liken this to the famous "twilight bark" in the Disney animated film *One Hundred and One Dalmatians* when a chain of dog woofs, yelps, yaps, and howls gets passed along from one dog to another to sound the alarm bells and work together to save Pongo and Perdita's Dalmatian puppies from danger.[13]

Members of a social media herd are generally honored, if not thrilled, to stop what they are doing and support others for a variety of reasons; they may genuinely want to help, or they want to show off how smart, connected, and resourceful they are. In the world of social media, however, providing information to someone doesn't automatically mean it will be accepted above the recommendations from other people. As with all kinds of influence, there exists a hierarchy of credibility and trust based on a host of factors surrounding the expert. By way of an example: As a doctor and researcher, I would have a high amount of trust among my followers when answering questions about health. But I doubt anyone would take me seriously if I were to start making recommendations on where to find the best bridal dress (although I've never actually attempted to do this, so who really knows? Don't worry, I'm staying in my lane).

The stakes don't even necessarily have to be astronomically high or dire for the herd to come to the rescue. A family might be new to a neighborhood and need to find a trusted pediatrician to care for their kids. Maybe the toilet has backed up and you need a reliable plumber. Or perhaps you just need a recommendation of a great TV series to binge-watch. Whether one needs a local restaurant, barber, or real estate agent recommendation—or a tip on how to get a red wine stain off a white blouse—there is probably at least one expert in your community who has the perfect solution (or knows someone else who does).

There have also been documented cases of people who have had diseases identified based on posted social media videos, photos, and other content.[14] Not to encourage everyone to hang up a medical shingle without earning the proper degree and license, but research is showing that it is possible to identify certain conditions based on the appearance of an individual or perhaps even the background used in a photograph. An individual who habitually posts backdrops with dark blue and gray on Instagram may reveal telltale signs of mental illness.[15] The usage of frequent incoherent phrases or certain expletives might be a sign of substance abuse, while an increasing focus on religious language has been linked to diabetes. That's not to say that we are qualified to diagnose sailor-mouthed Uncle Fred as a drug addict or Mallomars-infatuated Aunt Sarah who posts regularly about both her chocolate-covered marshmallow confection and favorite saints as a diabetic.

Certain language may, in fact, may be attributable to something entirely unrelated to health, such as a person's profession. Did you know, for example, that accountants swear more than people in any other occupation? It's especially difficult to glean any information from language used in posts when an influencer hires someone else to write them.

Siyamak (Siya) Saleh, MD, a primary health care provider in Cape Town, South Africa, told me about how he has helped educate and raise awareness on various medical issues and made a difference to specific individuals. As he described, "I posted a video on anemia. One woman had severe anemia and didn't know. She went, got tested, and received a transfusion. She is feeling much better and her quality of life has changed."

My field of ophthalmology offers many potential circumstances for disease discovery in photographs posted by people in their social media feeds—presuming that the pictures were taken under optimal conditions (the subject is looking straight at the camera, the flash has been turned on, and red-eye reduction has been shut off).[16] For example, an "abnormal red reflex"—when a black, white, or yellow reflection appears in one eye's pupil and the other pupil is red, as expected from the camera flash—may be detected. This may be an indicator of an ocular tumor or disease. It goes without saying, I would not recommend playing doctor and diagnosing and treating yourself and/or others. But you could potentially use your social media influence to sound the "twilight bark" and urge the individual in the photograph to consult an eye doctor right away.

In the next chapter, "Brain Cravings," we are going to explore what social media influence, sex, chocolate, cocaine, and gambling share in common. Although they are all things people did more of during the 2020–2021 COVID-19 pandemic, that's not where I'm going with this.

3

Brain Cravings

Are Smartphones Better Than Sex?

I Am Not Addicted to Chocolate, Chocolate Is Addicted to Me

—*title of a book by Marie Myriam*

One in five velvet monkeys in the Caribbean seek out and imbibe fermented sugar (in layperson's terms, sweet booze).[1]

Tasmanian and Australian wallabies' addiction to poppy seeds—a.k.a. opium—is so powerful that they can devour enough of a field to engineer a physical crop circle.[2]

In the Amazon rain forest, some jaguars have been known to supplement their carnivorous diet with the leaves of the hallucinogenic yage vine.[3]

While we're on the subject of the feline family, we all know that the domesticated house cat craves catnip, which is also known as *Nepeta cataria*, catswort, catwort, and catmint. However, you may not know the reason why a cat can't resist the plant. It contains an essential oil, nepetalactone, that stimulates the olfactory part of the animal's brain and triggers the amygdala to respond with odd behavior (i.e., your kitty cat acts like a wobbling junkie).[4]

What does all of this mean? Science has proven that animals—wild and domesticated—are just as capable as human beings when it comes to partying and getting drunk, stoned, and high. Some creatures are even more prolific than we are when it comes to caving to their addictions. A marsupial based in Australia known as the male brown antechinus (which strikes me as a fancy name for a mouse) has continuous sex for *fourteen hours straight* (a feat even Sting can't match). The poor critter exhausts himself so much in this time span that afterward his immune system crashes and he drops dead.[5]

In the introduction and chapter 1, I described the effects of dopamine—a tiny yet powerful neurotransmitter that stimulates the pleasure centers. For humans and most animals, the presence of dopamine is what drives behavior because the instant gratification provides a memorable reward that is too tempting to resist.

We can blame dopamine for a large part of why human beings are compulsively lured to sex. The same may be said for recreational drugs, such as cocaine. Ditto for gambling. The blast of dopamine from these activities makes us feel *really good*, which is why we crave more and overindulge, sometimes to the point of addiction.

When eaten in moderation, dark chocolate has various health benefits (including cardiovascular-related) and simulates the dopamine effect on our systems. Let's say you are among the vast majority of people who worship chocolate. (If you aren't or have an allergy, just play along.) To obtain the chocolate, you usually have to get in your car, drive to the market, park, enter the store, purchase the chocolate, and then eat it. (In my case, it's often gone before I've returned to my vehicle and opened the door.)

Now, what do you suppose were to happen if the chocolate were more easily accessible to you? For example, let's say you could open up a cupboard at home and extract your favorite bar of chocolate. You'd be pretty thrilled and devour it. After tossing the wrapper away, you remember having seen another bar of chocolate in the cupboard when you snatched the first one.

Hmm, you think to yourself, *How amazing is this? I don't have to schlep to the store or order online and wait for it to arrive to get my fix. . . . Would one more hurt?*

Before you know it, the second bar of chocolate is in your hand and being ravaged.

Your dopamine high is soaring but with minimal effort and without any obstacles getting in the way. On finishing the second bar, you remember having spotted a *third one* in the cupboard. And into the cacao cave you go.

When you are on your smartphone and browsing your social media feeds for hours, take a wild guess at what is driving you to keep scrolling. *Dopamine.* For many people, the head rush from the impact of their smartphones becomes so overwhelming they neglect important areas of their lives to get hits from one engaging post after another. A 2021 survey conducted by the Sachs Media Group revealed that twice as many people would rather give up sex than their phones.[6] What a travesty—but at least STDs would be down.

Can you imagine how empty our beaches would be if the frisky horseshoe crabs (which engulf beaches with their libidinous activities every spring) had smartphones? On the other side of the equation, would the male brown antechinus have a longer life span if it had the ability to use Instagram and TikTok?

BRAIN SEDUCTION

There are four reward pathways in the brain for dopamine: the mesocortical, the nigrostriatal, the mesolimbic, and the tuberoinfundibular. Each time we take a bite of that chocolate bar, the dopaminergic pathways are stimulated and the dopamine river flows, reinforcing the behavior that stimulated it. There aren't any calories associated with social media activity, so, unlike chocolate, people don't get full after consuming too much of it and therefore keep hammering away. When dopamine is stimulated at random—like slot machines in casinos—it has a stronger reinforcing effect. Similarly, social media provides an unpredictable environment of receiving different amounts of views and likes. It's the unpredictable payout of slot machines and social media that is the key to their magnetism.

Today's most prevalent indicator of peer recognition—the view and like counts—sends a frenzy of dopamine activity through the pleasure centers. We feel good when our posts and reposts receive many views, likes, and positive emojis (such as smiling faces) because of the dopamine deluge. I've been guilty of getting buzzed from dopamine when a video blows up with millions of views and likes. We react to these social stimuli in the same way as if we were popping Hershey's Kisses in our mouths one after the other. Each piece of chocolate seems to be better than the last and, before we know it, the bag is empty. Transfer that to time spent on influencer pages, and we can begin to realize where we are easily frittering away countless hours throughout the day—not only from activity on our social media pages but also from the influencers we follow.

What happens when a new post appears on one of our social media pages from an influencer? *Ding!* The dopamine bell rings, causing us to us to become giddy with excitement to check it out. We need the immediate gratification watching it, clicking to see how many *whos* clicked *which* button and *what* others wrote in the comment section. In the words of fashion model and TV personality Kim Stolz, "We get one of those little pings on our smartphones, and we get a little hit of dopamine as well. We get excited. We feel anticipation. As we feel this, we want it more and more. So we spend more and more time looking at our phones."[7]

In almost every TikTok video I post, I'm amazed at the charge of followers who jockey to plant a stake in the comment section with the word "First" to claim that honor. Often, many people do so simultaneously, which sometimes leads to a mini battle in which they vie to prove who was first. I imagine they experience a potent shot of dopamine, since I experience it when I'm involved in the fervor to place a "first" stake to someone else's post.

BRAIN DRAIN

Adults and children alike feel warm and rewarded when they receive more than one hundred birthday wishes in social media, along with dozens of additional likes, virtual balloons with confetti, happy emojis, and endearing comments. Whether we admit it or not, our brains are floating from dopamine sloshing around in our heads caused by so much virtual love. These responses serve as proof that we matter to people and have become increasingly more meaningful than an old-fashioned Hallmark card, even though clicking "Like" is a much easier gesture than traipsing to the drugstore and sifting through dozens of corny card offerings lining the shelves.

On the flip side, what happens if we don't receive the requisite volume of online social media birthday rewards? Or when we hear crickets in response to a photograph that we thought was our best selfie or a video that garnered an anemic reception? Our pleasure centers feel a void and become agitated. The result? Unhappiness, loneliness, anxiety, stress, and, in some circumstances, depression—especially for children and teens. I experienced that more times than I'd like to admit in my early days of social media.

In one video, I donned one of my long female wigs to depict a scene in which a girl mistakenly uses a slice of lemon on her face to treat acne. (For the record: *do not do this!*) The video was to promote a podcast episode of my *No Cap Health Show*, where Dr. Muneeb Shah was my guest. I expected it to be a home run viral hit. Unfortunately, it tanked. I felt bummed that my creation didn't fly, even experiencing some emotional distress regarding the failure. My expectations had been high, since my first video to promote this podcast episode with Dr. Shah had been a hit. While wearing the wig, I taped potatoes on my face to demonstrate a different homegrown acne treatment. (Technically, potatoes have salicylic acid, a substance that can help combat pimples. I advise that you only use approved cosmetics with it, not tater tots.)

It is ironic that dopamine—which is deeply associated with our pleasure centers—can potentially lead to such terrible outcomes. Unfortunately, the human compulsion to become drawn to the exciting world of social media influence can innocently lead adults, teens, and especially children down various treacherous paths.

THIS NOBEL PRIZE WINNER WAS DOPE

Somehow I doubt most people have heard of a Swedish scientist named Dr. Arvid Carlsson. His contributions to the science of the human brain are well worth celebrating. Not only were Dr. Carlsson's discoveries helpful in the advent of creating drugs useful in treating Parkinson's disease, but in the 1950s he was the first scientist to identify dopamine as the neurotransmitter that passes signals from neuron to neuron. Although his dopamine research wasn't hailed at the time, it has since been recognized as foundational to all current thinking on the subject.[1]

NOTE

1. Denise Gellene, "Arvid Carlsson, Who Discovered a Treatment for Parkinson's, Dies at 95," *New York Times*, July 1, 2018, https://www.nytimes.com/2018/07/01/obituaries/arvid-carlsson-who-discovered-a-treatment-for-parkinsons-dies-at-95.html.

Since social media interaction on smartphones is a relatively new phenomenon, the scientific data on the subject is still being generated and examined. However, we don't have to look very far to see that kids can be hooked on their smartphones and would often much rather spend time in their beds under the covers with them than be prompted by parents to "go outside and play"—the old standby activity for Gen X and baby boomers when there was nothing else to do. Now, instead of playing imaginative games in the yard or hanging around a playground or at the mall with friends, kids and teens are often alone in their rooms with their phones, roaming from one social media account to another. Their primary interactions involve posting, sharing, commenting, and perhaps texting each other. We've come a long way from decades past when teens used to babble with each other for hours on a telephone, hogging up one landline! (Yes, I'm old enough to remember the old days of rotaries, wall phones with cords, busy signals, and crank calls that couldn't be identified with caller ID.) Teens are often so unaccustomed to *speaking* on their mobile phones that it's not uncommon for anxiety to be induced from the prospect of doing so.

As a result of current modes of communication and peer engagement, today's teens are dating much less than prior generations (56 percent versus 85 percent for both Gen X and boomers), and fewer seem to be interested in cars and driving.[8] Whereas nearly every boomer had a driver's license by the time of their high school graduation, only *one in four* high school graduates have them today. Should we bring back drive-in theaters to restore both cars and dates, which were integral to society in previous generations?

There may be some upside here—at least for overprotective parents like myself—that kids today are having a lot less sex than previous generations; on average, they are starting in eleventh grade—a full year later than Gen Zers did. Even more encouraging news: teen pregnancies have been declining 7 percent a year.[9]

I'm sure you're starting to get that queasy feeling that I'm about to drop the other shoe—and you are correct. The early science reveals that, as children and teenagers continue to turn to social media to maintain their DBB, *their brains are changing.* A recent study at UCLA among teenagers ages thirteen to eighteen tested the impact of Instagram likes on their brains with functional magnetic resonance imaging (fMRI) that measures blood flow changes in the brain. (Brain neuronal activity is coupled with blood flow changes, making this an invaluable tool.) The results were eye opening: an area of the brain—the left nucleus accumbens, which is kind of like a rewards center—lit up with activity when their photos were liked.[10] In another study, also utilizing MRI, adolescents were far more inclined to click "Like" on photographs that already had a substantial number of previous likes (which relates back to the herd mentality covered in the previous chapter).[11] At the same time, activity increased dramatically in the visual cortex connecting to the precuneus and the cerebellum. When less favorable photographs were shown, the MRI revealed that entirely different areas of the brain were stimulated: the left front cortex, the precentral gyrus, the middle frontal gyrus, and the inferior frontal gyrus.

Note that these brain changes occurred for only a brief time during the study under controlled circumstances. Imagine what occurs when young people—whose brains are still developing—are exposed to positive and negative social media influences for hours on end while typically unsupervised. To compound matters, we know that our kids are multitasking with their devices while allegedly doing homework and studying. The data thus far reveals that these common adolescent habits lead to smaller gray matter density in the anterior cingulate cortex.[12]

What do all these brain changes mean for our kids? If they are choosing social media for their dopamine kick over having sex, you know we should be concerned. Don't worry, I'm not encouraging them to go out and engage in more sexual activity (although I do recommend more in-person socialization). Abstaining may be the best alternative from several other perspectives—pregnancy, STIs, religious beliefs, and so forth—but doing so as a result of smartphone addiction is proving to be unhealthy for their brain development, as their executive functioning becomes taxed and then distractibility sets in.[13]

You've probably heard the cliché that "watching too much television fries kids' brains." Studies have shown that this is more than just an urban legend, albeit with this caveat: the amount of negative influence is largely dependent upon genetics.[14] (For example, a child who has aggressive DNA will be more likely to act out on that behavior subsequent to watching a violent action film, whereas the behavior of a nonaggressive child would remain unchanged.) When it comes to social media engagement, however, multiply that impact by ten, as adolescent brain centers—regardless of their DNA—are flicking on and off while their dopamine gushes with the power of Niagara Falls. When the dopamine floodgates dissipate and the brain "dries up," the child withdraws into isolation and becomes despondent, potentially leading to more serious mental health issues (e.g., depression).

Although the research is still in its infancy regarding long-term ramifications, several studies have been conducted examining the effects of social media on adolescents. In one such study, it was proven that children who randomly received fewer likes than others developed negative thoughts about themselves. In a second study, negative responses to a low amount of likes on a regular basis led to increasing depressive symptoms over the course of a school year. In a third study, those children who already admitted to having been bullied were even more sensitive to receiving fewer likes and therefore more prone to depressive symptoms.[15]

I hope I haven't deflated you with these findings. As I've laid out throughout this book, there are many positives of social media influence. But it can be like pulling a tulip from the ground when it comes to the double-faceted mental health of our children; the flower is beautiful, but the roots are gnarly. Are they learning from social media and establishing healthy connections with peers—or are some spending *too much* time on social media sites that prevent them from engaging in genuine social interaction, good study habits, and proper nutrition and exercise? Are they reading a book outside of school every once in a while? Are they relying solely on the number of likes to determine their self-worth?

If you or your child is exhibiting any signs of being uncharacteristically or excessively withdrawn, isolated, or moody, it might be worth checking in with your family's mental health care provider to try to assess the root cause and search for solutions while there is still time for a reboot.

IF SMARTPHONES ARE A DOUBLE-EDGED SWORD, WHICH EDGE IS BIGGER?

Are modern kids— particularly teenagers—any happier than those of prior generations? Before you answer, keep in mind that that they have complete access to everything they could or should want right on their smartphones in their palms: unlimited facts, advice, communication, entertainment, shopping, delivery services, and so much more. I know, I'm dating myself again, but when I was a kid and happened to flip on the TV at 3:00 a.m., all you'd see on most channels was static, *The Late Show*, or a grainy informercial about a mystical knife that could slice through a soup can and deliver perfectly julienned carrot sticks. Today, kids have access to HBO Max, Netflix, TikTok, YouTube, Grubhub, and unlimited porn 24/7. What more could any right-minded (or wrong-minded, depending upon your point of view) teen need?

Monitoring the Future has tabulated data revealing that kids and teens who spend more time on their screens are far unhappier than those who do it less. The amount of unhappiness for all age groups seems to *increase* commensurate with time spent on social media. When immersion time becomes chronic, the rate of depression begins to soar. Technology doesn't seem to be paving the road to happiness for kids and adolescents.[16]

Parents, therefore, face a major challenge. Three out of every four kids have a smartphone, and they can't be without one for a variety of reasons, including to stay in communication with their parents, to build and maintain friendships, and to remain current with technology (e.g., apps) that are beneficial in their daily lives. Even a daily calendar with reminders can serve as an excellent tool for them. Checking in with social media every now and then is typically fine, as long as schoolwork, friendships, exercise, and a healthy diet aren't sacrificed.

The reality is that parents set boundaries and rules for smartphones, just like with any other potential risk. Based on all available research, they are justified in being sticks in the mud setting time limits on smartphone usage and making sure their kids are doing their work while unplugged from social media. The alternative—kids with potentially altered brains and/or depression—is far less desirable in the long run.

KNOW WHEN TO FOLD—AND LOG OUT

Influencers are equally susceptible to the allurement of a dopamine rush. As plastic surgeon and influencer Ricky Brown, MD, an influencer based in Scottsdale, Arizona, said to me, "There is an adrenaline rush and a euphoria [when a post] goes viral. I know we all feel it. It's nuts."

From personal experience, I can also attest to the propulsion one receives throughout the process, which, for me, starts to percolate right away with researching and preparing a TikTok video and studying a hit list of competitive posts to ensure mine will be on point. I can already visualize the follower reactions of likes, comments, and shares, which inspires my creative juices. Once the post goes live, the real fun begins. Throughout my day, I check up on the reactions. I admit that, in the beginning, I was hooked—no matter what the responses might have been. If it's high out of the gate, I imagine breaking through with millions and millions of likes (the McDonald's of TikTok!). If it's low to start, could it just be a slow ramp-up, or is it foreshadowing a dud? I may feel anxious and worry about whether I've slipped up and if there is anything to do to juke the engagement level (which is kind of like pressing an elevator multiple times, hoping it will get me to my floor faster).

Yes, it feels like I'm at a casino—I slip in my coins, pull the lever, and hope for three cherries to roll together in unison. My pulse races as I rub my hands together and salivate at the possibility that this one is going to be the biggie.

I'm getting close to reaching a milestone. Will it be the one to get me to the next million followers level?

The unpredictability of the reward is what makes it feel so exciting. I might bomb or hit the jackpot. People might send me heart and love smiley emojis or the opposite (make nasty comments). Either way, I am human, and the emotional highs and lows are certainly real and not beneath me. While I feel disappointed when I miss, the feeling is perishable as I get over it just as soon as my next TikTok video comes into focus, at which point I start all over again with a clean slate.

Detroit, Michigan–based Tony Youn, MD, a plastic surgeon, influencer, and author of the foreword to this book, describes it this way: "It's like gambling, you don't know when the next big one will hit. I think it becomes an obsession . . . getting that dopamine response when you are posting a video. [At first] you don't get a whole lot of engagement and, all of a sudden, by your fourth one [video], everybody's engaging in it, and you see a million views. More than that, you get all these comments and your follower count goes up . . . it really is a dopamine rush. And therein lies the challenge."

Karan Rajan, MRCS, MBBS, BSc, a general NHS (National Health Service) surgeon in London, experiences similar sensations: "[It's] like when you're gambling, and you're on a roll at the craps table. [You wonder] how long this is going to go—how much money are you going to make on that table? Where's the ceiling? And then, once that falls off, you're looking for that next dopamine rush."

One of the most exciting aspects of TikTok for me is the ability to prove or disprove facts. As a medical practitioner and researcher, I can help people in a lot of ways—such as helping them save money on a treatment that is ineffective, helping prevent them from doing something that is somewhat dangerous or giving validation to a natural remedy—but mostly clearing up myths and fallacies. There is a lot of bogus information out there. Once in a while, I'll manage to provide information and receive feedback that it will improve someone's life. For example, in response to one of my TikTok Live streams, a follower commented that she now wears sunscreen on her face. (Sunscreen has been scientifically proven to reduce wrinkles and the risk of skin cancer.) This comment certainly made me feel like I'm making a genuine difference to people as an influencer, which gives me another jolt of dopamine and inspires me to create more videos like that one.

A key difference from gambling, however, is that there are incentives that provide currency for a post. Views, likes, comments, and shares are wonderful, but there is an extra boost when people tag their friends in comments. Sometimes in TikTok people will create a *duet*. Followers (or nonfollowers) can also create their own reaction video follow-up and *stitch* it to mine before reposting. Influencers love this, as you gain even more notoriety for the post and continue to get the credit.

In the prologue, I came clean with my TikTok addiction and its impact on my family. Since then, I have done my best to make amends and straighten out my ways with them. That's not to say I'm perfect and haven't had occasional lapses. On one occasion, I took my daughters to a volleyball tournament. As time passed, I had such an overwhelming itch to do a TikTok Live that I squirreled out of the tournament toward my car. Once inside the vehicle, I slid on my TikTok doctor outfit—scrub top, hat, and mask around my neck—and aired a TikTok Live for about an hour. I changed and sneaked back to attend the rest of the tournament.

No harm, no foul—right? Wrong! What I didn't realize is that some of my daughters' teammates happened to follow me on TikTok. During the lunch break, they were notified that I was "live" on TikTok and informed my girls. You can imagine my humiliation at being caught ducking out of their tournament to satisfy my TikTok addiction. On the way home, the silence from my daughters made it clear that the roles were reversed and this time I was the guilty child who had been caught red-handed.

In September 2020, BusinessInsider.com published an article titled "Social Media Is a Parasite, It Bleeds You to Live." The premise is that the sole purpose of social media apps is to simulate the effect of casino slot machines on the human brain. As the author writes, "They entice with promises of validation and reward. Your work is shared widely. Your cause is amplified. You get a dopamine fix from positive reactions, or even any reactions."[17] In other words, social media sites leave candy crumbs at every turn to lure the user back.

It's been reported that 80 percent of phone users check their smartphones within fifteen minutes of opening their eyelids in the morning.[18] In the spirit of full transparency, I admit that I am one of them, largely because I use it as my alarm. I say to myself, *Since I now have my phone in my hand, let's see how it's going on TikTok.* Such addictive behaviors can make you anxious—especially if you start your day with them—distracted, less productive, and inattentive to your work and people around you.

When I silenced social media apps from my phone, I found myself newly endowed with several extra hours in my day, renewed mental bandwidth, and freer imagination that would have been lost to *doom-scrolling* (spending an inordinate amount of time on apps and sites that usurp your time, often focus on negative news, and can be misleading and sometimes even dangerous). You don't need to go medieval on abstinence; rather, you can selectively delete certain apps and stop giving the social media sites so much of your lifeblood. If you must stay tuned to certain influencer feeds, at least silence the whiplashing notifications and alerts about the most recent viral dog or cat videos and celebrity scandals. (I can neither confirm nor deny that my wife is guilty of falling into the dog video black hole.) All of that constant buzzing, dinging, and bleeping is flooding your brain with dopamine, as you can't resist checking out the latest tidbit. Once you are hooked and Pavlovian, you feel as if every sound and vibration that your phone makes is a matter of life or death, since you likely have come down with a serious case of FOMO (fear of missing out).

Fayez Ajib, DO, an emergency physician and influencer based in Miami, Florida, made a conscious decision to silence notifications for social media apps during certain times of day to avoid distraction. "You know the saying 'out of sight, out of mind'?" he asked. "That is really true because I'll work out or do work. When I finish, I'm say to myself, *Oh man, I haven't checked TikTok in [something] like seven hours.* So that's helped me bring down the amount of time I spend on these apps. It can become time consuming and, right now in residency, I want to spend the majority of my time focusing on becoming an emergency doctor. It's all about prioritization."

Naturally, there are some forgivable areas when it comes to staying attuned to one's passions. If you are a sports fan, it's probably fine to get alerts of your team's scores, the standings, player injuries, and such. If you want to keep abreast of major news headlines, a single reputable news source is probably all you need. No matter which side of the political spectrum you are on, avoid alerts containing any smack of political propaganda, as they are intended to rile you up.

Now that we have identified what social media influence can do to our brains, we are next going to investigate why children and teens have a greater propensity to be lured by influencers who have nefarious intentions.

4

Easy Prey

Why Are Our Young So Susceptible to Influencers?

It is morally as bad not to care whether a thing is true or not, so long as it makes you feel good.

—*Edmund Way Teale,* Circle of the Seasons[1]

I don't in any way pretend to be a parenting guru and will not attempt to use this space to convert this book into a parenting guide. Having twin teenage daughters may earn me an annual Father's Day card and, someday, a well-deserved Purple Heart, but I am far from an expert and don't intend to offer any parenting advice here, except for two things: (1) never pretend to know more about social media than your kids, as they can outclick you under and over the table; and (2) avoid corny dad jokes—guaranteed, they will hold this against you.

Instead, we're going to investigate the brain chemistry, neuroscience, and psychology behind why our young are such easy prey to social media influencers. The influencer universe provides acceptance, feelings of being special, and a false sense of close proximity to fame. Influencers provide the additional lure of being cool—but beware if they tout the joys of irresponsible activities, such as overindulging in alcohol and junk food.

We'll also investigate how parents accept at least some ownership of their children's lost innocence when it comes to having created their digital footprints so early on, often before they have even taken their first step. Lastly, we'll probe what might happen to young, famous influencers themselves when they grow up: Will they be able to make the transition to a successful career, or are they headed toward a bleak future?

This is not to suggest all influence for kids is bad, is irresponsible, and/or conveys empty content. Quite a few influencers offer rich educational information that can improve young lives. Australian former medical student, newly minted doctor, and influencer Sarah Rav, MD, for example—known as the "Queen of StudyTok"—provides entertaining tips and hacks for students on subjects such as "The Best Way to Take Notes for Online Classes" and "The Best Music for Studying." Dr. Rav, who started on Instagram when she was fifteen, says she aids kids who "might not have otherwise had access to a tutor or access to additional help from outside of school . . . and so they don't fall behind or fall through the cracks."

Another positive impact of social media for kids is how easily it provides connectivity to people with access to content all over the world. Josh Otusanya, an influencer and comedian based in Seattle, Washington, who happens to be first-generation Nigerian American, is able to reach family and friends in London, Dubai, and all over the globe. As he describes, "We're in an age where anybody can have access to infinite amounts of information [that people] didn't have access to before. A lot of kids don't realize how much free information is being delivered to them. In some areas around the world, this enables them to be more educated than the generations before them."

That said, we all need to become informed, on guard, and vigilant against the potential short- and long-term repercussions of what may occur to our young when it comes to the uncontrolled world of social media influence. We have a generation born between 1997 and 2012—known as Gen Z—who have had constant influencer exposure during their formative years at a time when there have been virtually no guardrails in place and they are neurologically most vulnerable. What could possibly go wrong?

THEY'RE A PISTOL

What weighs twenty-five grams (.06 pounds), is four centimeters long (1.6 inches), lives in coral reefs, and packs a killer punch?

This isn't a riddle or joke. Pistol shrimp, part of the Alphidae family, are tiny folks that have a special power to influence their prey, which include small crabs, other shrimp, gobies, and marine worms. Pistol shrimp have a large pincer—sometimes as big as the body—that creates a massive force. When the claw "snaps," it fires off a nasty shock wave of bubbles (well, powerful for a creature that's only four centimeters long) that is as scorching hot as the sun (8,000 degrees Fahrenheit) for just a fleeting moment. The energy produced is louder than a gunshot. Through this sonic targeting, the prey is immediately incapacitated. Then: dinner time![2]

I bring up pistol shrimp superpowers not to imply that influencers literally paralyze and consume anyone, but rather to paint a metaphorical picture of what they can do to our children. Children and teenagers have flocked to social media as their go-to source for maintaining DBB (as explained in the introduction, as well as chapters 1 and 3), which correlates with distractibility and increased prefrontal activity among adolescents and young adults. (We'll get into more about the role of the prefrontal cortex soon enough.) A reduced sense of delayed gratification was observed among a group of heavy smartphone users, reflecting heightened impatience. Researchers found that this result correlated with structural white matter connectivity in the brains of the participants—an area of the brain implicated in reward processing and executive control over behavior.[3] These changes are occurring at dopamine levels that could pickle any child's brain. The end result for our kids is analogous to getting hit by a pistol shrimp every few seconds, except that it feels good, and they want to do it again.

Even just the advance thought of an impending dopamine hit can drive certain behaviors. In one study, rhesus macaque monkeys were provided with information about a reward involving water. Although they didn't need the water at that particular moment, their dopamine rose just from the simple knowledge that the water—not something more enticing, like bananas—exists for a later time.[4]

The same may be said for kids and teens before they begin surfing influencer pages; they have an idea of what might be in store for them, so they may have a dopamine rush preceding the actual one that draws them in. Once they see the title of a particular video, they get an even greater sense of what is coming, and the dopamine begins its assault. TikTok's FYP (For You page) is extremely potent in terms of building this massive sense of anticipation. When a follower swipes up on a current video, a new, seemingly unrelated one—but, in reality, based on the user's click history—pops up that can feel irresistible to the viewer.

THE DEVELOPING ADOLESCENT BRAIN

Are children and teenagers most susceptible to peer opinions and influencers because their brains and identities are not wholly developed? The answer is an emphatic *yes*. It's been known for some time that certain parts of the human brain develop at different times—from birth through young adulthood. Scientists have proven that the prefrontal cortex, which resides just behind the forehead, sprouts again just before puberty (age twelve for boys; eleven for girls) and does not finish maturing and pruning until age twenty-five.[5]

Why is this fact so important? The prefrontal lobe is the control center of the brain, managing and coordinating many functions—organization, decision-making, social behavior, and mood. The time frame before and during adolescent growth of the prefrontal cortex is tantamount, as this is when the brain matures and soaks up important information. Whatever the brain retains during this period has the potential to stick forever as learned. By the same token, whatever is discarded tends to go *poof*!

In his acclaimed book *Before You Know It*, John Bargh, PhD, describes what happens to the human brain subsequent to a stroke.[6] Victims of this medical event suffer losses in one or more of several important functions: memory, speech, vision, or emotion. Take a wild guess which part of the brain has been damaged—the prefrontal cortex. Surprised? Stroke victims have essentially lost their brain's CEO, which had provided purpose and direction for myriad functions. When the boss calls it quits, the corporation becomes aimless. Dr. Bargh refers to various cases in which stroke patients seem capable of performing routine tasks utilizing parts of their bodies but then perform them without any rhyme or reason. For example, stroke patients were able to drink a glass of water without difficulty. However, when patients' empty glasses were refilled in front of them, they continued to drink nonstop—even though they were full and not the least bit thirsty.

A healthy, maturing adolescent might be incredibly bright and talented, receiving straight As in school and raves for maturity. At the same time, as the prefrontal cortex is expanding, certain aspects of judgment might be clouded—like the stroke victim who has lost some control in that area. The teen might not be guzzling unlimited glasses of water, but the CEO in the brain would not yet be experienced or knowledgeable enough to think critically about information imparted by influencers. Kids and teens are consuming glass after glass of influencer recommendations, ideas, opinions, and miscellaneous content, even if they are unnecessary and or unsuitable. Their Perceptual Intelligence is already at a serious disadvantage due to the timing of their brain development.

This may help explain extreme trends that have no logic whatsoever and yet somehow find a way to catch on among kids in the social media space. During our conversation, influencer Krysten Mayers informed me about girls who "were going around saying that they have to cut off a piece of their genital area every month to stop it from growing. I think it was originally done to trick boys. But, you know, some girls actually believed it and harmed themselves."

For those parents who think their adolescent kids are "going dumb" when they have unexpected lapses in judgment and decision-making—or you simply don't understand why they are drawn to certain things you consider too dangerous and/or mature for their age—cut them some slack. Their prefrontal cortexes are going through a makeover at the same time their hormones are raging—which can become a dangerous combination, don't you think?

THE INSECURE ADOLESCENT BRAIN

There are other major changes that occur during adolescent development, including hypothalamic-pituitary-adrenal (HPA) axis reactivity, which, when flared up, leads to an increase of stressed-out hormones.[7] As if kids don't have enough challenges, let's make them more anxious and insecure by raising their sensitivity response levels!

As adults, when we lack confidence addressing an issue because we don't have enough time to research it, we take a shortcut—sometimes trusting the opinion of an authority figure, who may be a celebrity. Imagine what happens to insecure, anxious children and teens in these situations, who rely heavily on influencers as their primary information source.[8] Are they walking around with an extension cord looking for someone to plug into?

Swedish researchers probed this phenomenon by studying the influence of YouTube personalities on kids. By examining the impact of a particular Swedish YouTuber (a young girl named Misslisibell, who provided a tutorial on makeup), the researchers found that kids were more likely to adopt influencers' attitudes and beliefs, even when they were unrelated to products and brands.[9] They determined that YouTubers helped construct identities among children and serve as their role models, impacting what personas they wished to take on and project themselves. Once influencers have established this type of relationship with young followers who have low self-esteem, it becomes even easier for them to earn their followers' trust as an information and product recommendation source.

Question: *Who usually becomes class president?* Easy answer: *the most popular kids.*

Our children, who usually have no desire to spend time researching a product or service, take the most expedient shortcut when making a purchase: they do not hesitate to follow the recommendations of a popular influencer to get that powerful, immediate shot of dopamine and find any way to fill their buckets with self-confidence. This is especially true when a child is insecure and part of a peer group that follows the same figure and goads each other into making the same trendy purchasing decisions.

THE ILLUSION OF BEING SPECIAL

Children can also become seduced by the charms of influencers because they may not yet be sophisticated enough to discern reality from orchestrated fantasy. They may have no idea what's real or not while flitting from one social media site to the next; reality can be blurred. It is not easy for children to recognize whether an influencer is who they say they are, which means children can literally be taking the experience at face value.

When kids develop an emotional connection to an influencer, a dynamic known as a parasocial relationship (PSR) forms. This is not a true social relationship, and yet it seems like one to the individual being influenced because the brain interprets the strong emotional connection as if it were the real thing. Children yearn for companionship even more than adults, which is why they are so drawn to these parasocial relationships.[10]

Who are the people serving as role models and making our children feel special today? Where might they be found? What lessons are they imparting to our children? Are these individuals the same people in real life as they appear on smartphones, laptops, and computer screens?

The fact is, influencers may or may not have any legitimate credentials whatsoever, except for one or more of the following: a certain visual look and appeal; online charisma and passion; a semblance of knowledge in a niche area; an unusual skill or talent; a creative ability to make videos or take selfies; an opinion or perspective that engages others to follow; or a flair for writing posts consisting of 280 or fewer characters.

In chapter 1, I introduced the concept of *authenticity*. What does this mean for our children when it comes to their influencers?

Way back in 1969, a young Presbyterian minister in a cardigan sweater and tie named Fred Rogers hosted a children's program on PBS: *Mister Rogers' Neighborhood.* Rogers's reassuring smile and gentle manner enabled him to educate, entertain, comfort, and, in his way, influence young people with social lessons. Parents and children alike implicitly trusted this nice man on the TV set.[11]

How did Rogers do it? Authenticity. He was a genuinely caring individual who sought to make children feel special. Many of the songs he wrote and performed on his television show, such as "You're Special" and "I Like You as You Are," were intended to produce that experience for his young viewers.

I don't have any doubt that "what you saw was what you got" with Mr. Rogers. He had no agenda, except to introduce universal values and help kids feel good about themselves. I'm sure he had to wear some typical stage makeup and hair product, but, other than that, he was the real deal (and his cardigans were his own; his mother knitted them for him).

As for today's social media influencers . . . we simply don't know. Each one is different and, as of this writing, there isn't a network (such as PBS) or a governing body (such as the Federal Communications Commission, a.k.a. FCC) to vet influencers, review their content, or, when necessary, provide parental warnings (although all social media platforms have community guidelines). They have proven virtual authenticity to their followers.

It's reasonable that large numbers of today's influencers make themselves up for the screen; after all, their images appear on millions of devices in the blink of an eye. What personality in any medium wouldn't want to look their best and relatable in front of such a wide audience?

The difficulty for kids and teens is whether they possess the ability to distinguish between what is real and what is online illusion. Once again, their Perceptual Intelligence becomes challenged. It's one thing for an influencer to look spectacular, but we run into problems if that individual is made up to resemble someone they are not and pretend the façade is real. The goal is not only authenticity but also to "look like us" in a natural—albeit glamorized or conceptually ideal—way. What would kids think if they knew the great lengths some influencers went to in order to create this convincing illusion? In some cases, they are spending as much time preparing their physical appearances as actors in a film or on a TV show. Some meticulously plan hair, makeup, and outfits for what *feels like* an organic video or photo. Are they really using each and every product they have recommended on their accounts? Do the children watching and clicking realize that their heroes and heroines may be merely pretending and are being paid to advertise those products?

It was clear to everyone who watched *Mr. Rogers' Neighborhood* that his universe was pure fantasy, although the living room itself was far from anything fancy. It's doubtful any child past or present would believe that Mr. Rogers's actual home was filled with colorful sets, a trolley, a castle, and talking and singing puppets.

The world of an influencer is a different story. Influencers typically invite their communities into their homes, revealing what appears to be an intimate glimpse into their private lives—sometimes directly inside the sanctity of their bedrooms. If the on-screen background is indeed the influencer's legitimate inner sanctum, could it still be a staged set? The followers see what the influencers and their handlers (some have them) wish viewers to experience. Everything contributes to the brand in some manner, shape, and form.

How does this make the children feel? Special. Accepted. Privileged that they can get so close to celebrity on a regular basis. To be sure, regarding the last benefit, such perceived proximity to a star is simply not attainable through a television or film screen, which lacks the intimate feel of social media.

In this instance, the specialness of being accepted into the influencer's world provides a feeling of immediacy, connectedness, and intimacy that has never before been experienced between a celebrity (influencer) and a fan (follower). Imagine if we were to go back a few decades and have had such special pseudoprivate access to Hollywood starlets such as Marilyn Monroe, Rita Hayworth, and Jayne Mansfield; the paper tabloids wouldn't have stood a chance. On the one hand, the studio-built mystiques of these personalities would be gone; on the other hand, viewers would feel as if they were personal friends with Marilyn, Rita, and Jayne—people previously considered so distant and far out of reach that the word *star* was aptly applied to them.

No matter which way we examine it, however, the influencer/follower dynamic is a one-sided emotional relationship providing the illusion of closeness and friendship. The literal meaning of the word *follower* in of itself implies a passive stance. The likes, the purchases, the gushing comments, and so forth are the equivalent of preferential bows in deference to the acknowledged leader. Such dedication becomes liquid currency for influencers, product marketers, and advertisers.

COOL RECOMMENDATIONS

Believe it or not, Ryan Kaji of Ryan's World is a ten-year-old YouTuber (a.k.a. "vlogger") who presently has more than *thirty million subscribers*. His usual video involves taking viewers along his daily routine, including eating breakfast. He opens toys and then reviews them in what appears to be an organic manner—not in a traditional type of staged commercial. Kids feel they have a special relationship with their "friend" Ryan and implicitly trust his recommendations. The emotional feelings that children have when an influencer's relationship connects them to a product in this way is known as *meaning transfer*.[12]

Ryan has the ability to tap such follower emotions to the tune of *$29.5 million earned* in one year. He now has a line of his own branded toys, clothes, and home goods that are offered at Target, Walmart, and

Amazon. He has even starred in his own TV show, *Ryan's Mystery Playdate*, on Nickelodeon since 2019.

Few people have questioned the integrity of Ryan, his family, or his bank account. But . . . are his recommendations 100 percent legitimate? One must wonder, especially since Truth in Advertising filed a claim on August 29, 2019, asserting that "nearly 90 percent of the Ryan ToysReview videos have included at least one paid product recommendation aimed at preschoolers, a group too young to distinguish between a commercial and a review."[13] So, to paraphrase the earlier question: Does Ryan genuinely use all those toys? While we don't know for sure in his case, interviews with teen influencers reveal that they often use brands they fully support, but there are always exceptions.[14]

ADVERTISING AND THE MODERN FAMILY

It wasn't so long ago that suburban family shopping took place primarily in the local mall. The mom would drag her tykes from store to store and maybe give the little ones a ride on an electronic pony and reward them with ice cream at the end of a long day browsing the aisles.

The dynamic has now completely—and perhaps permanently—changed. The influencer kids dictate what is cool (such as clothing and toys), and then the followers beg their parents to click the links and make the purchases. (One can only hope most children don't have unlimited access to credit cards!) For busy parents, this may be a something of a relief, if not a blessing. They no longer have to deal with driving to the mall, battling over a parking spot, trudging through stores, hunting sales, scavenging the shelves and racks for the right sizes, waiting for the kids to try things on in the fitting rooms, and dealing with cashier lines. Best of all, they might save themselves the embarrassment of their kids throwing tantrums in the parking lot.

It's not a news flash that online shopping has been gradually overtaking the brick-and-mortar retail marketplace—the COVID-19 pandemic and social distancing have added jet fuel to that trend. Now, for better or for worse, it's been reported that "73% of kids ask their parents to buy something after seeing recommendations online by kids influencers."[15]

In addition to previously mentioned issues related to brain development, hormones, and self-esteem, children are particularly vulnerable to influencer advertising because of underdeveloped advertising literacy—the ability to recognize and critically evaluate advertisements.[16] Advertisers (including on influencer pages) know this fact all too well and can target their advertising to exploit the developing—all right, I'll just say it, *naïve*—adolescent brain.[17]

The world of influencer advertising is already huge business, estimated to exceed $16 billion by the end of 2022.[18] Since we are only at the beginning of this phenomenon and very little of the advertiser/influencer relationship is monitored or regulated, the ocean floor is bottomless. Online marketing platforms, such as One Impression, have become the new advertiser talent scouts, scouring the universe for the next appealing kidfluencer to make the coolest choices (meaning their clients' clothing, toys, and other products).

WHAT DOES THE FUTURE HOLD FOR CHILD INFLUENCERS?

Has anyone seriously asked the following questions:

Q: What child labor laws exist protecting young influencers?[19]

A: *None.*

Q: What will become of all these wealthy young social media influencers?

A: *Your guess is as good as mine.*

Q: Will they grow up and learn to take selfies, post videos, and recommend products on screens?

A: *Wait—don't they already do this?*

Q: Will their followers stand by them as their voices change and they age to adulthood?

A: *Lemme consult my crystal ball.*

What will become of child influencers if they ever fall from grace (e.g., scandal), become prey to capitalist marketers, or, worst of all, end up irrelevant? (Speaking from my adult experience, this is the greatest fear for any influencer.) Without unique skills, what do they have to fall back on for the long term? Given the trials and tribulations of young Hollywood celebs maturing into adulthood, I foresee a rocky path for at least some of them, unless the supports are put in place from their families for career plan B (including a proper education).

We can only hope that their inner circles have their best interests at heart and that they are factoring in the long term lives of their children in their decision-making. If the stage moms of the past are any indication—everyone from Rose Thompson Hovick (mother of burlesque star Gypsy Rose Lee) to Patsy Ramsey (mother of JonBenét Ramsey, the young child beauty pageant winner who was murdered)—it is in our best interests to pay attention to the future welfare of our kidfluencers. This is especially worrisome when we consider that it's now common-place for parents to present their offspring to the world when the little ones are too young to have a say in the matter; in fact, they may not even be old enough to speak. Allow me to explain. . . .

TO *SHARENT* OR *OVERSHARENT*—THAT IS THE QUESTION
In one important respect, our children are by no means at fault for how they have been sucked into the world of social media influence. Children are introduced into the virtual world long before they have been delivered into the real world. It's been estimated that at least one-quarter of sonogram images are posted online. The online attention for babies accumulates over time: one-third of all parents share photos of their newborns from hospital rooms. If you're a parent, can you relate? At least you're in good company. These posts are followed by the myriad obligatory pix of them being welcomed home by friends and family. It continues over the years through pictures of birthdays, the first day of nursery school and grade school, communion or bar/bat mitzvah, graduations, summer camp, prom, and on and on. . . .

Consider this statistic: In the United States alone, 92 percent of two-year-olds already have an online presence.[20] This all seems great and wonderful for friends and family, but what of the children themselves? How much of this digital footprint has been disseminated among marketers and product advertisers without permission? What will happen in the next wave of advancement when facial recognition technology extends to social media? How many targeted lists do these two-year-olds already appear on? This is only the tip of the iceberg when one shovels on the volume of scams and predatorial activity that is so pervasive on the internet.

We rightfully think of online predators as the worst kind of lurking evil, baiting and luring in our children online. These individuals are indeed terrifying; for all we know, they could be our seemingly harmless neighbors. But how did our children get hooked on the internet in the first place? Who is responsible for having created such an extensive, well-cataloged library for the entire public to browse?

The answer is obvious: *parents.* As harmless as it may seem, mothers, fathers, and perhaps other guardians are the ones responsible for initiating the massive digital profiles of their children and making it seem like the expected thing to do all along. This raises the question: *What legal rights and protections, if any, do children have from their own parents who innocently—and perhaps recklessly—post whatever they want?*

I'm not deriding parents for being proud of their children and wanting to share their beauty with others. This is an understandable activity, and, of course, my wife and I are guilty too, via Facebook and my patient newsletters. The dilemma—which no one has adequately addressed—is when parents overdo sharing (including to friends or followers they don't know), which causes the data and content to mount, circulate, and fester. In addition to being fodder for influencer marketers and advertisers—as well as predators of all varieties—there is the obvious simple and overlooked issue few parents consider: *a child's legal right to privacy.*

As with all new things, a fresh term has been coined to address this issue: *sharenting.* In short, this refers to the variety of ways that parents can share information, images, and other content about their children. The word exposes an inherent conflict between parents' right to dictate how and what they reveal about their children and the kids' right to keep their information to themselves.

JOHNNY B. GOOD

One notable story involves Johnny, an eight-year-old boy with ADHD who was suspended from school several times for behavioral issues.[1] His mother posted photos of her son, along with school reports of his misbehavior, on social media in the hope of finding tips and solutions from others and sharing her learnings with other parents facing similar situations. The posts evolved into a blog, which has now drawn in a substantial following.

Everything seems well and good, right? Johnny's mom has performed a valuable service for her son, while at the same time helping other moms. There is one tiny sponge left after the operation: As the years progress, how will adult Johnny feel about his entire childhood ordeal having been blasted across the social stratosphere? Will his digital footprint—which he's had zero input on—have an impact on his future college admittances, job applications, and relationships? Putting all those issues aside, what if Johnny's childhood becomes an embarrassment to him later on and, from an emotional standpoint, he just wants to put it all behind him? With a Bigfoot-sized digital footprint already out there, how will he ever escape it?

NOTE

1. Stacey B. Steinberg, "Sharenting: Children's Privacy in the Age of Social Media," *Emory Law Journal* 66, no. 4 (2017), https://scholarlycommons.law.emory.edu/elj/vol66/iss4/2/.

The law is now struggling to map out a policy that does not encroach on parental rights or their decision-making authority but at the same time protects the child's right to privacy. The challenging questions for lawmakers to answer: *At what age do children have enough authority to go up against their parents? How can the law weigh in on this subject when there is already so much gray area about what type of content might cross the line?*

Things seemed so much simpler prior to the internet. Newspaper and magazine articles lacked the immediacy and potential impact of a blog posting; in many cases, the editorial staffs of the publications would weigh in on what subjects were deemed appropriate for public consumption. Although such things did become public, there was less editorial space available for the average person than in today's limitless blogosphere, and the most extreme reportage was often saved for the *National Enquirer.*

Let's examine a more "positive" example from the past: A proud mom might have waltzed into a professional photographic studio with her beautiful newborn baby in the hope she might be recognized and molded into becoming a magazine model. The parent would sign all the requisite waivers and the photographs would make the rounds. One in a million of these cherubs would ultimately become famous.

Now, let's compare the above with a modern sharenting scenario: What if a parent were to post a photo of her child to shame the child for misbehavior? This is happening with alarming frequency. Some desperate parents have exposed their children's misdeeds in public online forums with the intent of embarrassing them enough to reverse their behaviors. Such online discipline rarely works; if anything, the children resent their parents and wear these displays as a badge of honor. A few enjoy the attention and become incentivized to commit worse acts of rebellion. They may encourage others to do the same.

Again, what will happen to these kids when they grow up and their youthful antics have already been seen by thousands or millions of people and still remain accessible via Google search? Should children have to pay their entire lives for what they did at thirteen years of age? The debates on this subject will continue for many years, long after parents have already disclosed volumes of information about their children. For now, parents have more immediate concerns about the welfare of their offspring, notably in terms of following adult influencers who act irresponsibly—sometimes driving their platforms without a clutch.

INFLUENCE AND UNDER THE INFLUENCE

It took many years—as well as legal battles—for it to happen, but regulators in the United States were ultimately able to clamp down on the advertising of harmful products, such as alcohol and cigarettes, that targeted minors. You'd think at least some of these laws and restrictions might have been applied to the internet; unfortunately, as with everything else, loopholes were created and work-arounds set in motion. While traditional ads and banners are closely monitored for such suspicious content, one thing tends to slip past scrutiny: influencer posts. This is especially alarming when one considers how—as we established earlier in this chapter—kids and teens are susceptible to these things because of their developing brains and highly impressionable psychology.

According to a study at the University of Amsterdam, there is a great deal to be concerned about when it comes to posts from influencers that toast the merits of imbibing.[21]

Kids are instinctively drawn to such risky content as vaping, and, as we all know too well, if it's out there, they are sure to find it.

The statistics from the aforementioned study are sobering: 64 percent of influencers surveyed posted favorable content about alcohol. In all likelihood, the influencers didn't think twice about the ages of their followers when they recommended certain alcoholic beverages and/or joked about the benefits of drinking and partying. Many posts included photographs and videos of people laughing, having a good time, and doing things they considered cool. The clear-cut message conveyed: drinking is a fun game, and there are no consequences to bingeing. Imagine if Mr. Rogers were to have ever recommended a martini instead of a glass of orange juice!

Additional studies are revealing that influencers are contributing to the continuing increase in preteen and teen alcoholism.[22] This shouldn't surprise you, since the influencers seem "attractive, trustworthy, and expert" and, as previously stated, their underage followers have a difficult time distinguishing between them and genuine, responsible authorities. Since social media influencers are not considered strangers to the kids and are trusted, the young followers are even more likely to listen to their alcohol recommendations than they would any warnings or cautionary tales from a pop star, film star, or TV star.

The pump-the-brakes-on-what-you're-doing-and-listen-to-this fact: one-third of all teens ages fourteen to seventeen search for product recommendations from their influencers. If they are not a drinker at the start of an online search, they are far more inclined to start doing it subsequent to receiving beverage suggestions from an influencer. If they already happen to drink, they are prone to raiding their parents' liquor cabinets with even greater frequency.

In their defense, adult influencers can claim they have the right to post whatever they want, and they can't control who is reading their content. Whether they are aware of it or not, this situation is becoming a boon to alcohol companies and their advertisers, who now have fresh pathways to go around regulators. Unfortunately, this is not the only potential pitfall of influencer recommendations on kids.

THEY ARE WHAT THEIR INFLUENCERS EAT

We all know kids love what's unhealthy for them: fast food, sugary snacks, and fructose-filled drinks. More than two hundred thousand children in the United States have either type 1 or type 2 diabetes.[23] The Centers for Disease Control and Prevention (CDC) reports that one in five American kids is overweight.[24] Add influencers into the mix and you have a recipe to potentially compound this situation.

Studies have only just begun to address the impact of social media influencers on children's food intake. In one recent study involving 176 children between the ages of nine and eleven, researchers examined the impact of influencers on the dietary habits of their followers. Posts involving healthy and unhealthy foods were tested.[25]

The results confirmed what every parent fears the most. Influencers who recommended unhealthy (high in sugar, fructose, fat, cholesterol, calories, etc.) snacks caused a much greater intake of those unhealthy foods. Posts about fast-food restaurants (e.g., KFC and McDonald's) received an unusually high volume of likes and comments.

One might optimistically be inclined to think that influencers who posted about healthy foods (high fiber, good nutrition, low fat/calorie/cholesterol) would have a *positive* impact on the diets of preteen followers. Nope. The healthy influencer suggestions did not alter the kids' eating habits one way or the other.

This brings us full circle back to my conclusion earlier in this chapter (which follows my example of pistol shrimp): Children often lack the essential critical thinking skills of adults to be able to distinguish truth from fantasy. Their brains are more dopamine reactive and not fully developed, which means they are highly susceptible to messaging in influencer posts and are at an increased risk of neurological changes due to social media use. In the aforementioned nutritional study, researchers concluded that preteen followers couldn't tell the difference between a sponsored (paid) advertisement and an unsponsored advertisement, and, if they did, they couldn't care less.

I hope my foray into the impact of social media influencers on our children was sobering. The onus is on us to be vigilant protecting our children from the potential dangers—whether intentional or not—from undue negative online influence. To reiterate what I stated in the beginning of this chapter: *dopamine is an extremely powerful neurotransmitter*. When it floods the brains of our children, their perceptions may become distorted and they are susceptible as easy prey to online influencers, who have an arsenal of tactics at their disposal for manipulation on a range of subjects.

As for grown-ups, make no mistake: there are areas where adults are also vulnerable to the illusionary world of influence, which we will tackle in the next chapter.

It's All an Illusion

How Some Influencers Misrepresent Themselves—and the Facts

Cap, it must be remembered, is an art which demands collaboration between the artist and his public.

—E. M. Butler, The Myth of the Magus[1]

More than a century ago, legendary illusionist Harry Houdini famously said, "What the eye sees, the ear hears, and the mind believes."[2]

It would be safe to say that, if Houdini were alive today and performing his eye-popping and death-defying stunts and tricks, he would make quite a social media influencer (albeit with many disclaimers along the lines of "Do not *ever ever ever* try this at home!"). It is important to note that Houdini was well aware of the fact that his art fell into the category of entertainment. While clearly his feats required an enormous amount of talent, skill, and practice, he never pretended that there was anything otherworldly to his accomplishments. First and foremost, he regarded himself as an entertainer.

By the way, I probably fooled you with the quote at the top of this page. The actual quote starts with "Magic" (not "Cap"). On social media, influencers and content creators can just as easily dupe us.

What, then, do we make of our present-day social media influencers? Do they fit into the category of illusionists and/or entertainers? Are they genuine authorities whose words and advice can be trusted by their followers? Or do they fall somewhere in the middle whenever it happens to be convenient for them?

I believe that influencers may be any combination of the above, as long as they clearly distinguish illusion from reality on-site, are honest regarding methodology and results, and offer information and guidance in a responsible manner. While there are many reputable influencers on social media who fulfill these criteria, there are also those who recklessly post information and offer so-called solutions that have no basis in fact and could possibly cause harm to the public.

Boston-based pediatric sports physician and influencer Jess Andrade, DO ("Dr. Jess"), expressed a similar sentiment to me: "It's critical that we do the research. I see it happening where people don't do the research and then make a video. The information goes viral and now you've misinformed a large group of people."

When I do a TikTok video while wearing my surgical cap, I am representing myself—a surgeon who underwent years of extensive study and training to receive my medical degree. Truth be told, anyone can put on a surgical cap and/or a white lab coat and pretend to be a physician on a social media platform. You don't even need the outfit. On social media, anyone can claim that any product or treatment treats any condition. It's deceptive and unethical. Ironically, the more shocking the claims, the higher likelihood the post will virally blow up. No one is out there serving as an official watchdog to alert and protect viewers against intentional or unintentional quackery and misleading information.

If you look closely at television ads and commercials involving health professionals, often you'll see a teeny-tiny caption that reads something like "actor portrayals" if the people involved aren't genuine health practitioners (or anyone else they may claim to be). The Progressive commercials starring "Dr. Rick" ("Parenta-Life Coach") are particularly amusing, as the white-haired, mustachioed actor attempts to cure people from acting out uncontrollable behaviors that closely resemble their own parents (e.g., tossing away cliché signs like "Live, Laugh, Love";

learning how to correctly pronounce the word *quinoa*; and discovering how to sit down without groaning).

While we all recognize that comic characters such as Dr. Rick aren't the real thing, it's not always as easy to distinguish on social media platforms. Disclaimers aren't required, so they rarely exist. How would someone be able to distinguish a charlatan from a real doctor or someone who is just having fun with a white coat or scrubs? As Dr. Jess said to me, "I've seen a few people put on lab coats and pretend to be doctors, but they're not. And I think that sort of stuff is misleading. When people intentionally misrepresent their credentials and mislead the public, it can be pretty harmful."

On many social media platforms, there is a growing epidemic of bogus duets in which advertisers steal social media video clips of real doctors and combine them with another video to stage a misleading product endorsement. Dr. Dana Brems was one such victim of this nefarious activity.[3] In the duet, a video was posted of her giving the thumbs-up to a weight loss product she does not endorse and, in fact, believes is potentially harmful and causes eating disorders. She reported the violation to TikTok, which essentially responded that the duet was fine and did not violate the platform's guidelines. Dr. Brems called out the platform in her own post ("Shame on you!") for allowing this to occur because, as she determined, they don't want to lose advertising revenue. To TikTok's credit, at least they tend to respond when doctors report similar abuses by advertisers. The platform now has a policy prohibiting any posted video from creator-paid advertising boosts if the doctor or influencer in the video is endorsing a product or service.

Mind you, such violations do not only concern health advice. The shenanigans might pertain to subject areas ranging from cooking to fashion to gardening and a host of other subject areas. (At least no one is likely to get sick or injured from these three categories—unless I were to start doing a "Cooking with Dr. Brian" channel.) But what about an area such as finance and investing? Would you really trust an amateur to tell you what to do with your money? And yet so-called financial

experts are rampant on social media, offering all kinds of misinformation that could drain your bank account with stunning alacrity. In the
world of Bitcoin, for example, everyone is suddenly as knowledgeable
on investing as Warren Buffett. In mid-2021, even Kim Kardashian
joined the craze, offering "Ethereum Max"—an alternative cryptocurrency. Ms. Kardashian may be phenomenally wealthy and successful in
her universe, but would you trust her for financial advice?[4] Well, many
people do.

When following influencers' prescribed advice, one might think
to ask, "Who's the source?" and "Who is behind the curtain (and the
makeup, wardrobe, and set)?" When it comes to seeing through the illusion, it's all too easy to be fooled because no entity has created a safety
net to provide warnings, and we all want to believe that solutions to our
everyday problems magically appear on our smartphones in front of our
eyes—which harkens back to the Houdini quote that opens this chapter.
This is how our Perceptual Intelligence can get torpedoed.

There is much more to influencer facades than meets the eye. Let's
blow all this smog out of the way, so we can pinpoint the source of the
illusion in our minds, understand how influencers can take advantage
and hijack our PI into accepting their illusions as fact, and review where
we stand in terms of monitoring the ethical behavior of influencers,
especially when it comes to advertising practices.

To begin, let's start with something as simple as how a first name or
surname can have connotations we rarely think about and yet reveal
a great deal about the human psyche and how viewers connect with
influencers.

WE ARE ATTRACTED TO OURSELVES—AND THOSE WE HOPE TO BECOME

Why do we like certain influencers? Is it due to a deep-seated, psychological fracture in our sense of self—or perhaps a lack of a secure
identity?

As it turns out, we like people who resemble ourselves—or how we want ourselves to be perceived. It's human nature and often this operates beneath our consciousness. Is it coincidence that the most common first names in a state are rooted in that state's name? Take Ken, for instance. More people named Ken live in Kentucky than anywhere else in the United States. The same is true for the population of Louises in Louisiana. Most guys named George reside in Georgia. Where do you suppose the greatest number of Florences live? Florida, of course. Keep in mind that most of these residents weren't born in these states; the majority relocated to these places without even realizing why they did so.

THE ILLUSION OF A NAME

Harry Houdini's name alone conjures images of a larger-than-life figure: a man who could perform miraculous feats on a trapeze wire, escape from inside a whale, swallow one hundred needles, and survive being buried alive. In reality, Houdini was five-foot-six Hungarian-born Erik Weisz.[1] That doesn't sound nearly as glamorous for an escape artist, does it?

Celebrities often shed their birth names to create personas to craft an illusion that is indelibly inscribed in your brain with a Sharpie. Can you identify these contemporary performers by their original names? Reginald Dwight, John Stephens, Jennifer Anastassakis, Alicia Augello Cook, Natalie Hershlag, Lea Michele Sarfati, and Eric Marlon Bishop.

Social media influencers can afford to be far more daring and obscure than actors and singers when it comes to originating their virtual alter egos. Try identifying the names of these top influencers by their birth names (I bet you can't get them all without cheating!): Jimmy Donaldson, Pedro Afonso Rezende Posso, Vlad Bumaga, Ariel Rebecca Martin, and Lucas Hauchard.

Answers to paragraph one, in respective order: Sir Elton John, John Legend, Jennifer Aniston, Alicia Keyes, Natalie Portman, Lea Michele, and Jamie Foxx.
Answers to paragraph two, in respective order: MrBeast, rezendeevil, A4, Baby Ariel, and Squeezie.

NOTE

1. https://www.biography.com/performer/harry-houdini.

Social media influencers develop profiles that evolve into established, recognizable online personas that are relatable to the Kens, Louises, Georges, and Florences, no matter where they live. They may tailor their platforms to attract the widest audience of people possible with an eye toward what that group identifies with and considers authentic. Self-identification is a powerful attractant for influencers. One study suggested that children's perception of being similar to their favorite influencers was related to PSR (parasocial relationship), discussed in the previous chapter. This bond translates to trustworthiness.

The notion that we prefer people who are more like ourselves goes back to our evolutionary past. Thousands of years ago, if a stranger approached a village and looked radically different from the group—blond hair versus brown; short versus tall—that person wasn't accepted as part of the group and deemed a threat.

Whether we admit it or not, we also tend to be drawn to attractive people. Scientific studies indicate that, when participants view pretty faces, the reward center of the brain—the orbitofrontal cortex—lights up (hello, dopamine!).[5] The unfair reality is that attractive people are more likely to be hired for a job and earn more money.[6] With all of this in mind, how do we come to terms with the truth to (a) and (b) below in terms of social media influencers?

a. We tend to be followers of people who look, think, and act like we do.
b. We tend to be followers of people who are beautiful, confident, and successful.

Yes, both (a) and (b) can simultaneously be true, since the illusion of similarity between influencers and their followers is purely aspirational. The followers may desire to resemble their influencers of choice, fantasize about transforming into them, or be delusional in thinking they already look like them. Since the illusion occurs on device screens that can maintain privacy, the illusion becomes something of an ongoing, self-perpetuating fantasy. To help us grasp this concept, let's take a look at today's top ten most popular overall influencers across all platforms combined (which can change in a heartbeat, but you'll get my point momentarily):[7]

1. Cristiano Ronaldo, 517 million+ total followers: soccer (ahem, football) star known for his good looks
2. Justin Bieber, 455 million+ total followers: singer and heartthrob
3. Ariana Grande, 429 million+ total followers: singer and actress considered beautiful even without makeup on
4. Selena Gomez, 425 million+ total followers: singer, actress, and beauty going back to her childhood pageant days
5. Taylor Swift, 361 million+ followers: singer who has been named one of the most beautiful women in the world by many publications, including *Maxim*
6. Dwayne "the Rock" Johnson, 342 million+ followers: former pro wrestler turned actor, whose screen fame was no doubt propelled to some degree by his masculine good looks and powerful physique

7. Katy Perry, 338+ million followers: singer with unique looks that are generally regarded as attractive
8. Kylie Jenner, 333 million+ followers: media personality known for her photogenic looks
9. Rihanna, 332 million+ followers: iconic singer with stunning looks (born in Saint Michael and raised in Bridgetown, Barbados)
10. Kim Kardashian, 319 million+ followers: How do we define her? Let's say she is an attractive "media personality" like her sister, Kylie (see above).

So, there you have it—not a single eyesore. While you may not find every single influencer mentioned above attractive to you personally, it's undeniable that they are all alluring and charismatic in some larger-than-life way to *their* respective audiences.

How can we use this intel to help ourselves? We can protect our PI from potential ambush by recognizing that we are susceptible to bias toward people who remind us of ourselves, consider attractive, and aspire to become. In doing so, we can hopefully identify when we start to be swayed on factors other than objective and accurate information.

Of course, not all influencer attraction is due to physical appearance, although good looks certainly don't hurt popularity. Some followers are spiritually or emotionally drawn to influencer pages for their content and authenticity (or at least the convincing illusion of it), both of which must always be present.

FILTER, FILTER ON THE SCREEN—HOW INFLUENCER ILLUSIONS ELICIT DOPAMINE

It's no secret that actors and performers of all types wear makeup and utilize a wide variety of products to conceal their flaws—no matter how miniscule, prominent, or even imagined. A good portion of well-known celebrities have also been known for their extreme attempts to reverse the aging process with multiple cosmetic surgeries from their faces down to their bums. One can hardly blame them for doing so, as the beauty standards in the entertainment business seem to be impossibly high and tabloid photographers have been known to go to great lengths to capture celebrities at their worst. This doesn't just go for women; actors Leonardo DiCaprio, Jason Momoa, and Vin Diesel are just a few guys who have been shamed as having "dad bods" over the years.[8]

No world is crueler on this front than social media, where one notable celebrity—American singer, rapper, songwriter, and flutist named Lizzo (Melissa Vivianne Jefferson)—was on the receiving end of some harsh shaming and bullying regarding her weight. Back in 2020, offensive memes circulated in which Lizzo was depicted as a literal "bomb" being dropped out of a military craft upon Iran.[9] The fallout became so widespread that the singer felt she had to shutter her Twitter account for a year and a half before returning in 2021.

In case it's not already apparent, Lizzo has always striven to present herself authentically. She expressly chooses not to manipulate her image. Her photographs and videos are genuine and not touched up with filters. What you see in her photographs and videos is what you get, so people have an opportunity to view her as she really is. Her social media persona is not an illusion—but as authentic at the titular character of the Netflix show *Ted Lasso* (played by Jason Sudeikis).

Given such harsh treatment doled out to some influencers, you can understand why they and others doctor photographs and add filters to images and videos on their social media feeds. Trolls—not the Scandinavian dwarflike characters, but rather those who post inflammatory comments on social media with the intent of provoking viewers into emotional responses—wield enormous power when posting; they can insult or undermine whomever they want without ever having to face their victims in person. In many cases, they will use pseudonyms or emojis as their profile names and/or images and therefore don't even need an ounce of courage to post something offensive targeting an influencer—or just about anyone, for that matter (especially classmates in grade school). The freedom associated with social media can turn everyday people into vicious trollers and bullies, like *Lord of the Social Media*

Flies. In a safe place, such as the comments section, people can trash an influencer or a follower without the threat of public exposure or other consequences. Multiple people can become drawn to the "illusion of belonging" to a group and hop on the shaming bandwagon without thinking twice about it; they become bonded by hate or discrimination toward a common adversary and don't feel a shred of guilt. (Sounds a bit like fans and their sports teams, don't you think?) Social media space has become fair game for such unprovoked attacks because so many people are doing it in some way.

Lizzo is hardly the only personality with an antifilter posture, which goes to show that having the looks of a supermodel is not the only way to inspire and attract followers and ramp up their dopamine levels. Dermatologist and influencer Dr. Muneeb Shah says he believes filters "create a false image of perfection to followers and set unrealistic expectations." Spencer Barbosa, a young influencer, headlines her TikTok page with the words "this shit is NORMAL" to stress her preference for portraying herself without any visual trickery. She sometimes skips her makeup routine and flat out refuses to use any beauty filters. She turns them off, even though by default the app already has them turned on at the onset of creating a post. As she explained to me, "Personally, I just like don't want to promote that. With every image, you don't see the way that someone's posed or how she's been edited. In my opinion. I feel like there should be a disclaimer for that."

Ms. Barbosa's commitment as an influencer to authenticity is much needed, especially among teenage girls. An internal Instagram company presentation revealed that nearly a third of adolescent girls said that when they "felt bad about their bodies, Instagram made them feel worse."[10] It's been conjectured that Instagram is more of a breeding ground on this front than other platforms—such as TikTok, Snapchat, and Facebook—because it focuses more so on the physical body through photographs and videos. In another Instagram company presentation, some alarming statistics were brought to light: 13 percent of British teens and 6 percent of American teens linked their suicidal tendencies to this platform.[11]

Since this is a common global issue, one would think there would be a worldwide outcry to do something about it. So far, no such thing has happened. However, a few countries, such as Norway, have taken a bit of initiative, enacting laws requiring labels attached to content with doctored images. The goal—to "raise awareness among people that the perfect bodies in advertisements do not show people as they appear in real life"—seems noble, but only time will tell whether the effort will have a tangible effect on preventing or reversing issues related to bad body image among social media followers and whether other countries will adopt similar legislation.[12]

I'm in the same camp as Dr. Shah and Ms. Barbosa, eschewing filters and any other technical manipulations that might make me look more like George Clooney. While I certainly try to create the clearest image and use basic lighting—my selfie light is a whopping 3.5 inches in diameter and clips to my phone, that's it—for a positive viewer experience, I don't wear makeup. Occasionally, I have donned a blond woman's wig. (Spoiler alert: It's for a character I play in one of my social media series.)

#CAP

Even successful, credible mainstream celebrities have fallen prey to false ideas on social media. In 2020, Lori Greiner—one of the sharks on *Shark Tank* TV show—inadvertently spread misinformation on a video post. She asked her hundreds of thousands of TikTok followers (at the time) to identify whether a sneaker she held up in her hand appeared as either pink and white or gray and turquoise (or teal). If you observed the former, she claimed, you are right brained; if you saw the latter colors, you are left brained.

Okay, what's the trick? you are no doubt asking.

The trick here is that there is no trick. I showed that this is 100 percent cap in one of my posts.[13] The color interpretation does not reveal anything at all about the viewer, except that the viewer has a different lighting setting on the screen, which causes the sneaker to take on a different color appearance.

This explanation is relatively innocuous, right? After all, no one got hurt (although a few disagreements over the different viewpoints broke out). Does it really matter that hundreds of thousands of people were unintentionally misled by Ms. Greiner about a sneaker color? Was anyone traumatized thinking they were right brained or left brained? Probably not, but consider the following: the source of Ms. Greiner's video was actor Will Smith, who has *megamillions* of TikTok followers. Suddenly, these numbers seem so stratospheric that it makes you think about what other pieces of so-called facts are unfounded—whether from Ms. Greiner, Mr. Smith, or myriad other influencers. Those other pieces of information may not be quite as harmless as misdirecting whether you are right or left brained.

Dr. Fayez Ajib believes that when any influencer spreads any kind of misinformation, they are automatically in the category of "bad influencer," particularly if "you chase views rather than provide genuine content." He believes, as I do, that influencers bear the responsibility of being accurate regarding all video posting—whether the erroneous content is intentional or not. This doesn't just apply to an influencer's viewers but also to the entire community, as you never know how far and wide misinformation will spread. As Dr. Ajib says, "It comes back to your moral compass and being honest with yourself and your audience."

An influencer has the burden of telling the truth and owning up to when falsehoods slip through, whether big or small. The sketchy act of one influencer may reflect poorly on a wide swathe of influencers, whose credibility gets dented by mistaken claims. When someone posts something inaccurate, every influencer pays a price in credibility, simply by association.

Medical practitioners who happen to be influencers find ourselves in something of a *capademic*. We've formed a loosely knit community watch in the neighborhood of social media in which we call out what is and what is not cap. We patrol by tasking our followers to alert us when they encounter suspicious videos and then tag us in the comments to get our attention. People with high PI question the veracity of outlandish claims, no matter who might be making them and how many people clicked "Like" on them. Those with low PI could lack critical thinking and accept cap at face value without asking questions and challenging it, often going as far as writing gushing comments and sharing the posts, which spreads the virus outward. The wider the contamination, the more space inaccurate information is granted to breed and be accepted as fact by unsuspecting viewers.

Fortunately, the medical community is not the only group that takes it upon itself to oversee influencer behavior.[14] One Instagram site, influencerstruth, exposes sanitized and augmented photos and those who spread misinformation, particularly about the COVID pandemic. The site, run by a woman who only goes by the name "C.," sets about its task without any monetization. In the world of news reportage, some sites—namely, Factcheck.org, Politifact, and Snopes—strive to keep the record straight about fact versus fiction. When it comes to tightly held political beliefs, however, it's doubtful their assertions make a dent in "fake news." People believe what they want to believe, especially when it comes to information regarding their party of choice. If they happen to be confronted by facts corrected by these sites, objectors might claim they are biased in favor of the other side. If we can't trust the fact-checkers, where should we look for the truth? People who support the notion of "alternative facts" are exhibiting low PI—or are twisting language for their own agenda in a deliberate attempt to confuse people— and need to go straight to the definition of the word *fact*: "something that has actual existence . . . an actual occurrence . . . a piece of objective reality."[15] It's best to keep emotions, which often cloud PI, out of the equation when it comes to distinguishing fact from fiction—especially regarding science. Evolution, for example, has been proven as fact by science and medicine, but there are those who don't wish it to be true because it contradicts their religious worldview (which by its nature is often emotional). As Dr. Jess remarked, "When you provide medical-based information, emotions shouldn't play into it because *fact* is not an *opinion*. Sometimes influencers have a lot of emotion and opinion in their information, which makes it difficult for them to be objective."

THE ILLUSION INHERENT IN INFLUENCER ADVERTISING

In the summer of 2015, Kim Kardashian wrote an enthusiastic post on Instagram touting the benefits of Diclegis, a prescription morning-sickness medicine. While holding up a vial of pills, she stated that "it's been studied and there was no increased risk to the baby."[16] While she did recommend pregnant women consult with their doctors about it, she made an error in judgment: she omitted the side effects of Diclegis (e.g., heavy drowsiness) and that it was untested with regard to preexisting conditions.

Guess who contacted Ms. Kardashian next? The Food and Drug Administration (FDA)—with severe private and public warnings for the influencer to cease and desist misbranding the product. The post was hastily removed, which is all well and good, except for the fact that Ms. Kardashian's relationship with Duchesnay Inc.—the drug manufacturer of Diclegis—remained undisclosed and vague at best. In her post, she stated that her doctor prescribed it and it helped her feel better, but it was not made clear whether it was a paid endorsement.

The matter suddenly shifts us into the opaque. In this circumstance, the illusion of influencer perfection has gone way past the authenticity factor. Ms. Kardashian may have been embarrassed by the FDA takedown, but of what substantive consequence was it to her? A post takedown doesn't require much effort, she didn't have to pay any kind of fine, and her following remained intact. What is to discourage her—or anyone else—from repeating such action? As will be discussed below, federal law has since been enacted for transparency in influencer advertising.

Ms. Kardashian aside, influencer fraud—in the form of illusion, if not outright lie—continues to be a troublesome concern for companies and consumers. Some influencers work around social media app policing and purchase fake followers, views, likes, and comments. Yes, you read that correctly: comments can be bought, to show successful engagement of their product advertising and be able to charge brands more for posts. Since even false, farmed views and likes have the potential to breed genuinely favorable responses, it becomes almost impossible to disentangle the two and prove what transpired.

Dr. Ajib described to me the trap that many content creators fall into once their following begins to increase. Brands entice them with cash for product placement in posts on their accounts. If the advertisement isn't identified as such in a post, how are followers to distinguish what the influencer genuinely recommends versus the items that are there and are paid advertising? They can't. Dr. Ajib challenges fellow influencers with the following questions: "Do you feel good about accepting an ad for vitamin gummies that you know yourself are overly expensive when there is a cheaper alternative? Do you feel comfortable pushing that out to your audience?"

Sarah Rav, MD, doesn't like to point fingers at other influencers, as she believes everybody's platform is their own. However, she also has her limits: "Personally, I wouldn't follow an influencer who sells out. I'm all for influencers promoting products that they love and use—especially if that's how they make a living. Sometimes it's a job and they need to pay for rent. I'm all for brand collaboration. What I don't particularly like is when they do anything to make a buck—like fitness influencers who sell weight loss products such as a detox tea—even though they know that it doesn't work."

In 2019, Entrepreneur.com reported another type of deception, unrelated to false product advertising: nearly a quarter of influencers intentionally misreport their engagement numbers to inflate their advertising value.[17] One UK-based influencer claimed to have 230,000 followers and worked with twenty-two brands; she charged $1,000 per post. On the surface, this doesn't seem to be a lot of money at risk—until you realize that 96 percent of the engagement was fake, which means that every advertiser unknowingly flushed $960 with every paid post.

The irony is that—in at least some cases—identifying an ad as such (with an #ad or some other identifier) may garner a more desirable result for the advertiser. In one study, researchers—with the help of an influencer—found that posts using advertising identifiers did not suppress the subjects' reactions.[18] If anything, the #ad seemed to improve the overall response by as much as 19 percent. Why would the subjects be more attracted to a product when they know it's an ad? We can only speculate that the disclosure boosts the perception of the influencer being authentic and transparent.

THE NEW SHERIFF IN CYBER TOWN

What responsibility does the government have in protecting people from such deception? Is there anything they can even do about it, considering they are already so far behind the curve understanding social media?

In November 2019, the Federal Trade Commission (FTC) issued special guidelines for social media influencers with the intent of cracking down on how they disclose information about their sponsorships.[19] A few months later, they sent ninety warning letters to various influencers—half of whom were celebrities—in an effort to get them to comply with the new rules—or else. In case you are wondering why they selected these ninety parties: All you need to know is that 93 percent of the top social media personalities violate the guidelines. So, they aren't chasing the little guy or gal (yet).

Here are the most important points of the *Disclosures 101 for Social Media Influencers* document:

- Disclose when you have any **financial, employment, personal, or family relationship** with a brand. [**Bolded** words appear that way in the actual document.]
- Keep in mind that tags, likes, pins, and similar ways of showing you like a brand or product are endorsements.
- If posting from abroad, U.S. law applies if it's reasonably foreseeable that the post will affect U.S. consumers. Foreign laws might also apply.

The above can be simplified even further. If you're scrolling through social media pages and see a post tagged with the hashtag #ad, #sponsored, #[company name]partner, or #paid partnership, then you know the influencer is working with a paid sponsor. With such policing in place, followers no longer need ponder if the influencer was compensated in any way to favorably mention the product.

The second bullet is considered the most onerous by sketchy influencers and marketers, who monetize through advertising and favorable metrics. Transparency may not exactly be their best friend. Naturally, many influencers are reluctant to identify their posts with the hashtags that denote sponsorship, as they fear it will annoy their followers and, possibly, cause a few to abandon ship. These concerns are misplaced, as transparency makes the influencer seem more honest and authentic and, therefore, more trustworthy to young people, as the above-cited study showed.

As with everything else related to influencer marketing, some people find creative ways to manipulate the system. For example, there are influencers who try the opposite strategy: instead of hiding that a product placement was paid for, they add tags suggesting they have a sponsor when, in fact, they do not. In one instance, fashion designer and influencer Palak Joshi's Instagram post featured a shiny photo logo of a prominent Chinese phone manufacturer (OnePlus) and tagged its Instagram handle.[20] The only problem was that the company was not an actual sponsor and had nothing to do with Josh's post. This is an attempt to create the illusion of a badge of success. If a prestigious company sponsors or partners with an influencer, it (presumably) boosts credibility in the eyes of that influencer's followers. Anesthesiologist and influencer Dr. Magnolia Printz provided this advice to know when to hit the brakes: "I think one of the things you have to be careful about is when sponsorships, brand deals, and chasing money become more important than your original goal."

Aspiring influencers will often go to great lengths to rev up their street cred and gravitas that might otherwise take years to nurture.

Another deception is for the influencer to post a "thank-you" to an established company for a product or service, even though they had zero relationship with that brand. Illustrator and Instagram influencer Monica Ahanonu once made an Instagram post featuring custom artwork promoting a Chanel cosmetics kit. What's wrong with this picture? Chanel knew nothing about it. It's possible the Chanel organization might let something like this go, because, after all, it's free advertising. However, there are many reasons they could object—namely, they might not approve of a falsely implied partnership with that particular influencer, especially if they believe it that influencer is not in line with their brand.

Moving forward, can a combination of guidelines, common sense, and self-regulation win the day so that influencers will arrive at the conclusion that they don't need illusion to entice and manipulate their followers? If they have content worth sharing—whether it's for knowledge building, problem solving, or pure entertainment—we can hope that they will take the high road and let their posts and reputations speak for themselves.

Dr. Tommy Martin, a resident physician and influencer in Little Rock, Arkansas, offers a wake-up call to some bad actors out there who threaten to damage the integrity of their influencer peers: "We have to realize that every interaction is permanent. It cannot be taken back. It will be with that person until they leave this world. This does not matter if it is the homeless person on the side of the road, the troll in the comment section, or your best friend. Every word—every action—leaves an eternal imprint, and it is up to us determine what it will be and whether it will be positive or negative."

As comedian and influencer John Otusanya puts it, "A bad player is acting from a position where she or he doesn't understand how much influence they have. If an influencer decides to start wearing some funky hat, or some kind of earring or necklace, there will be some people who are going to buy that because he inspired them. That's one thing. But if an influencer is acting recklessly, promoting harmful behavior, or making references or jokes that can be hurtful to people, it could potentially push someone over the edge in a really dark way."

In the next chapter, we'll probe to find out just how dark things can get.

6

Imminent Danger

What Serious Threats Are Hidden in Plain Sight with Social Media Influence?

I've never seen a human this close before.

—*Ariel, from* The Little Mermaid[1]

In chapter 2, we discussed how followers can at times function like "a herd," following their respective influencers down whatever path they choose to direct them. Sometimes, a much darker side of this tendency manifests when the influencer takes messaging or attention grabbing to extreme lengths without considering the potential consequences.

When you think about it, human beings are one of the few living creatures who can actively place one another in serious imminent danger—both intentional and unintentional—by coaxing them into doing self-harming things. A wolf pack leader, for example, is unlikely to direct its group to lap up chlorine to rid themselves of an infection.

Lemmings—small rodents native to arctic areas—have received undeserved bad press with regard to their intelligence. If you are ever referred to as a "lemming," rest assured it's not intended as a compliment; it's an insult meaning you lack individual thought and mindlessly follow a leader. However, the pejorative reference has no basis in fact when it comes to lemmings. The belief that the creatures are gullible and simultaneously "jump off cliffs" in succession is a myth based on footage of Norwegian lemmings migrating and dying as a large group. The species would be happy to learn that some know that's cap. According to a researcher in the Department of Arctic and Marine Biology at the Arctic University of Norway, they probably migrated because of "social stress, food shortage, or predators."[2] So, no, lemmings are not suicidal automatons.

Human beings, by our nature, elect to take far greater risks out of curiosity, impulse, thrill seeking, or just plain recklessness and foolishness. Some of us actively choose to jump out of a perfectly good airplane (skydiving), step off a five-hundred-foot bridge (bungee jumping), dash alongside one-thousand-pound horned beasts (running with the bulls), fling our bodies from a cable above ground (trapeze), scale steep bits of the earth's surface without safeguards (free soloing mountain climbing), escort a motorized bipedal through an earthly element (motorcycles through hoops of fire) just for fun, kicks, and perhaps peacocking.

RECKLESS ABANDON

Human beings have a long history of trying to attempt the impossible and draw immense crowds and create instantaneous fame for themselves. In 1974, a flamboyant American stuntman named Evel Knievel (whose real name, Robert Craig Knievel, was far less catchy) drove a rocket-powered motorcycle across Utah's Snake River Canyon, which was a mile wide. Knievel crashed but miraculously survived because his chute sprang open ahead of schedule.[1] While several others have occasionally been willing to risk life and limb attempting similar feats over the years—more recently, "Mad" Mike Hughes, who jumped nearly fourteen hundred feet across the Arizona desert on his motorcycle in January 2014—these acts are generally limited to the select few and to date haven't caused social media copycat fervors.[2]

Tragically, on February 22, 2020, in an attempt to prove the world is flat (yes, you read that correctly and more about that in chapter 10), Hughes shot up in his homemade steam-powered rocket and crash-landed to his death.

NOTES

1. "10 of the Most Dangerous Stunts of All Time," CBS News, July 30, 2016, https://www.cbsnews.com/media/10-of-the-most-dangerous -stunts-of-all-time/.

2. James Doubek, "Daredevil 'Mad' Mike Hughes Killed in Crash of Homemade Rocket," NPR, February 23, 2020, https://www.knau .org/2020-02-23/daredevil-mad-mike-hughes-killed-in-crash-of -homemade-rocket.

We do plenty of foolhardy acts on our own accord, but what happens when we add in the power of influencer suggestion and the susceptibility of suggestible followers joining the party? In this chapter, we'll see what can happen when influencers get carried away and incite their followers, starting with a trend that is becoming all too commonplace: people playing judge and jury and publicly calling out others for statements, written posts, photographs, practices, or other behaviors they do not feel are acceptable, often based on their own personal standards— sometimes without granting the accused parties a chance to defend themselves. Welcome to a world reminiscent of the Geneva, Switzerland, and Ingolstadt, Germany, depicted in Mary Shelley's *Frankenstein*, where the villagers become mobs with torches and pitchforks to take down "the monster."

WAKING UP TO WOKE CANCEL CULTURE

Certain controversies have erupted when popular influencers or every-day people with large communities flex their influencer muscle by attempting to cancel a person or product (usually to punish the company behind it). Social media has weaponized influencers and creators to take people down with lightning-fast venom. I'll admit there is something positive to be said for an influencer or creator who uncovers a clear-cut scandal that protects people in some fashion. For example, a witness may post a video of a corporation dumping toxic liquid into a town's drinking water, poisoning the entire community. An influencer—or social media user—might repost it, causing the video to go viral. The original whistleblower may have saved dozens of lives by using social media influence to shine a light on a crime that might otherwise have gone unreported. (By way of a specific real-life example, the murder of George Floyd by Officer Derek Chauvin on May 25, 2020, probably wouldn't have come to light had it not been for videos of the incident taken by bystanders on their phones.)

There are also gray areas when one person's "wokeness meter" challenges another's posted opinion, preference, naivete, or old-school values to the point of public shaming. In many cases, it is entirely possible for someone to agitate thousands of people with one innocent and/or ignorant post. We all know this to be true: words can have nuance and multiple layers; in the world of social media, it is all too easy for a person to inadvertently step on a land mine. One misguided post can lead to all kinds of labels that go viral and then stick—especially *sexist, racist,* and *homophobe.* Cancel culture can be a form of bullying.

Dr. Magnolia Printz is especially concerned with the amount of judgmental bullying that goes on through kids' social media. "I just don't think that teenagers and preteens have the frontal lobe developments or the impulse control to not post something that could permanently ruin their chances of getting into college or getting a good job." While she readily admits that there are people who have exhibited some egregious behaviors worth calling out, she firmly believes "there's a better way of addressing those things, instead of not giving that person a chance to explain what may have been taken out of context. And social media is forever."

UK-based surgeon and influencer Dr. Karan Rajan has growing concerns about cancel culture's increasing effect on a young person's mental health. "Kids can get hit hard really hard by negative comments. There can be a kind of gang mentality where you get a bit of a lynch mob attacking someone—it's a very aggressive thing. The whole cancel culture thing can become toxic. It can lead to depression and maybe even people taking their own lives."

The trending influence of wokeness and pile-on cancel culture in social media has become a particularly personal issue to comedians, writers, and entertainers who require creative freedom and boundary testing to produce their art. A wide range of celebrities—including British comedian John Cleese, Harry Potter author J. K. Rowling, talk show host and comedienne Ellen DeGeneres, *Glee* actress Lea Michele, singer Bryan Adams, and actor Chris Pratt, to name a few—are notable targets of social media cancel culture's Most Wanted. In 2019, comedian Shane Gillis was canceled just after he finally got his big break: joining the cast of *Saturday Night Live*. Why did *SNL* pull the plug on him before the first appearance? A Twitter posse unearthed some past videos of him making jokes about Asians and homosexuals. I'm not suggesting one way or the other whether his words were offensive, but, either way, let's take a few steps back and ask the question: Aren't comedians expected to push the envelope and be controversial? Where would Lenny Bruce, George Carlin, Richard Pryor, Joan Rivers, Don Rickles, and Dave Chappelle—as just a half-dozen obvious examples— have been if they hadn't satirized the controversial or sensitive topics of their day to get laughs and bring certain issues to light? Personally, I eschew the same things as the woke crowd: racism, bigotry, sexism, homophobia, political misinformation, and so forth. By the same token, I am concerned by the deluge of vitriol and punishment often shoveled out with zeal by cancel culture in social media. It strikes me that, in general, things are getting pretty uncomfortable for those who believe in the right to free speech and individual opinion. The herd mentality often has a fierce knee-jerk habit of presuming they know a person's meaning, intent, and personal beliefs and then lashing out to rile others up to leap on the runaway escalator. Unfortunately, once labels are out there, reputations, careers, and lives can be ruined with little to no chance of reclaiming them.

Social media has a nasty habit of turning on its own. An influencer named Isabella Avila, a.k.a. @onlyjayus, for example, had at the time built up a substantial following for her "Psychology Tricks" videos: 13.5 million on TikTok; 1.2 million on YouTube; and 169,000 on Twitch.[3] When some of the influencer's private old messages surfaced containing what was perceived to be a racial slur, she lost her Netflix partnership and various sponsors. Advertisers on her other platforms seemed to discreetly thin out, and she subsequently issued an apology. Her accounts continued to grow. At the same time, Change.org issued a petition to ban her from TikTok, which had garnered more than 436,000 signatures as of January 2022.[4] Still, she continues undaunted and has even fanned the flames by making the following hubristic statement in a TikTok video: "I'm so confident that's not going to happen [getting banned], I'll sign it [the petition] myself."[5]

Time will tell whether Avila—who now has over *sixteen million* TikTok followers at only twenty-two years of age—will have the last laugh. In the meantime, the ethical dilemmas continue to rage regarding whether one's exposed personal beliefs and/or private messages merit such mob social venom, replete with torches and pitchforks.

DEPRESSION AND COPYCAT SUICIDE

The world was stunned on August 11, 2014, when it was announced that beloved multitalented comedian and film/TV star Robin Williams had committed suicide. The circumstances of his death were gradually revealed in detail, as were the causes behind the tragedy. Here was a man who had achieved the greatest heights of accomplishment as an actor and comic and seemingly had everything to live for, including a family who loved him dearly. Yet none of this was enough to counter Williams's severe depression resulting from a rare disease, Lewy body dementia.

One might think that reports of Mr. Williams's tale would mean increased education about depression and suicide, which logically should have led to more discussion, available treatments, and preventive care for other sufferers of depression. To the contrary, media coverage—especially *social* media coverage—caused the opposite to occur, with more people following suit and taking their own lives. After Robin Williams's suicide, there was a *10 percent bump* in suicides, which wasn't unique in just the United States.[6]

In *Perceptual Intelligence*, I outlined "the halo effect" in which fans accept the facades of celebrities (e.g., actors) at face value and believe that their on-screen personas are true in real life. By way of an obvious example, is comedian/actor Bill Cosby—who was imprisoned for nearly three years on three counts of aggravated sexual assault—the same person as Dr. Huxtable, the father figure character he portrayed for years on *The Cosby Show*? Years before Cosby was accused of mistreating multiple women, millions of people would have proudly invited him over to a party, as if the comedian had been a symbolically virtuous man like his TV alter ego—hence, the halo effect.

I believe there also exists an even darker halo effect. The stark statistics say it all: media coverage of a teen suicide sparks a copycat suicide rate that is 400 percent higher than that of adults.[7] The controversial 2017 Netflix series *13 Reasons Why*, which depicted the details of a teen suicide, is estimated by the *Journal of the American Academy of Child and Adolescent Psychiatry* to have been responsible for a 28.9 percent increase in suicide among Americans between the ages of ten and seventeen.[8] Studies are revealing that girls who start spending two to three hours a day on social media and then increase that over time are at much greater risk than boys, although the reasons for this phenomenon continue to be explored.[9]

The sobering point is that young people, in particular, are more susceptible to modeling both positive and harmful behavior of characters in the media, especially when it comes to influencers who are presenting themselves in their "true form." When social media influencers display self-harm in any form, the immediate result is a correlated surge of that copycat behavior. Nearly *one-third* of teens and young adults who reported seeing self-harm on Instagram admitted to doing the same or similar behaviors.[10]

Dr. Siyamak Saleh from South Africa informed me that he has "seen a few people with huge followings suggest to people that they can go kill themselves." While TikTok and other platforms have strict community policies against this and have taken down certain videos as soon as the violations have been brought to light, there is always concern that one will slip through or have a long delay before being removed and inflict harm to people through the power of suggestion. The platforms and the influencers themselves always need to stay vigilant and guard against any such reckless recommendations.

TRAGIC COPYCATS

For some copycat responses to social media influence, critical thinking has checked out; therefore, PI is unfortunately nonexistent or challenged at best. Imagine this scenario: Two people approach a friend and ask the friend to jump in the air. When the unsuspecting individual cheerfully takes a leap airborne, both friends kick out each of the person's legs while they are in midair. What do you suppose happens next? Once the person's spine hits the ground, the head is snapped back with tremendous force and the back of the head smashes against the surface (usually concrete). The result? Concussions, facial wounds, broken bones, split-open heads, and, sometimes, death.

Yes, the above type of injuries and many more actually happened. A lot. Some resulted in fatalities. In 2020, the "skull breaker challenge," as it became known, was a TikTok prank that often led to serious injuries and deaths among kids. (TikTok later removed all those videos.) *How could two people do such a terrible thing to their friends?* you ask. The dark halo effect convinced the herd that this was a cool and acceptable thing to do and looked funny on video as their friends' heads smacked against the pavement like cartoon character Wile E. Coyote or Homer Simpson.

In May 2021, thirteen-year-old Destini Crane of Portland, Oregon, paid a steep price for attempting to reproduce a viral TikTok video. Hoping to create a cool effect, she wrote a message in a bathroom mirror with rubbing alcohol and then set it on fire with a lighter and candle. Her attempt backfired, and a blaze roared through the bathroom. Destini suffered severe burns to her face, neck, and body, a few of which are permanent, despite three skin graft surgeries.

Kids seem to be finding all kinds of creative ways to goad each other into burning themselves. Dr. Jess Andrade brought to my attention the "salt and ice challenge" in which kids shake table salt on exposed skin (such as the arm), place an ice cube against the area, and then hold on for as long as possible.[11] The result of the science experiment? Searing pain and second- and third-degree burns that require trips to the ER and, sometimes, skin grafts. After all is said and done, scars may remain forever as a lasting tribute to a seemingly harmless act gone south.

As I mentioned in chapter 4, TikTok star Krysten Mayers recalls having seen a trend in which girls cut off a piece of their genital areas every month to stop it from growing. What might have begun as a gag to trick the boys became a real method of self-mutilation, as some girls went ahead and started harming themselves on a regular basis and then recommended it to others. One 2018 research study found *nearly thirty-six thousand* videos on YouTube with some association to this barbaric act.[12] They boiled these down to 150 comments related to such videos for analysis in the study. So far, it seems, condemning the act may have almost as many detrimental results as condoning it, since bringing this issue to light creates a stigma around it for those who have done it to themselves—while also drawing in the curiosity of newcomers. Until conclusive preventive methods are developed, the best ways to curb such acts are to ban remotely similar references in social media and for parents to monitor their kids' accounts and whom they follow as closely as possible and have proactive discussions before things have a chance to get out of hand.

BODIES AND FOOD

Dr. Andrade reports having "seen more eating disorders and new onset eating disorders than ever before." Poor body image, less emphasis on human interaction, feelings of exclusion, and cyberbullying are among the main causes attributing to the increase. In fact, 65 percent of those who suffer from eating disorders state that they have been bullied in some way—largely in social media. A 2016 study in Australia revealed that social media has had a particularly negative impact on body image.[13] Dr. Andrade describes what eating disorder patients have said to her: "I was watching too many videos of other people's body types of body images, and I just went down this rabbit hole, and I developed an eating disorder that I couldn't get myself out of."

Comedian and influencer Josh Otusanya has seen cyber fat shaming firsthand: "I saw a video in which an overweight person posted a video about self-love. She was proud of herself. For some reason, a lot of people started ragging on the person, making fun of her. That turned into *thousands* of comments. The dark side of it to me is when you have access to a lot of people and a mob turns on you. That can be dangerous and negative to your mental health."

The good news on this front is that several popular influencers, including Maleah Whitten, Ve'ondre Mitchell, and Spencer Barbosa, are taking action to help neutralize body image issues on social media. In a partnership between TikTok and Dove—producers of soap and skin care products—the influencers have teamed up in a concerted effort to post content designed to boost self-esteem.[14] Spencer, who has deep passion and commitment to this issue, said to me that her efforts have been paying off: "I've gotten a lot of messages from girls telling me that they went to the beach in a bikini for the first time ever because I've influenced them to love their body. They have realized that their bodies don't have to be perfect. Hearing younger girls telling me that they feel confident in a bikini is the best feeling ever. I wish someone would have told me that I [looked] good in the bikini when I was in high school."

Harmful food-related trends can originate anywhere in the world and virally spread to any country. *Mukbang*—an amalgam of the Korean words *mukja* ("let's eat") and *bang song* ("broadcast")—is a dangerous trend that began in South Korea and has become a worldwide phenomenon.[15] The act involves people binge-eating tons of food—usually of the most unhealthy variety possible (e.g., French fries, fried chicken, buffalo wings, deep-fried sticks of butter—you get the idea)—while others watch on social media.

Influencers have found ways to monetize the gluttonous act. One influencer, Nicholas Perry (a.k.a. "Nikocado Avocado"), gets paid to gorge on pernicious foods on his YouTube channel. Viewers seem to receive a vicarious thrill watching him prepare and then consume dozens of containers of spicy ramen soup (among other foods) in one sitting. Perry may be a poor choice for a role model, but, to his credit, he is a poster child for self-awareness, honesty, and transparency. He clearly announces his intention right from the get-go on his video post, while also assigning blame to his viewers: "If anything crazy happens here, it's gonna be *your* fault. Just for the record, should I be doing this? Probably not. But we're doing this because guess what? I need *views*. I need *money*. I need to be *famous* on the computer. This is what everyone comes to you for. Don't sit there and lie and say, 'Oh no, they come for *community*.' People come here to get *famous*."[16]

There can be a steep price for this obsession with views, money, and fame, however. Studies are already revealing that "watching mukbang worsened their diets rather than improved them" and that "PMW [problematic mukbang watching] was positively related to loneliness and PYU [problematic YouTube use]."[17]

EXTREME DANGER

Are these the most extreme instances of imminent danger instigated by the behaviors of some influencers? Unfortunately, I am just getting started. Months after I thought I'd documented enough examples of dangerous challenges, I read about a new one that emerged and went viral in August 2021: "the milk crate challenge."[18] The setup is much the way you are probably visualizing it. Once milk crates are piled high into the form of a pyramid, thrill seekers must climb to the top without, well, tumbling down and breaking their neck (or at least various useful bones). Although TikTok banned the hashtag for the challenge and medical practitioners have begged people to stop participation, people continue to do it, undaunted.

Dr. Rajan has observed myriad unhappy endings in which people have attempted the most alarming things to garner page views. "I've seen people doing all sorts of hard-core-type stunts. They'll scale high-rise buildings and then fall off and die. Or, while pretending to have tongue piercings, they'll swallow magnetic balls. They reach the intestines and then cause a bowel obstruction or perforation—and then, you know, they have major bowel surgery and come close to losing their lives."

The "see one, do one" mentality isn't relegated to just physical challenges. Dr. Andrade sees kids in the hospital with afflictions having direct correlations to things they were copying from social media: "There was a Benadryl challenge where kids would attempt to overdose on Benadryl for the effects. We saw extreme amounts of ICU admissions from Benadryl overdoses." The over-the-counter drug contains diphenhydramine, an antihistamine that can also be found in Sominex and Tylenol PM. When taken in extreme amounts, Benadryl is poisonous and can attack the bladder and kidneys, the heart and blood vessels, the nervous system, and the stomach and intestines. Complications can include pneumonia, muscle and brain damage, and heart rhythm disturbances (which sometimes can lead to death).

Is fame and popularity worth the risk? If you ever think it might be, just visit the kids and adults in the hospitals who attempted these stunts—or google the obituaries of those who tragically didn't survive them. While we can't completely turn off the spigot to prevent dangerous new trends from happening, we can proactively engage our children in conversations about the potential hazards of such activities to help strengthen their PI.

MISINFORMATION, DISINFORMATION, AND MALINFORMATION

Andy Pattison, the team lead for digital channels in the Department of Digital Health and Innovation at the World Health Organization (WHO)—who routinely holds meetings with the leadership of all the social media platforms—said to me, "When somebody is posting misinformation, it might kill somebody—like drinking chlorine to cure you. If I say it might kill someone, I don't mean it as a threat. I'm giving them advice. But if they choose to go ahead and post that anyway, then someone may really die as a result. . . . There's too much *misinformation* and there's too much *disinformation*. The difference is that *mis*information can be accidental. *Dis*information is deliberate."

Mr. Pattison sums up the reality of the situation well, while also distinguishing the primary difference between misinformation and disinformation. Both are rampant in social media and can be equally dangerous. Either way, viewers with low PI are inclined to believe such falsehoods—whether they are intentional or not—and then indiscriminately spread them as fact. There are circumstances in which the social media platforms could take much tougher stands and guard against erroneous information, but all too often they look the other way for a variety of reasons: controversy breeds page views and can lure advertising dollars; they do not wish to be perceived as Big Brother censoring freedom of speech; they do not want to get caught in heated political debates; and the obvious one: it's an awful lot of extra work and headaches to be a watchdog—which costs time and money. And, despite the efforts of some social media platforms—such as YouTube, Facebook, and Tik-Tok—to crack down on COVID vaccine misinformation, instances of antivaccine propaganda continue to sprout up.

For the record, there are three types of potentially wrong content:

1. *Misinformation:* These are pieces of information that are unintentionally incorrect. They might include things such as spellings, translations, dates, and statistics. Humor also sometimes falls into this category when someone takes a joke seriously or misinterprets satire as fact. The trouble here is that it becomes all too easy for someone to post misinformation and then claim, "Oh, I was only joking," or omit the qualifier because of the assumption that viewers understand that it is parody.

2. *Disinformation:* This is where things take an even sharper ethical turn. Disinformation, which involves doctoring facts and/or visuals (such as photographs) to suit an agenda, vendetta, or whim, can cause emotional, physical, and perhaps reputational harm. It may include starting up rumors about a person or entity, manipulating or cherry-picking data (such as medical information), or even spreading conspiracy theories.

3. *Malinformation:* This act—which we can think of in terms of being overcaffeinated dark intentions—is when private information about an individual or organization is intentionally made public. This might involve a leak from a whistleblower, sabotage by someone in the victim's inner circle, or hacking from an outside source. The motivations can vary but are usually sparked by revenge or a desire to spark major controversy or cause chaos.

If the COVID pandemic taught us nothing else, it's that it can be imprudent to trust social media influencers who don't have medical or scientific credentials for our health information. Misinformation and disinformation can spread illness and death among innocent citizens. Between 2019 and 2021, we heard it all: COVID-19 was a hoax; the chemical on COVID testing swabs causes cancer and/or changes your DNA; vaccines cause autism;[19] and the infections were being spread through 5G wireless networks.

One thing we know for certain: Misinformation, disinformation, and malinformation breed mistrust—and I don't just mean in terms of the social media influencers and followers who spread this. I'm referring to mistrust of medical practitioners, researchers, scientists, and educators who devote their lives to uncovering scientific fact, treating those who are ill, and preventing the spread of disease. The medical community has more than enough to deal with under ordinary circumstances; throw in a pandemic, mass prevarication, and political controversy, and our entire civilization starts redlining. We have come too close to the edge in recent years to allow low PI to continue to cause tragedy.

EVEN INFLUENCERS CAN BE DUPED

Influencers are not immune to certain social media hazards, as the doomed Spring 2017 Fyre Festival concert (a.k.a. "the Greatest Party That Never Happened") proved. The "luxury" event, scheduled to take place on April 28–30 and May 5–7 on the Bahamian island of Great Exuma, became a multimillion-dollar scam that ended in disaster for everyone concerned.

Billy McFarland, the man behind the debacle, defrauded people to the tune of $26 million for an overhyped, overpriced event that had zero *"there there."*[20] McFarland dragged down the reputations of several powerful Instagram influencers—including Bella Hadid, Hailey Baldwin, Emily Ratajkowski, and Kendall Jenner—who became unknowing accomplices when they were fooled into appearing in videos advertising the event.

The Fyre Festival was a firestorm of disappointments for the guests, who paid a fortune to attend what had been pitched as a "VIP event." Instead of gourmet meals, attendees were served cheese sandwiches and salads. The rock band Blink-182 was scheduled to perform but backed out prior to the event. The accommodations—which had been described as eco-friendly domes and villas—were cheap tents that hadn't even been assembled by the time the guests arrived.

Justice was served when McFarland pled guilty to wire fraud and was sentenced to a six-year prison term. Several of the influencer models who appeared in the advertising campaign (including Ms. Hadid) settled lawsuits and returned a fraction of the $1.7 million fees they received.[21] Hopefully, lessons were learned all around from the debacle.

FAKING IT

A *deepfake*—sophisticated 3D AI technology that enables a person to create a video of oneself as someone else, often a celebrity—is yet another potential threat to civility in the social media space. The technology is progressing so rapidly that it is ever so simple to put out a convincing, realistic deepfake.

Between February and June 2021, ten videos of Tom Cruise doing day-to-day goofy things (such as a coin trick) popped up on TikTok. The favorable reactions to the posts went thermonuclear into the tens of millions. No one had seen Tom Cruise behave this way on TikTok before, so it became something of a surprise treat for fans of the star. The only problem? Although the person in the videos looked and sounded exactly like the original, this was not Tom Cruise. The poser was Tom Cruise stand-in actor Miles Fisher, whose basic appearance bore such close enough resemblance to the real thing that special effects artist Chris Umé was able to accentuate the impersonation with precision through CGI.[22]

While some viewers were wowed by the simulation, others didn't care for being fooled by "deepfakegate." To date, Tom Cruise—the real actor, that is—hasn't publicly weighed in on what he thinks of it, which may mean that either he's a good sport and thought the videos were amusing or he was able to shrug it off. But what happens when the next deepfake target disapproves of being represented without permission? Does this individual have protective rights? Is this free speech and comedic satire—or a new form of identity theft?

The issues become even more complex when you consider the volume of disinformation and misinformation already prevalent in social media. A lot of users are inclined to believe what they see at face value and not even realize it's entertainment. Imagine if someone could convincingly utilize CGI to do a deepfake of the president of the United States locking in the codes on the nuclear football to launch a nuclear strike against China. Or if someone chose to create a deepfake of a politician in a compromising sexual situation to ruin that person's career? On a personal level, what if someone has a grudge and wants to enact revenge by creating a deepfake that ruins the victim's career or family life?

Maryland law professor Danielle Citron is convinced that deepfakes can cause concrete, extensive harm. They can potentially determine the outcome of an election, sink an IPO, be used to commit fraud, or bully or extort people. "The threat landscape is pretty significant," she was quoted as stating. "Deepfakes are a huge jump in the technology. They let you manipulate existing video or fabricate from digital, whole-cloth, video and audio showing people doing things and saying things they never did or said."[23]

On the other side of the argument, there is the ever-important right to free speech. By way of comparison, aren't politicians and other public figures fair game for performers who do impersonations of them on TV (such as *Saturday Night Live*)? The difference, of course, is that the audience is in on the joke and knows the portrayal isn't real, which isn't the case with deepfakes. There are laws presently being discussed to pressure social media platforms to be on the lookout for deepfakes and remove them as soon as they are detected. Unfortunately, once the video is out of the bag and shared by even just a few viewers, it may already be too late. If the video has gone viral, it's inevitable that people with low PI will take it as real on face value and spread it as a conspiracy theory. One can only hope that, moving forward, CGI companies will be wise enough to embed their products with strict piracy violation rules and even watermarks to prevent such deepfakes from happening without approval from the party being depicted.

We began this chapter by examining how rare it is for creatures in the animal kingdom to lead themselves toward imminent danger. By contrast, as we've established through numerous examples, human beings have no qualms about venturing down an ill-advised path that could cause irreparable harm to themselves or others. And yet, no matter how many people end up in the hospital or worse, we never seem to learn from our mistakes.

With that in mind, for the following chapter, we are going to steer away from the wolves and lemmings and head toward different animals—grazing deer and cattle—as we seek to understand why we are drawn in by celebrity influence for a supersized portion of our decision-making. For now, I leave you with the famous line by *Good to Great* author Jim Collins: "Bad decisions made with good intentions are still bad decisions."[24]

Celebrity Sells

How Social Media Influencers Are a Different Breed Than the Traditional Celebs We've Loved All These Years

I love show business. I wake up every morning and kiss it.

—*Richard Pryor, comedian*[1]

Successful entertainers—actors, musicians, dancers, and other types of celebrities, including models—attract and win over fans through a combination of talent, honed skill, good looks, and charisma. Sometimes there is the addition of the elusive "it factor"—the special something that makes a celebrity even more attractive and desirable—which has the potential to overpower all of the other aforementioned traits (or possibly compensate for shortcomings). For some contemporary examples of superstar "it factor," consider Jennifer Lawrence, Bradley Cooper, Angelina Jolie, Ryan Reynolds, Lady Gaga, Kanye West, Taylor Swift, and Justin Bieber.

While some of the aforementioned entertainers will be known for some time—perhaps on par with the likes of Audrey Hepburn, Gregory Peck, Marilyn Monroe, Steve McQueen, Aretha Franklin, Frank Sinatra, Janis Joplin, and Elvis Presley—the jury is still sequestered and deliberating on the longevity of fame for social media influencers and what legacy, if any, they will ultimately leave behind. Many influencer posts are timely, topical, and zeitgeisty but may date poorly over time. Dr. Sarah Rav told me she has her doubts about how long they will last but does believe that some "will probably be remembered like the Kardashians for being famous for just being famous."

Several important questions come to mind when comparing the relationship between social media influencers and traditional successful entertainers:

> *Can an established celebrity (e.g., film actor) become a true social media influencer?*
>
> *How can we tell the difference between a celebrity who is "on social media" and one who has metamorphosed into a fully grown social media influencer?*
>
> *Is it possible for an influencer to go on to achieve film, television, recording, stage, or other type of fame?*
>
> *Is crossover success a desired goal among social media influencers?*

As we address the above questions, we distinguish between a mainstream celebrity who happens to use social media as a hobby, curiosity, or necessary device and one who also qualifies as a bona fide influencer. Here are my criteria to help make the distinction, which may apply to varying degrees in each category, depending on the individual:

1. *Viral content:* There is no influencer without a veritable cornucopia of hits. As stated earlier, one rose does not a bouquet make.
2. *Authenticity:* The star is being true to themselves on the platform with no deception that would rile the community. Posts credibly reflect the genuine thoughts and beliefs of the influencer, not what they want people to perceive. If it's revealed that the influencer doesn't hold those tenets to be true, the trolls may line up for a snarly takedown through vicious comments.

3. *Personal space:* Some talented performers are private people by nature and create precise boundaries between their personal and work lives. They may have popular social media feeds but don't share intimate aspects of their lives. By contrast, a celebrity who presents their true self to the public has the potential to be a social media influencer.

4. *Consistency and commitment:* A social media influencer posts regularly and keeps their finger on the pulse of the community while also wowing them with surprises and quality content to keep them engaged. They are not simply communicating outward while promoting a new film release or spreading the word of fundraising activities. (Not that there isn't anything inherently wrong with either; it simply means that alone doesn't qualify as a pure social media influencer.)

5. *Uniqueness of content:* Social media influencers seek to post content that is fresh, relevant, topical, and feels as if it connects directly to their followers in some tangible way. It's as if the posts were tailored for their audience, not the other way around. They accomplish this feat through a variety of potential creative methods, including, but not limited to, original, profound, witty, topical, informative language; entertaining or instructive videos; or selfies (which are sometimes seductive). By contrast, celebs (including fashion models) who rotate old heyday shots throughout the day (e.g., "Here's me in 1998 on the set of _____") don't necessarily fit the influencer criteria because the content isn't specially created for the platform or unique.

6. *Treating social media influence like a professional job:* If a celebrity dabbles in writing posts and making videos irregularly and inconsistently—such as with incongruous content and in different writing styles—they may not be a true influencer. Influencers may test different themes or styles to see whether there is traction, but typically there is a core presence weaved through their content. There is a level of commitment and intent involved—or at least the public's perception of these factors.

Did you happen to catch the one thing not listed among my criteria? *Number of followers.* While this point obviously matters a great deal, it's inconsequential when separating popularity from influence. Tom Hanks, Sofia Vergara, Halle Berry, and Tom Cruise are enormously popular stars with over-the-top social media follower numbers that equal their salaries, but are they "pure, factory, matching numbers" influencers? I would say not, as they don't score high enough on the six requirements.

Now, for comparison, let's consider the case of Will Smith. He is a film and television actor, a rapper, and still a star despite slapping Chris Rock at the 94th Academy Awards in 2022. Mr. Smith boasts millions upon millions of TikTok followers; in fact, he has more than the population of any state in the United States. He's a MLI (macro-level influencer, pronounced "m'lee"), defined as an influencer whose follower counts exceed the populations of some large countries. While that in and of itself doesn't qualify him as an influencer, he checks off all the other boxes. His videos are tailor-made for social media, and, as a result, they consistently go googolplex viral. He uses his TikTok platform to reveal a lot of his personality, is convincingly authentic, invites people into his personal life, creates unique content, and is diligent with his posts. His creative and funny TikTok posts range from illusion and animation (a sword-wielding miniskeleton carving a face into a pumpkin that swats him away after the job has been completed) to practical jokes (nearly dropping his chewed gum into the open mouth of a sleeping friend on an airplane) to rapid book signing, and so on. It is evident to anyone viewing his account that there is a great deal of thought, effort, and care put into them. He invites fans to step into his life, cerebral cortex, and imagination in a much deeper way than Hanks, Vergara, Berry, and Cruise, whose looks alone would garner massive numbers of followers. Mr. Smith's social media influence is tsunamic compared to their tide-pool-like influence because he has succeeded as both a traditional megastar and a communicator on the platform.

Moving onto a completely different galaxy, let's probe the extraordinary life and career of one George Takei. If you happen to be a fan of the original *Star Trek* series, which first aired in the 1960s, and its subsequent feature films, you'll know him well as the actor who portrayed the swashbuckling helms officer Lieutenant Hikaru Sulu—most often referred to as plain "Sulu." The beloved role has granted Mr. Takei a tremendous amount of recognition and gravitas among the sci fi community. Prior to 2011, however, few people outside that world would be able to identify his name, unless they happened to be exceptional at television trivia.

What happened that year? you ask.

In March 2011, at the distinguished age of seventy-four, Mr. Takei joined Facebook.[2] He was an early adopter of social media as a vehicle for sharing his thoughts and opinions. Mr. Takei openly posted about his gay marriage and support of LGBTQIA+ rights. His humor and honesty—including his now famous catchphrase "Oh, my!"—resonated among a much broader range of people than just the sci fi community. His reach multiplied when he revealed that, as a young boy, he and his family had spent three years in a Japanese internment camp during World War II—*in the United States of America*.[3] As time went on, he amassed a considerable following for one who played a supporting character on a TV series that ran for only three seasons more than five decades ago. Takei's sustained fame has enabled him to focus his platform on addressing major social and political issues.

Does George Takei qualify as an influencer? He unequivocally does on a number of fronts, especially since his social media community has bolstered his Hollywood recognition, if not surpassed it. Every day he brings serious subjects to light in an intelligent, informative way, and many of his posts go viral. He brings an authenticity to his platform that has created awareness and even led to striking change. As Mr. Takei has described about his social media style, "I took the approach that social media should be more about what the fans want to talk about rather than just me. I never wanted to post things like my workout routines or what I had for breakfast. It's really not that interesting. But with the rise of social media, we have an opportunity to discuss together, laugh together, and take action together."[4]

Whereas George Takei went from modest Hollywood fame to breakout social media influencer and activist, there are many influencers who use their platforms to head in the reverse direction. Being TikTok famous may be good enough for some entertainers but not others. Charli D'Amelio, for example, sought to expand beyond her hundreds of millions of TikTok followers (putting her in the top ten of country populations in the world—more than Japan, the Philippines, and Egypt), so she has since added film (*StarDog and TurboCat*) and television actress to her résumé. Dunkin' Donuts has even named a coffee after her—Charli Cold Foam—and offers her merch (vernacular for merchandise—that is, products) in the shops. Addison Rae has attracted more than one hundred million followers with her dance videos but has been transitioning to movie star with *She's All That*. Singer Nessa Barrett gained popularity on TikTok before expanding her career to become a full-fledged stage performer and recording artist. Many people don't realize that Justin Bieber's career genealogy traces back to viral YouTube videos that opened the music industry's doors.

It's therefore entirely possible for a traditional celebrity (such as Will Smith) to cross over and crush it as a MLI. It's equally viable for a Hollywood personality of lesser renown (such as George Takei) to discover an even broader audience as a social media influencer. Numerous all-time great entertainers (such as Tom Cruise) may be popular on social media but don't necessarily get a callback as influencers. This brings us to the "organically grown" native influencers—such as MLI Swedish YouTuber extraordinaire PewDiePie (Felix Arvid Ulf Kjellberg)—who have risen up primarily in the digital space. And, as mentioned, we are seeing other influencers (such as Addison Rae, also a MLI) who view social media influence as the first step on a much longer and winding trail to mainstream superstardom.

Even now, there are everyday adults and kids out there who are just beginning to post on TikTok, Instagram, Twitter, or Facebook and will someday become "overnight social media sensations" from one breakout video that goes megaviral or a steady stream of strong content that builds a community. Are these natural-born-and-bred influencers also celebrities? In many cases, the answer is *yes*. While they may have started out as normal people posting everyday (or extraordinary) things in their feeds, they have emerged from their humble origins to become celebrities to their followers; they may remain complete unknowns to everyone else, unless something remarkable happens and they are catapulted into the mainstream. Another difference between this type of influencer celebrity and a Hollywood-famous person is that the former is expected to maintain authenticity, no matter what. This means that if their brand is that of a "regular person," they typically stay in that lane. Dr. Muneeb Shah believes that the role of this everyday influencer will continue to evolve and grow in importance: "I think we will see more of a focus on the individual creators of content and platforms, prioritizing them over traditional celebrities. Those who have been successful on TikTok, they were all normal people by all stretches of the imagination, right? I think people want more of that than mainstream celebrities."

The top influencers may share the same half-dozen criteria I laid out earlier in this chapter, but their digital gestation, areas of focus, talents, methods, and backgrounds generally share little in common. My signature CAP hat is wildly different from that of Zach King—who performs extraordinary visual feats of magic in his videos—and on a whole other spectrum from dancer extraordinaire Charli D'Amelio. (I dare not ever attempt to perform a split.) Another key distinction among established influencers is whether they are in the game to "make money." As the saying went on the *Seinfeld* TV show, "Not that there is anything wrong with that"—just as long as their practices are above board and ethical.

THE BUSINESS OF INFLUENCE

In distant fields and hills around the world, grazing deer and cattle exhibit behavior that isn't much different from how we respond to celebrities strutting down the red carpets of award shows. Research has substantiated what ranchers, herdsmen, and hunters have known for centuries: during feeding times, deer and cattle are drawn to align their bodies to the magnetic north through a sense called *magnetoreception*. In similar fashion, social media influencers can lure us in their direction with their content: line up, eat up!

By the words in its own name, show business is a business. Celebrities are often required in their contracts to promote their films, TV shows, Amazon web series, and so forth via "press junkets" to maximize viewer consumption to justify their salaries. If Bradley Cooper has been paid $15 million for a movie but fails to promote it, and then it doesn't break even, he probably won't bank the same fee the next time around.

When hiring a star for television, radio, or even what remains of print advertising, savvy marketers consult the Celebrity DBI, which is, essentially, an index that measures honesty of more than seven thousand celebrities. They want to know: Who has made the top ten on the list? They search for a perception of the pitch person's credibility and trustworthiness relevant to the product or service.

While there isn't an equivalent DBI for influencers (not yet, anyway), the appearance of their authenticity already puts them high on the honesty index in the perception of their followers and brands—especially when their numbers are at MLI level. When influencers promote a product or service in their feeds, the target audience is organically present and measurable, in contrast to a traditional television, radio, or print ad with a TV or film celebrity. The likelihood of success is, therefore, more predictable because the influencers' connection to their respective communities is deeper; they are built on authenticity, trust, and a shared interest in the subject area. As a result, influencer marketing DNA is typically stronger than that of traditional celebrities. Hence, the explosive growth of influencer marketing firms and traditional firms that add influencer divisions.

The PI of the follower is constantly being tensile strength tested as the trusted influencers offer seemingly free heartfelt product recommendations. In some cases, a follower may be more accurately referred to as an influencee. I liken this to an apartment rental situation, where there is a lessee (the tenant) and lessor (landlord). Some of them truly believe in what they are pitching and, hopefully, are speaking from personal experience and usage of the product or knowledge of efficacy. If it's the influencer's own brand being pitched, it's easy to figure out the inherent bias, which might not matter to the followers. If, however, the influencer is getting paid to sell the wares of others—like the pitch people on QVC and celebs in car commercials—there is no way to know for sure, unless it is disclosed with #ad, as we discussed in chapter 5. The followers have the task of distinguishing between an objective influencer recommendation and a product endorsement that has only been posted because a brand paid the influencer. Those with high PI will be able to tell the difference and perhaps save their credit card balances from mass purchases.

Here's one insider tip to identify whether a sponsored post is also an authentic endorsement: When you see a paid post with appropriate identifiers, look at the influencers' prior content for genuine, nonsponsored posts that reference the product or service. Prior nonpaid posts predating the paid one are a potential indicator that the influencer uses the product for its implicit value. For example, I created nonsponsored posts involving the usage of a derma roller to stimulate hair growth. I was subsequently approached by a company that produces a derma roller and struck a deal to do a paid video. I agreed, since I had previously vetted derma roller technology and the existence of published studies supporting how the product can help increase hair growth. After posting the video—which I labeled with #ad, as is commonly accepted practice—a few people commented that I had "sold out." To my pleasant surprise, a greater number of followers defended me with comments along the lines of "He's done many videos about derma rollers before." This firsthand experience taught me an important lesson about how to assess the authenticity of influencer endorsements.

INFLUENCE: A GAME CHANGER IN TV ADVERTISING

No matter which football team a fan is rooting for to win the Super Bowl, everyone can agree on two things to be excited about: the halftime show and the lit commercials (*lit* is Gen-Zese for cool). Many of the latter have been boosted by marquee superstars, including Mila Kunis (Cheetos), Bruce Springsteen (Jeep), Nick Jonas (Dexcom), and Cardi B (Uber Eats).

If you think back to past Super Bowls, Coke and Pepsi have sponsored many of the star-studded spectacles with elaborate production values. Pepsi commercials included celebrities such as supermodel Cindy Crawford and singers Michael Jackson, Beyoncé, Christina Aguilera, Mariah Carey, and others. Meanwhile, in 1979, Pepsi's rival, Coca-Cola, delivered what stands as one of the most memorable commercials of all time with NFL Hall of Famer "Mean" Joe Greene ("Hey kid, catch").

Moving forward, it's clear social media influencers will play an increasingly important role in Super Bowl advertising, particularly when it comes to cola commercial combat. Pepsi, for example, has paid untold millions to sponsor recent Super Bowl halftime shows while mobilizing social media influencers to boost the effort on Twitter.

With a Super Bowl TV spot now in the high-rent district of $6.5 million,[1] Coca-Cola and Pepsi may think twice about producing expensive fizzy commercials with superstar entertainers when they can potentially get a lot more pop from a social media influencer post for much less buck.

NOTE

1. Brian Bonilla, "12 Keys to Making a Super Bowl Ad Worth $6.5 Million," Ad Age, November 8, 2021, https://adage.com/article/special-report-super-bowl/how-to-make-super-bowl-commercial-worth-several-million-dollars/2377806.

As I've stressed many times throughout this book, there is nothing wrong with influencers recommending products—as long as the items deliver on what they promise. Given their bonds with the communities, influencers take great risks to their reputations if the quality is inferior or if it is later revealed that they use a different product in their personal lives.

To be sure, influencer authenticity doesn't always translate to success. Some products have been known to backfire and even cause harm. Influencer Jaclyn Hill—who had multimillions of Instagram followers at the time—launched her own cosmetic line, Jaclyn Cosmetics. Sounds like a slam dunk, right? There was one slight complication: consumers began posting photos of the lipstick tubes smattered with items that would have been more at home in a medical lab—fungus, hair, and sharp pieces of plastic. A negative social media frenzy erupted. The company denied the negative claims by stating that the irregularities occurred in only 0.1 percent of products, but the travesty didn't end there.[5] Another beauty influencer took to YouTube to post an hour-plus dissertation video about how she had worked with the same lab as Jaclyn Cosmetics and was dissatisfied with the quality control, which had produced the same defects. Shortly thereafter, Hill's brand posted on Twitter, "Jaclyn Cosmetics takes consumer feedback seriously. We've reviewed the quality issues related to our Rich Lipsticks and believe our production did not meet our brand standards. We'll be issuing a full refund [including] shipping charges to everyone who purchased the product."[6]

Later, the influencer posted an apology video on YouTube. Ms. Hill seemed authentic, admitting to having been overconfident about the product's quality and not having hired enough quality control experts. Many of her fans seemed satisfied with the solution and continued to stick by her. However, a petition was filed—with many thousands of signatures—demanding recalls and investigations. When it comes to the conflicts of interest that arise when influencers create and recommend their own products, at what point can we discern a legitimate mea culpa from a brush-off? Time to bring in the body language experts.

Some influencers fail to see the approaching light as a train speeding toward them when it comes to recommendations in certain product categories, such as weight loss. On social media, it seems every week a revolutionary new diet supplement, concoction, pill, drink, powder, bar, or candy emerges promising to suck, dissolve, or sublimate excess poundage off anyone in less than ten days. In 2020, Kim Kardashian touted the benefits of appetite-suppressant lollipops produced by Fat Tummy Co.[7] There was nothing unusual about that; the influencer has recommended countless weight loss products over the years. This advertisement was different, however, as lollipops hold an even greater appeal to children than adults, and Ms. Kardashian's massive following happens to include legions of young girls. Were these lollipops safe for them to consume? No one knew for sure, as the FDA hadn't approved them for either adults *or* girls (as noted on the company's website). Let's think this through for a moment: Should young girls be taking *any* appetite suppressants, given the body image insecurities social media can foster, as discussed earlier in chapter 6? Ironically, prior to the pitch for the lollipops, Ms. Kardashian stated that she would be a protective mother when it came to the safety of her own children: "Gosh, I'm definitely gonna be that mom that's monitoring my kids as they grow up and want to get on social media."[8]

For all the wonderful entertainment, information, instruction, and personal connections made in social media, the world of influence is still a business, just like show business. Even if influencers aren't seeking to get you to open your Apple Wallet, the platform they are on most certainly wants its advertisers to get hold of it. As with television, radio, and print advertising, social media platforms are endemic with advertisements promoting a magical Main Street electrical parade of lures. Caveat emptor, right?

As I've mentioned in earlier chapters, there are plenty of social media influencers who put on white coats and play "make-believe" as doctors to make a buck. This practice is highly objectionable, especially when the influencers could be recommending untested products that are ineffective, unsafe, or both.

Rapper NLE Choppa (Bryson Lashun Potts) has a TikTok following that dwarfs the population of many cities. Many of his posts feature his music, style, or dance moves. He's also shared some things about his personal life, his interest in a vegan lifestyle, and his efforts to help various communities. All good, right? Yes—up until NLE Choppa presented a video (that went massively viral with more than 7.5 million views) endorsing a "concoction" (as he stated) that he made in the kitchen with claims of it being a "Viagra naturally made from herbs" with benefits, as he explained, to treat erectile dysfunction, raise testosterone, help grow the "mid-section," control early ejaculation, boost sperm count, and make you a "beast in bed."[9]

There were three ingredients cited that I researched on pubmed.ncbi .nlm.nih.gov (one of my trusted sources for searching studies published in the medical literature). First, *Mondia whitei*.[10] According to actual studies, there is research that it can improve the motility of human sperm, but there's no data to support the contention that it increases sperm count. There are studies in animals that found it could increase libido, testosterone, and erections. One animal study found it caused lesions in the testicles that reduced sperm counts.[11]

Second, burdock root (*Actinium Lappa L.*). One animal study found it increased sperm count and libido, while another animal study revealed that it caused atrophy of the testicles, along with damage to the heart, lungs, kidney, and lungs. Some of these complications were permanent, even after stopping use of the supplement.[12]

Third, blue lotus flower (*Nymphaea caerulea*). While there weren't any animal studies, there was one human study that reported toxicity.[13] This manifested as altered mental status changes (brain functioning), requiring the individuals to go to the emergency department.

A number of my followers tagged me in this NLE Choppa video to weigh in. I duetted it, accurately declaring it as *cap*.[14] At the end of video, I shared the names of some natural men's health supplements (that have human studies to back them up): L-citrulline, fenugreek, and ashwagandha. L-citrulline increases nitric oxide production in the body, which improves blood flow and helps mild to moderate erectile dysfunction (ED). Fenugreek is an herb, the seeds of which have been known to improve sex drive. Ashwagandha is a medicinal herb that can increase testosterone. As far as data from research studies goes, all three are these are *not cap.*

TikTok's response to my duetted video? Oddly enough, *I* received a community guidelines violation, and my video was taken down. They claimed my post contained "inappropriate sexual content," even though I never used "sex" or any related words—just "men's supplements." If my video had been a violation, why did NLE Choppa's video with the words *ejaculation, sperm,* and *erectile dysfunction* still remain? I couldn't understand why I had been penalized, especially since I was performing a public health service against inaccurate and potentially dangerous information that was viewed by many millions of people. I filed an appeal with TikTok. I lost. I can only speculate why my video crossed the line and NLE Choppa's did not with its sex-related language. Perhaps more frustrating and concerning is that the platform is not censoring based on potentially harmful misinformation, but rather on its self-selected guidelines.

IS BEING AN INFLUENCER A FUN HOBBY, A SERIOUS JOB, OR BOTH?

Picture this: You've diligently built up your social media accounts for two years with exceptional content. You have amassed enough followers to fill many NASCAR and NFL football stadiums and feel like you have only scratched at the full potential. Most of your posts have received high engagement numbers in terms of views, likes, and favorable comments, and several have gone viral on other platforms. You've even been interviewed by a couple of leading newspapers and blogs. Your inbox is now beginning to blow up with DMs from advertisers that want you to pitch their products and will make it worth your while financially.

One day, you have a family event at your house. A relative says to you, "I hear you are causing quite a stir on . . . what is it? Instagram? I haven't seen what you do yet, but I hear you are wonderful."

"Thank you," you say with a smile, careful not roast your relation for lack of social media IQ that might cause insult or embarrassment.

"Now that you've had your fun, what are you going to do as your job?"

Your eyes roll. You know what's coming next, but you imbibe a slow breath like you're assuming a downward dog yoga posture. "What do you mean?"

"Oh, come now, you know that's not a real career, right? At some point you'll have to become an adult and get a real job that makes money."

Hold up, right there. For many influencers, social media posting is, in fact, a fun hobby and nothing more. Even so, they take their efforts seriously and spend a lot of time creating their influencer posts. For many others, such as myself, it's an important supplemental activity to their full-time roles in their respective careers. As for the rest of the influencers, it's a full-time job that generates earnings. It's a career—and one that requires constant attention and development.

For Dr. Rav, this is 100 percent the case. As she described to me, she considers it her time-consuming "full-time job." She has reached a point at which she has monetized it and treats it like a real business—which it is.

Canadian-born influencer Spencer Barbosa started out on a different path when she was a ten-year-old girl. Initially, she wanted to "make it" as a television star. She earned a role on a Canadian show, *We Are Savvy*, and appeared in a few commercials. She said to her mom, "Oh, my gosh, Mommy, I want to be an actor!" By the time she reached high school, her TV career faded out because she was too occupied with schoolwork. Then she discovered an interest in content creation. "When I first kicked off," she recalled, "I had a bet with my sister that by the end of the pandemic I could get to fifty thousand followers on Tik-Tok. I was just joking around with her. But then it actually happened."

Ms. Barbosa didn't imagine her following would continue to grow or the hefty time commitment the tasks demanded. All along, she thought she was going to become a real estate agent until being an influencer turned into a "full-time job. . . . I'm spending my whole life on a phone. And I'm living on my own and paying my own bills. I have to take this seriously."

Dr. Tony Youn and I have a somewhat different relationship with social media than Dr. Rav and Spencer Barbosa. As it happens, the two of us share (at least) four things in common: we are physicians, we have demanding full-time jobs, we have children, and we enjoy binge-watching Netflix shows. Additionally, the "night job" of being an influencer has cut into one or more of those first three things for both of us at one time or another, and we've needed wake-up calls to rein ourselves in. As he describes, "There are times in which I have felt that maybe I've been neglecting my family. There are times where she's talking to me, and I've wanted to finish reading something or watching something related to my feed and it becomes a minor irritation for her. So, I realize have to shut down for a while and pay attention."

At a certain point, however, both Dr. Youn and I began to share something else in common: our social media feeds were starting to make money. The revenue hasn't been enough to quit our day jobs—not that we would do that anyway, due to our commitment to medicine and our patients—but it was something unexpected and extra. Another motivator, perhaps. Both of us now look at our social media feeds as having a business facet, even if it's not our primary job. Dr. Youn put it this way: "Social media has now become another revenue stream for me. One that's fun and has a lot of other possibilities associated with it."

For me (as with Dr. Youn), I will continue to take my role as an influencer seriously and balance it with my professional and familial responsibilities. I doubt it'll ever become my full-time job, but just a few years ago I never would have imagined I would be spending chunks of my time crafting and posting TikTok videos and tracking engagement numbers. As long as I can continue to educate, inform, and entertain with purpose—as well as keep it fun—I will press on with it and evolve along with the platforms.

In chapter 8, we will investigate a different kind of business on social media—the sexverse. A good portion of sexually related things that were pervasive on the internet have now spawned all new fruit on social media platforms. There is something appetizing for everyone—adults, that is—which has its benefits, I suppose, as long as people are capable of doing one thing: *turning it off before they get hooked.*

8

Sexual Solicitations

Are Influencers Turning Us into Sex Addicts?

Hey! Do me a favor and grab my butt!

—*Olaf, from* Frozen[1]

Human beings aren't the only coitus-captivated creatures on the planet. Our closest relatives, male and female primates (monkeys, apes, etc.), masturbate—a lot.[2] Male and female cetaceans (whales, dolphins, porpoises) do, too—except they manage it without any hands. Walruses, which are frighteningly well endowed, use their flippers when flying solo. Animals throughout the kingdom are instinctively "going at it" (though none like the brown antechinus mice mentioned in chapter 3). Animals crank away whenever and wherever they can—whether they have partners or are by themselves passing the time. They are not shy— so what if voyeurs happen to be in the vicinity? They also do not require much in the way of additional outside stimulation to get things going.

Renowned sex therapist and best-selling author Dr. Ruth Westheimer once said, "It is a catastrophe all of this virtual being together. I think there are people who get hooked on the Internet. If they need to look at sexually explicit material to be aroused, there is a problem."[3]

Dr. Ruth was not being sarcastic, nor was she exaggerating the extent of the issue. Today, it is estimated that anywhere between twelve and thirty million Americans have the condition known as sex addiction.[4] This seems like a tremendous range—which it is—mostly because it is impossible at present for researchers to tally a more accurate number. Many sex addicts don't view it as a problem (or not as enough of one to do anything about it). There are also those who are embarrassed and feel there is a stigma associated with it, which may be an accurate reflection of public perception. All you need to do is imagine a scenario in which you reveal to a partner, spouse, friend, or relative that you think you might be addicted to sex. How do you think this person will react at first? I would bet bedsheets that the responses would be along the lines of laughter ("You're joking, right?"), dismissal ("Come on, that's not a real thing, is it?"), or utter derision (the person suspects you are a "perv" and ghosts you). Then there are those who might keep to themselves their real sentiment—that the label is just an excuse to indulge.

Here's a sobering fact: Sex addiction is real and, unfortunately, getting worse every day. A few celebrities, notably actor Russell Brand and golfer Tiger Woods, have checked themselves into clinics to treat their respective sex addictions, which had torched their relationships at that time and tarnished their reputations.[5] In these instances, the sex addiction manifested in the form of promiscuous sex with multiple random partners. Internet porn can be like being hooked up to a coffee IV for someone who is sex addicted, while social media porn—still in its infancy by comparison—can seem even more intimate and real, like a dive into a vat of Devil Mountain Black Label coffee beans (the world's strongest coffee with 1,555 mg of caffeine per twelve-ounce cup).[6]

ENTER—THE SEX WORKERS

As the worlds of big-screen, VHS, and DVD porn films faded, the content diffused into the digital universe. The roles of sex workers evolved with the simple shift in content delivery method. Many of them have created their own interactive websites, thereby cutting out the producers, directors, and camera crews, which means 100 percent content control, improved personal safety, and more lucrative financial rewards for the performers without concern of being exploited by filmmakers or pirating because the activities are being recorded live. These webcam "girls" and "guys" can livestream (or photograph selfies) at home with just a mobile phone, so the costs to the content creator are negligible.

A significant number of professional sex workers—or amateurs—have realized they can get a much wider mainstream audience venturing into the world of social media and use their influence for advanced marketing: lead generation. When they post on traditional social media sites, such as Instagram, they seem more legitimate, as the distinctions between sultry model and porn entertainer become fuzzy. The freedom, luxury, and privacy of this new entrepreneurial model typically makes this a better lifestyle for them all around. One sex worker said, "At least I'm not waiting tables." (Ironically, some servers say, "At least I'm not doing porn.") Some sex workers consider their trade a path for female empowerment, entrepreneurship, and upward mobility. You might not want to view powerful entrepreneurs in the sex industry with disdain, as they might be "laughing all the way to the bank." And the more exposure they get on social media, the more appealing they become as product pitch people and opportunities arise for them to monetize it by selling merch, such as sex toys.[7] Even mainstream celebrity influencers, such as singer/actress Lily Allen and model/actress Cara Delevingne, have entered the adult novelty product arena.

Lena the Plug started out in the traditional porn industry but shifted over to social media and now boasts multimillions of followers on Instagram and YouTube. It shouldn't be surprising that she has created a successful business; she is a college graduate of the University of California, Santa Cruz, with a degree in psychology. Her business deploys social media influence to feed her base of subscription customers who pay for exclusive content.[8]

There are thousands of other influencers and content creators on Instagram, YouTube, and TikTok who straddle the fence when it comes to modeling and acting versus porn. Many selfies and seductive poses leave little to the imagination, except perhaps covered nipples, pubic hair, and other visuals that might violate the platform's community guidelines. Some influencer photos and videos entice viewers—known as *thirst traps*—which can include individuals striking seductive poses baring skin or dressed in minimalist outfits. In others, the thirst trapper teases and leers at the thirst "trappee." Why post a thirst trap? The reasons include seeking attention, temporarily pumping up self-esteem, adding new followers, wanting a catharsis during a stressful time, or promoting personal branding. Most often, the thirst trapper implies, like a person in a bar waving a hand in the air who announces, "Dopamine for everyone here, it's on the house."

BEYOND MEASURE

Despite what is often seen on computer screens, the average erect penis size of an adult male according to most sources is approximately 5.2 inches.[1] This stat went viral in a number of TikTok videos, along with popular videos reporting a recent study's finding that penile length correlated with nose size; people with bigger noses tended to have longer penises.[2]

NOTES

1. Adrienne Santos-Longhurst, "What's the Average Penis Size?" Healthline, April 17, 2017, https://www.healthline.com/health/mens-health/average-penis-size.

2. Hiroshi Ikegaya et al., "Nose Size Indicates Maximum Penile Length," *Basic and Clinical Andrology* 31 (2021).

ONLYFANS—SOCIAL MEDIA GOES EXCLUSIVE

OnlyFans was founded in 2016 on the premise of monetizing content without advertising. Unlike the free model of most social media sites, OnlyFans is subscription based, which can either be free or have paid monthly membership fees to fans (users). Creators with free subscriptions can charge fans to "unlock" or view select videos, photos, and join livestreams. OnlyFans can create a more 1:1 experience between creator and fan. In addition to not having to be subjected to paid social media ads, fans receive access to exclusive content that distinguishes it from most other social media sites: the content is largely uncensored, although there are protective community guidelines, as with other platforms.

While OnlyFans began in 2016 as a site for mainstream creators, its lenient content policies attracted adult entertainers and sex workers, which widened its membership[9] and forged its reputation as the app for this content. The business model caught on during the COVID shutdown in 2020, enabling the site to grow at a rapid clip. Interestingly, the greater freedom for content creators and wider monetization opportunities have attracted some superstar traditional performers, such as rapper Cardi B.

The site's liberal policies have captured the attention of museums and artists whose provocative works were banned from other social media sites. In October 21, 2021, the *New York Times* reported that the Vienna Tourist Board posted photographs of paintings and sculptures that didn't pass the community guidelines of other sites but were welcomed on OnlyFans. A photograph of a twenty-five-thousand-year-old limestone figurine of a woman titled *Venus of Willendorf* may have been deemed inappropriate for Facebook, but it was not a problem on OnlyFans. Similarly, the algorithms of Instagram and Facebook blocked a video post celebrating the anniversary of Koloman Moser's early twentieth-century painting *Liebespaar*, a painting that depicts a man and woman having intercourse while standing upright. (It's tame compared to some of the sexual content on OnlyFans.)[10]

In the summer of 2021, something unusual occurred. Due to increasing pressure from its banking partners, OnlyFans announced that it intended to ban pornography from its site on October 1. The outcry from subscribers and creators who post sexual content was so immediate and vehement that the London-based company shifted gears and reported its plans to maintain the site's prior content policy. OnlyFans was able to leverage the massive responses from its community to coax the banks into backing down and allowing the site to conduct its business as it deemed best.[11]

Influencers on this platform have the luxury of being able to set their own subscription rates. Actress and singer Bella Thorne charges $20 a month for a fan subscription (or $102 for six months) to her feed, which includes seductive videos that might have been restricted on other sites. The liberating tone and focus of the platform also provide her with a forum to speak her mind without feeling the wrath of trolls. As she described to *Paper* magazine, "OnlyFans is the first platform where I can fully control my image; without censorship, without judgement, and without being bullied online for being me."[12] For the performer, this has proved profitable, especially when she became the first influencer on OnlyFans to earn $1 million in one day.

Influencer Dr. Magnolia Printz said to me she has been following the rise of OnlyFans with keen interest. "Instead of making TikToks, I should post on OnlyFans, so I can pay off my student loans," she remarked. Of course, she was only joking. (It happens she's already paid off her student loans.) Her comment is telling, however, in the sense that mainstream influencers on TikTok, Instagram, and everywhere else are taking notice of how profitable the subscription model can be.

While Dr. Printz isn't opposed to OnlyFans' sexual content, she does have specific limits to how far it should go. "Do I want my eight-year-old and twelve-year-old children to see content from porn stars? No, obviously not. I just don't think that is an appropriate conversation at that age. When they are older and can afford their own cell phone, drive a car, maintain good grades, and have all those responsibilities, then it's time to have the conversation about what's out there. We can discuss things like the dangers, the legal ramifications, and their rights. I think that's a conversation parents need to have with their kids when they are old enough."

MY ONLYFANS INFLUENCER EXPERIENCE

While conducting research for this book, I reached out to OnlyFans, as I wanted to have firsthand understanding of the platform. One of their relationship executives onboarded me as a verified influencer on the platform. I set my subscription up as free and incorporated some select paid posts.

What did I think about it? Overall, I did enjoy the freedom to post anything I wanted—especially cap or no cap videos on topics such as the myth that masturbation stunts growth (employing *Snow White and the Seven Dwarfs*), how online porn addiction can cause erectile dysfunction, and the unfounded claim that the Ashwagandha herb can enlarge the penis. Had I posted this content on TikTok, it is likely I would have received a sexual activities community guidelines violation.

How would I best describe OnlyFans experiences at the time of this writing? *Thirst Trap City*. I observed three types of verified influencers (types one and three are featured on the official OnlyFans app feed, whereas type two is not):

1. *Mainstream influencers heavily laden with thirst traps:* I found they often have free subscriptions and feeds that offer free lifestyle photo and video content (such as yoga postures, exercising, cooking, mixing drinks, and outdoorsy pics and videos) with varying generous helpings of thirst trappy content. Some thirst trap posts are locked, and payment can provide access to additional thirst trappish content (which sometimes includes nudity). Once I subscribed to many of these accounts, the influencers sent welcome DMs, which can be broken into three categories: (1) a pleasant welcome message; (2) a pleasant welcome message with locked or free thirst traps; or (3) a pleasant welcome message with an upcharge invitation to "tip" (pay a fee) to be a "VIP" for exclusive content (which may or not be X-rated; it may be included or require additional payment).

2. *Sex worker influencers:* These accounts are explicitly sexual in nature based on their profile pictures and bios. They can have free

subscriptions where fans pay to unlock content on their feeds; other accounts are paid subscriptions.

3. *Mainstream influencers with minimal or no thirst traps:* I fall into in this category. These influencers, which appear to be the minority, post content like you would find on any other social media app from most influencers.

THE BENEFITS OF SEX EDUCATION

In an episode of the hit British Netflix show *Sex Education*, Otis (Asa Butterfield), the main character—a self-appointed sex teen therapist following in the footsteps of his mother, Dr. Jean F. Milburn (Gillian Anderson)—consoles a friend by saying, "Everyone has bodies, right? It's nothing to be ashamed of."[13]

Where are kids today receiving most of their information about sex? Is it from TV shows such as *Sex Education* and from the internet? Schools, churches, and community centers have been effective for one out of five children between the ages of nine and twelve, at least in terms of messaging regarding abstinence. Unfortunately, this stops when they hit adolescence. While teens are primarily learning about STIs and safe sex from parents, parents seem unprepared to effectively discuss expanded sexual topics with their teen children.[14] Often omitted are the positives, such as love, pleasure, and solid relationships. Important topics, such as abuse, exploitation, contraception, and pregnancy, also tend to get overlooked or purposefully skipped. Schools aren't faring better: sex education classes have had no effect on reducing teen STIs, nor have they reduced teen pregnancies. Social media seems to show some promise in this regard. In one study using correlation analysis, teens were about two and a half times more likely to have used contraception or a condom after seeing sex health messaging on social media.[15]

If you look carefully and objectively, there is a substantial amount of responsible, beneficial sex education on social media platforms. Dr. Karan Rajan believes that some influencer feeds are beneficial. "It can raise awareness about difficult and taboo subjects. Some TikTok and

SEX IS GOOD FOR YOU!

Sex—*safe* sex, that is, with willing, loving partners of legal age—does wonders for mind, body, and spirit. All the available research data concludes that sex isn't just about procreation and a lot of feel-good fun. Numerous research studies have shown that sex burns calories, battles colds and flu, reduces the risk of heart disease, regulates hormone levels, helps resolve headaches (putting a dent in the "I have a headache" excuse), reduces physical pain, lowers blood pressure, lowers stress, reduces risk of certain cancers (breast and prostate), boosts mood, improves self-esteem....[1] Wow—as Dr. Ruth might say, it's time to get busy!

NOTE

1. "12 Ways Sex Helps You Live Longer," Healthline, September 14, 2016, https://www.healthline.com/health/ways-sex-helps-you-live-longer#burns-calories.

YouTube videos offer really good stuff everyone should know about their bodies and reproductive health—particularly in areas where sexual health information is lacking."

As I discovered, there are quite a few influencers who post informative, entertaining, and sometimes even empowering videos and blogs, while being mindful that kids might be browsing their feeds. Sexuality doula and sex educator Ev'Yan Whitney runs an informative podcast, *The Sexually Liberated Woman*, and blog, *Sex Love Liberation*, along with her social media feeds. Whitney (identified as they/she) educates her followers on a wide range of subjects—from understanding asexuality to reclaiming their bodies.[16]

There are several other reputable influencers who impart sex education knowledge from a feminist perspective to large audiences. In her

YouTube videos, sexologist and author Shan Boodram (a.k.a. Shan Boody) offers practical tips on subjects, such as finding female-friendly pornography, using the hands more during sex, navigating dates, dealing with sexual assault, and more. Shelby Sells, who refers to herself as a celebrity sex therapist and sexologist, conducts sex-positive dialogues in her feeds intended to enable people to experience greater intimacy.[17] Pink Bits, run by Christine Yahya—an Armenian Australian graphic designer and illustrator based in Sydney, Australia—has become popular on Instagram for "illustrating the bits and shapes we're told to hide."[18]

Dr. Printz referred me to two additional influencers who engage their millions of followers on issues pertaining to sexual health: Dr. Jennifer Lincoln and Dr. Staci Tanyoue (a.k.a. dr.staci.t). As she describes, "They're both OB/GYNs. Dr. Lincoln is in Portland, Oregon, while Dr. Tanyoue is based in Florida. I met them in Dallas a few years back, and they're killing it on TikTok. Really good medical and educational information. They discuss important subjects like periods and tampons while busting myths about feminine washes."

From a personal viewpoint as a parent, while I might be open to my teen daughters hearing straight talk about sex from the above authorities, I wouldn't start celebrating if they were venturing through a sex worker's account, even if the feeds are benign. While these influencers may seem harmless, they are not the best role models for kids. It's important that parents always be aware of—and have approval over—what their kids are watching, the sites they are visiting, and the influencers they follow. It's important that parents have these conversations with their children.

TO FAP OR NOT TO FAP—THAT IS THE QUESTION

In *Perceptual Intelligence*, I underscored how, throughout history, societies have frowned upon masturbation; some even took drastic measures to condemn people who were caught in the act. Going back to the Bible, Onan was slain by God for "spilling his seed." Since then, many religions have taken extreme measures to prevent, if not ban, the touching of oneself.

At the beginning of this chapter, I cited just a few animals that masturbate with frequency. We don't like to think of ourselves as being similar to animals, but the fact remains that we share more DNA with other creatures than people realize. Masturbation is normal and natural, and all the science points to the human inclination—if not necessity—of performing the function as a regular and healthy practice, unless it's done to excess, in public, or in a way that impacts other parts of one's life (e.g., sex addiction, as noted earlier in this chapter). Research studies have revealed the potential positive impact of masturbation on the human body, including reducing the risk of prostate cancer among men. For women, it can improve their sex lives and even ease postmenopausal symptoms.[19]

As with many other subject areas, social media is rife with misinformation and disinformation about this normal human practice, causing a lot of people to feel unnecessary guilt and shame. Influencers have coined new terminology for abstaining from the practice that is far removed from the *Seinfeld* euphemism "master of my domain." For men, the act has been newly dubbed *fapping*.[20] In 2012, the *NoFap* movement was formed by Alexander Rhodes, a web developer from Pittsburgh, Pennsylvania, to curb porn addiction with emphasis on quitting masturbation. Male members of the group are known as *fapstronauts*. Women, who are allowed admittance into the movement but only make up about 5 percent of membership, are referred to as *femstronauts*.

One of the motivators of NoFap is the theory that abstinence increases testosterone levels in men. Proponents cite two studies: the first involved only ten men, which is too small of a pool from which to draw any dogmatic conclusion; the second did reveal a 45 percent spike in testosterone seven days after abstinence but then a sharp return to the original levels thereafter. Does this blip for one day have any clinical benefits and outweigh the other benefits of fapping? There is no data to support this and one subsequent study of thirty-five men revealed that testosterone levels rose after self-stimulation. Additionally, it's believed that, if anything, public misperception and ensuing guilt over masturbation may cause psychological issues such as anxiety and possibly reduced testosterone that are far worse outcomes than anything related to the physical act itself.[21]

Some influencers who peddle NoFap confuse the issue by intentionally or unintentionally omitting that excessive porn watching is the cause of the side effects they cite. It's as if you were to scarf down a huge tin of cookies, and then someone attributes the spike in your blood sugar levels to excessive salivating in your mouth. (Salivating is a secondary effect; the cookies are the actual cause of the elevated blood sugar.) Hence, while porn addiction in general may be a genuine problem for a significant number of people, closing down the masturbation shop is not the solution. We need to start decoupling porn addiction from auto-gratification and cease blaming masturbation as the culprit. Most reputable therapists and medical practitioners who have studied these conditions and treated patients believe that people addicted should enter a twelve-step program as if they have any other addictive condition.[22]

Contradicting established facts and practices, some influencers have not only pushed the NoFap movement but also boldly started their own unfounded variations. One such influencer, Netherlands native Rob Mulder, gained a following on TikTok and YouTube that includes recommending his "NoFap challenge" to go one week without watching porn or masturbating. As he states, "If you think this will be hard then you probably have an addiction and you are the exact person that should be doing this challenge."

According to his online profiles, Mr. Mulder is not a medical practitioner, scientist, or researcher. In one viral video, he states that fapping is a bad thing because it (1) "messes up your sexuality" and (2) "kills your motivation and ambition." He goes on to recommend that if you want to be someone who has the motivation to work toward goals and has a healthy sexuality, "then NoFap is the thing for you."[23]

Published medical studies do not back up these claims about the harms of fapping (masturbation). While his intentions might be coming from a good place, I believe Mr. Mulder may be referring to online porn addiction, which involves compulsively watching porn and fapping at the same time. (It may also include engaging in other sexual activities instead of, or in addition to, fapping while compulsively watching porn.) To be clear, porn addiction is distinct from fapping with or without watching porn (but not compulsively), which is generally not considered dangerous. Regarding the rationale for his NoFap recommendation, this is my response: that's cap.

Dr. Kunal Sood, an anesthesiologist and influencer, posted a video in which he pointed to captions above his head along with music to answer the following phrase "why you should not participate in No Nut Challenge November"[24] with the statements about how masturbation can "reduce anxiety, increase endorphins (relieve pain), and improve skin."[25] To drive it home, a follow-up video addressed whether masturbation in moderation can "reduce confidence, cause oversexualization of women, decrease motivation and energy." His summary: *cap*. If that wasn't enough, Dr. Sood hit the trifecta with this video: he took the opposite position of "you should participate in No Nut November if you are" and then filled in the blank at the end with "addicted, [have] negative thoughts toward the act, religious reasons."[26]

While I would still recommend checking with a therapist or medical practitioner and looking into a twelve-step program before entering such a challenge for porn addiction or sex addiction, Dr. Sood's balanced approach counters misinformation without risk of offending people or lighting up the platform with unnecessary controversy.

Given that social media platforms are still in their relative infancy, time will tell how much long-term impact all this sexual content will have on children and adults. One thing we know for certain: it is unlikely the amount of suggestive material will decrease in the foreseeable future. If anything, influencers will become even more creative with virtual reality content and find ways for viewers to feel they are in the middle of it.

We've covered porn in relation to influence, but there are myriad other ways—both visible and hidden—that time spent on social media can hamper our ability to focus on the most important things in life. Since this holds true for influencers as well as followers, I suggest that you pay close attention to the chapter that follows.

9

Driven to Distraction

Are We Unfocused and Unproductive because of Social Media Influence?

Technology is a useful servant, but a dangerous master.

—*Christian Lous Lange, Norwegian historian*[1]

You don't have to be a PhD student in zoology or a research scientist to know that members of the animal kingdom, especially predators, are blessed with an extraordinary ability to focus. It's unlikely a tiger, wolf, hawk, or shark would ever be too preoccupied to put off stalking and hunting down delicious prey for the predator's dinner special of the day. Meanwhile, the animals lower on the food chain—fish, deer, cows, pigs, rodents, and so forth—are equally homed in on the opposite end of the spectrum, survival; their senses and instincts are heightened to be on the alert for danger and to bolt on a split second's notice when they intuit an entrée is afoot: them.[2]

There are occasions when even the most tuned-in animals become distracted, however, leading them to miss being the snacker (the one doing the snacking) or snackee (the creature serving as the treat). Sometimes, this is not a predicament of their own doing. For example, the roar of a motorboat on a lake might jolt a hermit crab enough to fail to realize that a seagull is about to swoop down and add it to its family's clambake.[3] Animals can be distracted by other externalities. Certain foul scents, such as chemicals from a factory, can hinder the mood of a hot and heavy evening between two consenting animals, who otherwise would have followed their natural procreational instincts and gotten busy.

Human beings are also distracted by outside forces, as well as by problems of their own device. The internet has made finding information on any subject matter easy and fun with a few taps on the keys. Social media has reignited dormant friendships and facilitated swift sharing of data and images—some relevant and/or educational; others nonsensical, trivial, nostalgic, and/or entertaining. For all the benefits and good the above online advancements have done for society, we have also caused a number of maladies to fester without astringent self-care—namely, some things I've previously discussed: porn addiction, racism/hatred, shaming, misinformation/disinformation, predatory and other criminal behaviors, and more.

The one thing noticeably AWOL from the above list: *time*. How much of this precious commodity has been engulfed by social media? Can you recall how you spent your time in the last century prior to the arrival of these platforms? One thing that probably came to mind was that back then you did a lot of conversing one-on-one with others on your landline, rather than the current primary usage of your mobile phone—texting and scrolling through feeds.

Just how unfocused and unproductive have we been due to social media influence? How much are we being controlled by social media and its influencers? Let's find out.

THE SOCIAL *MEDIA* DILEMMA

On January 26, 2020, Netflix released the documentary/docudrama *The Social Dilemma*. By happenstance, this was aired one and a half months prior to the COVID-19 shutdown when millions of people were forced to stay at home. The number of people on social media during this time rose to a whopping 57.6 percent of the global population—a 10 percent increase from 2020 to 2021. The average time spent on platforms per day rocketed to an average of *two hours and twenty-seven minutes per day*—a 43 percent increase—across 6.7 platforms per internet user.[4]

Let those statistics marinate for a moment. People around the world have been spending *two and a half hours of each day* on social media. To put it in perspective, the average individual only exercises twenty-three to forty minutes per day.[5] According to the Archives of Sexual Behavior, couples across age groups only have sex once a week (or fifty-two times a year).[6] To salt this sore more, the duration of sex lasts from an efficient thirty-three seconds to the "Olympic" forty-four minutes.[7] People are engaging in social media fifteen more hours per week than they are having sex.[8] It seems—based on what was discussed in the last chapter—we are far more addicted to viewing carnal acts and related activities than physically performing them.

The Social Dilemma brought to our attention how these platforms paradoxically connect us and polarize us, while also doing everything in their power to Gorilla Glue us to our screens. Instead of turning to friends, family, and professionals for personal comfort when we face emotional crises and feel isolated, we more often turn to social media to lick our wounds with quick fixes, to busy ourselves, and to escape from the real world. In the film, Tristan Harris, a former design ethicist at Google and cofounder of Center for Humane Technology, contributed this alarming statement: "We're training and conditioning a whole new generation of people that when we are uncomfortable or lonely or uncertain or afraid, we have a digital pacifier for ourselves that is kind of atrophying our own ability to deal with that."[9]

Through interviews with technological architects of algorithm-based technology—which provides the bait, or cheese, in the social media matrix that attracts users, increases their dopamine, and leads them into scrolling and clicking into black holes—the film exposes just how dangerous social media can be in terms of masterminding addictive behavior. The goal of every platform, whether they volunteer this information or not, is to mine users' data and click behavior patterns to confine them in their digital domains for as long as they possibly can. Users need not even buy anything for their activity to be valuable, as simply consuming content from creators and influencers generates enormous bytes of consumer data that can be exploited by advertisers, marketers, and the platforms themselves.

Under the tutelage of unsuspecting users, algorithms "learn" users' behavior patterns and psychology, thereby enabling them to predict their actions. Users are perpetually served such powerful boluses of customized content that breaking social media addiction can be as difficult as kicking a drug habit. Those two and a half hours per day spent on social media will likely continue to exponentially increase while challenging our ability to discern fantasy from reality (low PI), communicate and empathize well with others, and hone interests and skills outside the digital framework. At the same time, we are being hammered by online advertising, which erodes our individual and collective mindshare. A recent study revealed that influencer advertising generated "277% greater emotional intensity and 87% higher memory encoding in participants than TV ads."[10]

There is a tangible price tag on what we are paying for the avalanche of distraction, and I'm not just referring to how much money is being spent. As you'll discover in the next few pages, productivity has suffered to such an extent in schools and in the workplace that it makes us question whether we accomplished more back in the days of pen and paper.

ARE STUDENTS CHECKED OUT—BUT CLICKED ON?

Social media has attracted a wide age group of young people from preteen to college years. It's estimated that 90 percent of students between the ages of thirteen and seventeen have used at least one platform.[11] According to the Pew Research Center, 81 percent of teenagers are active users. This same Pew study identified reduced academic behaviors as a result of social media, such as "completing homework and attending class, lower academic confidence and more problems affecting their schoolwork, like lack of sleep and substance abuse."[12] The challenge for young students is that they get such a powerful dopamine hit from scrolling the feeds of influencers, creators, and friends that it's difficult for them to resist while trying to concentrate on homework or study for a test, which is unlikely to give them the equivalent DBB. For preteens and teens, clicking through their feeds becomes a perpetual itch that needs to be scratched. Once they launch into the social media universe, reentry back into schoolwork becomes harder, especially picking up where they left off.

College students don't fare all that much better. According to a 2019 Canadian research study, half of college students surveyed readily admit that their phones and laptops involve them in off-topic activities in the classroom.[13] A separate study involving 675 undergraduate and graduate students spanning twenty-six states revealed that 97 percent of students use their phones in the classroom and a stunning 70 percent of these students said this phone usage was spent on social media.[14] These stats—along with the collateral damage from overuse discussed earlier in this chapter—are likely well known to all the platforms, but are they making any effort to de-throttle? Even beer companies spend millions of dollars a year on "Drink responsibly" PSA (public service announcement)-ish commercials.

Influencer Krysten Mayers summarized it best to me: "I know a lot of people who are being productive . . . but then they take a break. They pick up their phones and go right to TikTok. They believe they will scroll for, say, five minutes. Fifteen minutes pass by, then twenty minutes pass by—and soon it becomes addictive. They don't really know how much time is passing by as they're scrolling through something that they are enjoying. . . . It can be very distracting, especially if you're in school and you're supposed to be doing a project that has a deadline in a couple of hours."

ARE WORKERS ACTUALLY WORKING?

In the last chapter, we discussed how porn addiction and sex addiction have become increasing problems for adults as a result of the internet, including social media. Do adults have the superpower necessary to resist social media distractions while they are at work? Of course, they are adults—right? According to a study by CareerBuilder, the answer is a definite no: 44 percent of employees consider the internet a major distraction while on the job; 36 percent are keeping tabs on their social media feeds. Dopamine will be dopamine.[15]

Is checking Facebook, Twitter, Instagram, or TikTok pages during office hours part of anyone's job description? Well, sometimes—if you happen to be in the marketing department working on the company's social media sites or if you are conducting genuine market research for your employer. LinkedIn makes a great deal of sense if you work in a Human Resources department or for a recruitment firm.

As we all know, however, these situations are not the case for the majority of employees, who cannot resist the tempting sirens of social media to find out what is happening in their feeds and what their favorite influencers have to offer on a daily, if not hourly, basis. While most business leaders and human resource professionals acknowledge the benefits of social media and employees can spot-check their feeds during breaks, lunches, and downtime, they also see firsthand how addictive it can be and how much company time gets swallowed up by excessive browsing—even among those who are considered good performers. Compounding the problem for organizational leaders is how many workers are thinking about what is happening on social media even when they aren't actively immersed in it.

One corporate HR leader, Steve Todd, AVP, global head of workplace at Nasdaq and founder of Open Sourced Workplace, identifies additional areas of concern. He believes social media could harm individual and company privacy issues and damage reputations, especially among employees who are prone to oversharing and post too much personal information about themselves. Taken a step further, this situation can be detrimental to a work environment when certain comments, photographs, and/or videos of a controversial (including political) nature circulate among the work population, which can impact company morale—or, worse, leak to clients and customers who might be offended by the content. He also believes that some adults develop cravings for immediate attention and gratification that are not realistic in the business world, setting them up for disappointment when that doesn't materialize in the workplace.[16]

Our challenged ability to resist social media at inopportune times and suffer the consequences reminds me of *Speed Racer*, a popular cartoon series that aired during my childhood. The fantastically fast GRX race car (that blows away Speed's Mach-5 supercar) requires its drivers to consume a designer beverage to sharpen their senses and, more important, suppress their fear of high speeds. However, the drink induces intense dehydration, but water will dilute its effects. If they can't resist the water bottle that is within arm's reach, a severe case of tachophobia (a fear of speed) overcomes the drivers and they can crash. Social media can become that water, which can derail users and influencers alike.

INFLUENCERS ARE NOT INVULNERABLE

At the beginning of this book, I made a confession about my own social media experience having crossed the line and how I devoted excessive time to the influencer part of my life, at the expense of my family. I liken my situation to a sex addiction specialist who ends up in a twelve-step program for that exact malady. Like any recovering addict who longs for the dopamine fix, I must be vigilant about getting too caught up in my influencer efforts. Fortunately, some sense was knocked into me early on, and I was able to turn things around and balance my TikTok efforts with other important parts of my life and work.

While I don't raise a celebratory glass for clinkage when I hear other influencers share tales that bear similarities to my own story, it does give me some consolation to know that we are all human and face common struggles. Influencers are by no means bulletproof against the dangers of social media—especially the drain of precious time.

Nearly all the influencers I interviewed for this book have had at least some experience with their platform work interfering with some aspect their personal lives, families, day jobs, or all three. Before we cover a few of their specific challenges, let's first take a look at how they responded to the question "How much time do you spend on your social media platform every day?"

Dr. Sarah Rav: A minimum of two hours a day to edit and to create, edit, and consume [be a user]. And then I'd spend the entire Friday filming.

Dr. Tommy Martin: Two to three hours per day.

Krysten Mayers: During the week, I'd say maybe two or three hours total. I usually make all my videos for the week on the weekends because my weekday schedules are so busy. I spend six to eight hours on Saturday making the videos, researching information, and editing them. I might have around four or five videos to post throughout the week and spend the rest of the time responding to comments.

Dr. Karan Rajan: Two to three hours a day. I will be the first one to say I probably spend too much time on social media, given that I'm a full-time doctor.

Dr. Magnolia Printz: It could be two to three hours a day on the weeks that I'm off from work.

Dr. Ricky Brown: A couple of hours a day.

Josh Otusanya: At this point, it feels like a full-time job. I feel like it's almost every hour of the working day, every single day—so, six to eight hours every day.

Dr. Jess Andrade: Three hours a day.

Spencer Barbosa: It's probably ten-plus hours a day. What I normally try and do is work as hard as I can Monday to Friday. I won't go out with my friends on those days. I try to take weekends off as much as I can, so I film extra videos during the week. But sometimes I have to create a video by the next Sunday, so I do it.

While being an influencer may appear effortless, it's anything but. These successful influencers expend an enormous amount of time, energy, and thought on getting their content just right for their followers and, ideally, creating posts that will be high octane and take off. The pattern I glean from their schedules is that those who have other "day jobs" (e.g., medical professionals, such as Dr. Rajan and myself) typically devote two to three hours a day to content generation and monitoring reactions across platforms. For the influencers who consider their social media platforms full-time jobs (such as Josh Otusanya and Spencer Barbosa), they are toiling around the clock like serial entrepreneurs and putting in six-to-ten-hour workdays and sometimes working weekends, days off, and holidays too.

There isn't a set blueprint, as the amount of time varies as needed to get things done. Unless an influencer has a pressing deadline for a sponsored post for an advertiser, influencers generally have flexible schedules within their control. I can say from personal experience that it's all too easy for influencers to get consumed by the platforms, just as users get caught up in the content that has been produced for them.

As is the case with any "job"—even one that is rewarding—it's entirely possible for the constant labor involved to take a serious toll on influencers, especially younger ones. Cases of burnout seem to be escalating. What initially was fun and gratifying for Gen Zers sometimes becomes a stressful chore that can take away from their educations, social lives, and other career pursuits. TikTok influencers such as Jack Innanen, Sha Crow, and even MLI Charli D'Amelio have all been vocal about the heavy burden they feel to keep producing content without a break and, as a result, have lost some enthusiasm for it over time.[17] Another creator, Josh Ostrovsky, once said to a reporter, "We're probably heading into a period of social media burnout. It's just too much. The noise is really hitting critical mass."[18] This issue has not deterred Mr. Ostrovsky from continuing to sprint in this marathon to maximize his content and engage his followers.

Spencer Barbosa candidly described her challenges as a full-time influencer to me: "My parents are always telling me that I need to have fun—that, as much as I love my job now, I still need to live my life and have a life outside of my job." Ms. Barbosa attempts to take weekends off, but often other people don't care about her schedule, so she caves in to requests that end up placing greater strain on her. "Sometimes," she admits, "I wish someone else could do this for me. But no one else can be Spencer Barbosa."

How addictive can the work become for content creators? For influencers, this has become an escalating problem because, once we have determined from data (number of views, shares, likes, comments) what type of content has the most appeal, we are carrotted to keep producing posts at a frenetic pace to capture the momentum while it's hot and fill our perception of demand.

According to Dr. Dana Brems, social media has become increasingly difficult to resist because the algorithms on every platform continue to become refined—which, for influencers, translates to "a much longer amount of time on social media than we did in the past." Dr. Brems arrived at the fascinating conclusion that "the platforms are pushing users away from content from their own friends in preference of influencers, or just videos that you'll just generally find entertaining. Back in the day, when we were just starting on social media, we were consuming stuff from our own friends. But now there's no end. It's like an infinite scroll." It's like trying to slurp water from a fire hydrant.

Dr. Sandra Lee (a.k.a. "Dr. Pimple Popper") described the situation this way to Dr. Tony Youn (who relayed it to me): "'Somebody who literally has no following makes a TikTok video and, all of a sudden, gets a million views. Then, on the next video, she'll get nothing. It's like gambling.'"

That dopamine rush and I are intimate; I know how exhilarating it can be. You refresh, refresh, and refresh to bear witness to your talent, which feeds your ego—at least for the moment. You watch the views go nuclear. You get giddy seeing gushing comments rush in like a tidal wave. Finally, you feel showered in dopamine as the shares hit the big league of 10K and then 100K. Every new benchmark drenches you in more dopamine until you're supersoaked like a towel in a hot midsummer rainstorm.

Then . . . the video climaxes and drops in a day or so. Now what? Influencers are compelled to scurry and create a follow-up post that tries to exceed the success of the last one. In other words, they might shove a lot more chips (translated to time and energy) into the pot. If that subsequent video doesn't achieve the same level of success, the influencer's emotional and mental state may come crashing down.

Dr. Brems has endured all the highs and lows. While she knows the posting spigot can be turned off anytime a break becomes necessary, it doesn't diminish the sense of loss an influencer experiences going cold turkey. "It's really difficult to deal with the fact that I might not be 'that guy' anymore—like maybe my time has passed. At times, I can get bummed. I miss that dopamine release."

My story of influencer addiction is a cautionary tale, but nearly all the influencers I interviewed provided their own version of how the obsession manifested and came close to spiraling out of control at one time or another. Dr. Tommy Martin confirmed how being an influencer has been known to take his attention away from people who are important to him. "Initially," he said, "when TikTok grew rapidly, I was having a hard time keeping up with it and not neglecting family time. I have definitely felt addicted at times. The need to make content, the need to respond to every message can hurt and damage other relationships."

Dr. Jess Andrade described to me the slight toll being an influencer has taken on her personal life: "I would spend the day by myself at my house doing content creation in a quiet space where I could film. Then I would try to find ways to create content when nobody was around, which also interfered because I wasn't able to do other stuff, such as go to the gym and do some of my chores. I was constantly on my cell phone responding to messages because you're supposed to do that within the first half hour after posting videos. I think this strained the relationship between my significant other and me. Since he's in internal medicine, we weren't seeing too much of each other because we were both working so hard in the ICUs. On top of that, I was doing TikTok in all of my free time. There came a point where I needed to face the fact that it wasn't working for me. I had to figure out a better way because this is a secondary thing for me; the primary thing in my life is my personal relationship."

Dr. Andrade needed a wake-up call to jolt her out of social media immersion. She and her significant other were unable to see or speak to each other much, so they were like two ships passing in the night. "I realized this was not sustainable in any way, shape, or form and took steps to rework things."

Ms. Barbosa became so laser focused on boosting her numbers that it impacted her mental health. "When you have a video blow up [go viral], it's an adrenaline rush and you get so excited. I kept refreshing to see how many views I had. I had to take a good look at myself in the mirror and say, 'People like your content. People like you. You're making good stuff. Why are you so worried about the numbers?' Sometimes you have to sit back and look at yourself in the mirror and prioritize what you want in life. You have to find out what makes you happy—numbers on an iPhone should not make you lose your mind."

Every influencer—including me—will acknowledge that the phone itself is often the biggest distraction. The device offers so many functions, apps, and things to search—not to mention neck-snapping notification bells, rings, and buzzes—that it often becomes impossible to put the phone down, especially for those among us who rely on it for most of our content creation, posting, and engagement. It becomes even more complicated when you have kids who demand and deserve your attention. Dr. Ricky Brown knew this was happening with his children, except they wouldn't specifically say anything to him (as my daughters did to me). "They saw me checking my phone and making posts all the time. I could hear them talking to me—but without actually talking to me, if you know what I mean. It was like I could hear them saying in their heads, *Dude, put it down and be present.* I realized this is not okay. This isn't who I am. It's important for me and my business, but I need to treat it so that it's business time work, not personal time work. I made a conscious effort to start putting my phone down in front of them. And I still battle with that."

Meanwhile, Dr. Shah sometimes needs to be distracted from social media content creation by someone else to find personal balance and prevent it from consuming him. "I don't take a break unless my wife makes me take a break," he admitted. "When I hang out with her, I don't spend time on social media."

Ms. Mayers and I concur that sometimes you need to shut the phone down as if you are placing a lock on it. She knows both influencers and social media users who put timers on their phones to establish scheduling parameters and limit screen time. "It all comes down to self-discipline. Otherwise, you don't really know how much time passes by where you're just scrolling. . . . Social media pulls you in and tailors your content, so you want to see more things. I know people pull who pull out their phones [while driving] at red lights, which I think is very bad."

DRUNK ON SOCIAL MEDIA

When you're driving on the road, your radar must be constantly scanning for all kinds of hazards: the recklessness and/or carelessness of drivers, potholes and unexpected objects or animals on the road, harsh weather conditions, and other dangers. For years, two threats to drivers were at the top of this list of preventable things most likely to cause an accident: drunk driving and mobile phone usage.

Initially, the problem with phones concerned people distracted while speaking on the device—phone to ear. This issue subsided when Bluetooth came on the scene, so people could talk hands-free, reducing danger. Then texting was ushered in, and thus began the era of drivers tapping away while blazing down the highway or knee-steering in traffic.

Now we have mounting numbers of people who are single-handedly scrolling through their social media feeds—and perhaps even posting and chatting on the platforms—with the other hand on the wheel. According to the Virginia Tech Transportation Institute, "distracted driving" has officially become the number one cause of road accidents at 90 percent.[1] More than ten people a day are killed by distracted driving with thousands more injured.[2] In one high-profile case, a Beverly Hills plastic surgeon named Frank Ryan crashed off the Pacific Coast Highway in Malibu and died because he was posting a photo of his border collie on social media while driving.[3]

This is all preventable. Some quick and easy rules of the road: Never drive drunk. Never text or email while driving. Lastly, *never* look at your social media feeds while driving. The influencers and your social media friends will just have to wait until you to arrive at your destination for you to view, like, and comment on their posts.

NOTES

1. "VTTI Impacts Transportation Policy," Virginia Tech Transportation Institute, May 14, 2013, https://featured.vtti.vt.edu/?p=197.

2. Joel Feldman, "Social Media Apps Are Too Dangerous to Use While Driving—EndDD.org Joins with the Partnership for Distraction-Free Driving to Launch a Petition to Save Lives," EndDD, June 6 (no year), https://www.enddd.org/end-distracted-driving/enddd-in-the-news/social-media-apps-dangerous-use-driving-enddd-org-joins-partnership-distraction-free-driving-launch-petition-save-lives/.

3. Kate Linthicum, "Celebrity Plastic Surgeon Apparently Tweeted Minutes before Deadly Crash," *Los Angeles Times*, August 18, 2010, https://latimesblogs.latimes.com/lanow/2010/08/frank-ryan-twitter-crash-heidi-montag-text-malibu-.html.

Over the years, I've picked up a few valuable tips on influencer work/ life balance from my own experiences, as well as from listening to my peers. I'll provide these solutions in chapter 12. In my mind, being able to be a responsible, balanced, well-rounded person who has their priorities straight and knows how to prevent and curb social media addiction is part and parcel of becoming a healthy, successful, accomplished influencer.

We have a couple of chapters to go before we get there, however. Next, we venture into the sinister world of cults, which can lure in and devastate the lives of innocent people of all ages, genders, races, creeds, and colors. The key similarities between the world of cults and that of influence?

A sense of belonging. Acceptance. Like-mindedness. Instant gratification and reward.

And . . . both situations involve followers.

10

Clicks and Cults

When Does an Influencer's Following Become a Cult?

All that glitters is not gold.

—*William Shakespeare*, Merchant of Venice[1]

Social media has become the new breeding ground for influencer-led cults and cultlike groups. There seems to be little the platforms can do to police them, unless they break the community guidelines. Sometimes the threats aren't identified and taken down until it's too late and the damage has already been done.

In 2017, a self-proclaimed spiritual guru named Bentinho Massaro lured in massive followers through his social media influence on Instagram, YouTube, and Facebook. Massaro claimed that he "vibrated at a higher frequency" than other mortals and goaded people into believing he was something of a godlike figure. Then came the hopeium financial pitch. For a meager $1,199 fee, a follower could gain access to a twelve-day cleansing retreat with Mr. Vibration himself in Sedona, California (dubbed "the Sedona Experiment II"). For a lesser amount, one could discover the enlightened path on Massaro's livestream feed. The event came to a screeching halt midway when Brent Wilkins, a longtime member of Massaro's herd, committed suicide.[2]

A TikTok influencer named Melissa Ong referred to herself as a "Mother Hen" to her following, whom were dubbed "Step Chickens." In May 2020, the *New York Times* reported that the Mother Hen enticed her flock—which numbers in the millions—and spread conformity by encouraging them to adopt her blue selfie profile picture. She subsequently cajoled them into flooding the comments boxes of Phil Swift, the creator of Flex Tape. Caving into the massive pressure, Mr. Swift adopted Ms. Ong's blue avatar as well.[3]

This may seem benign—even playful—at first, but there is an underlying issue here: How can one influencer wield so much power and influence that they can infiltrate and overrun the comments sections of someone's feed with a mob mentality, pressuring the target into doing their bidding? This turns pernicious and striking when we consider that Barack Obama and Mark Zuckerberg have been on the receiving end of the Mother Hen's trolling efforts. Whether you like or despise the individuals who were locked in her sights is not germane; it creates a cultish culture that can potentially incite racism, anti-Semitism, homophobia, political hatred, and a cornucopia of other antagonistic beliefs, widening our already splintered social divides.

Social media cults have a major edge over cults from the past. Whereas it used to take many years to recruit and indoctrinate new members, cult influencers today can accomplish the same feat with minimal effort and just a few manipulative posts. Social media algorithms can inadvertently infuse the onboarding process with steroids. The platforms curate and circulate posts based on the patterns set into motion by the users, so, if a follower is prone is engaging with certain types of content, that individual will probably continue to receive videos and articles on related subject matter. The feeds of antivaxxers, for example, are likely to be irrigated with posts that reinforce their beliefs.

The political world is well basted for this kind polarizing behavior, making it difficult for individuals to be receptive to others' views. Why would they be open to ideas that contradict their own when they see posts that confirm what they already believe to be true? People with liberal predilections tend to be deluged with content on feminist and civil rights–related topics, whereas conservatives are likely be exposed to continuous content about government control and overspending. In both extreme instances, the users enthusiastically engage with their feeds because they have more ammunition to support their arguments. The algorithms ensure that the singers are in front of their choirs. When a post is shared, a follower might comment something along the lines of "I agree. It proves everything I've been saying all along." Of course it does! As Dr. Dana Brems said to me, "They don't even realize that what they're seeing is catered to them. They think what they're seeing is the standard—the normal—but they don't realize that the content is one sided and directed *to* them. They don't understand that they are being fed this content because the algorithm has predetermined they would agree with it." We are all in the echo chamber, but only some of us are aware of it.

THE NORMALIZATION OF CRAZY

Cultish behaviors have permeated world history for centuries. Thousands, if not millions, of lives were lost during the Crusades (1096–1272), when European Christian soldiers sought to conquer the Holy Land. The invaders attacked Muslim and Turkish peoples because Pope Urban II egged them on with the words "God wills it" (or "It is the will of God"). You know someone has sprung a leak when one individual claims to have received DMs from a higher power to launch a mass attack on another civilization.

History seems to have forgotten the widespread, erroneous belief in witches that spread throughout Europe from 1300 to 1850, leading to public trials and the deaths of thousands of innocent people. In Germany alone, nearly 16,500 people—mostly women and girls—were tried and 7,000 were executed during this time frame. In 1642, Connecticut—then part of the British colonies—made the practice of witchcraft punishable by death.[4] Fifty years later, in Salem, Massachusetts, the infamous witch trials took place in which nineteen citizens were publicly hanged.

In total, hundreds of thousands of women and girls were murdered through rigged jury trials. Who originated this practice? A different pope. What prompted being arrested as a "witch suspect"? Merely an accusation from a man who was a true believer of the church's doctrine.

Cults may form for a variety of reasons: in the name of religion, due to a fear of the unknown or unexplained, or as a result of the founder's misperceptions, ill-conceived theories, or personal biases. As the rise of Nazism in Germany in the 1930s and 1940s proves, cultish thought can become embedded in an extreme political movement and catch on like an arsonist's handiwork—especially when the right conditions exist (e.g., a poor economy) and a specific group (such as the Jewish people during the Holocaust in which six million lives were exterminated, in addition to other groups) is targeted and blamed for the world's ills.

Misinformation, disinformation, conspiracy theories, prejudice, hatred, and/or a general desire to incite chaos fuel cultish thought. The more outlandish the concept, it seems, the more intoxicating the fervor.

Holocaust denials . . . UFOs . . . Antivaxxers . . . The 1969 moon landing was fake. . . . Dinosaurs never existed. . . . 9/11 didn't happen. . . . Election fraud . . . Crusades against evolution . . . Sandy Hook school shooting conspiracy theories . . . The world is flat. . . .

Let's pause right there: All the above theories seem ludicrous, right? None perhaps is as eyebrow raising as the belief that our planet isn't round. Is there really a group of people alive today who insist on this? Yes—and, in fact, they are quite serious. *Forbes* reported a survey in which one-third of all millennials believe the world is flat.[5] Rapper B.o.B (real name Bobby Ray Simmons Jr.) initiated a crowdfunding campaign in 2017 to raise money in support of the "earth is flat" theory.[6] Even NBA star Kyrie Irving was temporarily on that flight. (He later apologized.)[7] The ultimate goal was to launch a craft into space to help B.o.B "find the curve"—meaning, pinpoint the planet's edge. (Spoiler alert: NASA has been up there many times over and just can't seem to find that wily edge of earth.) The movement, spawned by batches of YouTube videos that went viral into the millions, grew to the point of some six hundred people attending its first national conference, which was captured in the 2018 documentary *Behind the Curve*. The biggest proponent of the theory, dubbed "the King of the Flat-Earthers," is a former software analyst turned competitive gamer named Mark Sargent (who does not have a scientific degree of any kind).

KINGS OF THEIR JUNGLES

Some dubious narcissists have royal titles bestowed on them (or dub themselves). David Koresh, leader of the 1980s Branch Davidian cult in Waco, Texas, was born Vernon Wayne Howell. He changed his name to Koresh, the name of an ancient Persian king. The "David" part added extra grandeur, as that harkens back to King David, the leader of the United Monarchy of Israel and Judah (a.k.a. Israel) circa 1010 BCE and the fellow recounted in the Old Testament as having slung down a certain infamous giant named Goliath.[1]

NOTE

1. No author, "Biography: David Koresh," *Frontline*, PBS, n.d., https://www.pbs.org/wgbh/pages/frontline/waco/davidkoresh.html.

While Mr. Sargent and his posse pose a greater threat to science, education, and collective PI than they do to anyone's physical or emotional health, their retrograde thinking takes humanity back eons in terms of intellectual progress. In addition to spreading misinformation, groups such as this one also resemble cults in terms of their ability to appeal to and assimilate people who feel isolated and separated from their families and communities. They welcome newcomers with open arms, serving as a place for them to feel safe and accepted. In other words, people who see themselves as outsiders to society suddenly feel like they fit in and belong—key ingredients for cults.

WHEN A FEED FEELS LIKE A CULT

There isn't a formal rule stating that physical group interaction is a requisite for a collective to be considered a cult. Cults can easily originate in the virtual world; in fact, they can operate in stealth mode and go under the radar in the digital universe, which primes social media for recruitment. Once the group has been established and amassed a following, in-person meetups and events ("conferences") may be held to tighten the knot.

DIGGING FOR THE MEANING AND ORIGINS OF *CULT*

You may already have guessed that the etymology of the word *cult* traces back to the ancient Romans (the term *cultus*). The initial meaning of *cultus* was along the lines of "care and worship." The word morphed into *culte* in French before being added to the English vernacular sometime in the early seventeenth century sans the *e*, as plain *cult*.[1]

So far, so good—right?

Next, we examine the Latin word *cultura*, which referred to farming. How does cult "care and worship" get laced with "growing crops"? For cults to survive, they must methodically be nurtured over time, as is done after planting seeds.

That still doesn't explain how the word *cult* has taken on a negative connotation distinct from *religion* to signify a *tainted fringe* or *unorthodox* group. One reason may be that, in the seventeenth century, William Penn (later the founder of Pennsylvania) used the word *cult* in writing about his ardent belief in the Quaker religion, which bought him an all-inclusive two-year stay in the Tower of London prison. Since being a Quaker was considered fringey back then and outside the Protestant "norm," the state founder's use of *cult* may have caused it to absorb a pejorative flavor.[2]

NOTES

1. Egor Kotkin, "What Is, Really, the Difference between a Cult and Religion (and the Origin of the Word 'Religion') Explained," Medium, January 6, 2019, https://medium.com/@EgorKotkin/what-is-really-the-difference-between-a-cult-and-religion-and-the-origin-of-the-word-88b36dda887f.

2. Editors of *Merriam-Webster's Collegiate Dictionary*, "Joining the 'Cult' of Word Etymology," *Sun Journal*, January 2, 2005, https://www.sunjournal.com/2005/01/02/joining-cult-word-etymology/.

Influencer feeds can occasionally come across as "cultish." Not only do some fringe influencers provide an inviting familial and community feeling for new followers (a.k.a. "recruits"), but they also share the following tendencies:

- Seek to build a mass following isolated from others.
- Provide the mantra and teachings of a central identified leader.
- Demand conformity in terms of a consistent "look" (e.g., avatars/ profile pictures for online followers).
- Focus on a similar member profile: vulnerable and lost young people (which is especially true during our era of social distancing).
- Procure money from their members. (For example, Ms. Ong sells vast amounts of merchandising.)

- Command followers to blindly do their bidding. (In the case of social media, it could mean something as simple as trolling the comments section of a public figure.)
- Wield enough power to intimidate, frighten, embarrass, or humiliate people whose views differ from their own.

Lastly, cult leaders—whether they originate online or on a physical campus—have a predisposition for thinking they are connected to a higher power, if not serving as a god themselves. Despite his moniker, "Medical Medium," influencer Anthony William has not received a whit of formal medical training. He asserts that his information comes to him through "a spirit" and that he has received personal messages from God. *Mr.* (not *Dr.*) William recommends celery juice ("the global celery juice movement") to heal fibromyalgia and provide relief for illnesses such as diabetes and cancer.[8] I suppose there are far worse things to recommend than celery juice, but it raises ethical questions about posting misinformation that has the potential to fill some people with false hope and perhaps lead them to forgo their physician-prescribed treatments and medications. (Celery does happen to contain some valuable nutrients and antioxidants; it is also low on the glycemic index, although it won't reverse diabetes.) It's often not beneficial to raise patients' hopes on theories that haven't been proven by science. The blind religious fervor for Mr. William's videos has gained him hundreds of thousands of followers across TikTok, YouTube, and Instagram and caught the attention of numerous celebrities, such as tennis pro Novak Djokovic. He even popped up on an episode of *Keeping Up with the Kardashians* on television and appeared on Gwyneth Paltrow's website Goop. Validation from other influencers and Hollywood celebs only boosts his public stature.

Dr. Rajan explained it like this: "Wherever there's a platform, there will be a yin and yang and a good versus evil. There will be the kind of power struggle between empirical evidence and pseudoscience. The Jedi cannot exist without the Sith and balance the Force, right?"

How does one distinguish a true influencer from someone who has ulterior motives? "In general, you shouldn't trust anyone," Dr. Dana Brems warns. "You don't know people from the content they post online. People who post things that make themselves look like a good person—honestly, that's kind of suspicious."

YOUTUBERS UNHINGED

In the world of social media influence, mischievous puerile humor can sometimes easily tip over to coming across as cultish behavior. What seems amusing, edgy, and irreverent to the influencer/leader can be taken seriously by their young followers and can lead to people getting physically, mentally, or emotionally injured.

In 2018, an irreverent young YouTube star named Logan Paul videotaped entering Japan's Aokigahara Forest (a.k.a. the "suicide forest") with an entourage of his friends. The group discovered an actual corpse dangling from a tree. Instead of shutting off the recording and contacting the authorities, Mr. Paul decided to videotape close-ups and other angles of the body and intersperse them with reaction shots of himself. A monsoon of outrage poured down on the influencer, including from suicide prevention groups and YouTube itself, which demoted him from its top-tier monetization system. Mr. Paul issued an apology, but his vlogs continue undaunted as he inveigles followers to "join the movement and be a maverick."[9]

Another influencer who casts a cultish shadow is David Dobrik, the leader of the Vlog Squad, which initiated frat boy–type pranks and stunts while he and his followers looked on and giddily reacted like an amped-up laugh track. Mr. Dobrik's subscription base ballooned into the millions, and his popularity crossed over to animated films (*The Angry Birds Movie 2*) and television (*Dodgeball Thunderdome* on the Discovery Channel).[10] He became embroiled in controversy when sexual assault accusations (including rape) were leveled against him from former female and male Vlog Squad members, along with reveals of risky antics in which Dobrik placed his squad in harm's way. In April 2021,

YouTuber Jeff Wittek posted a two-part video docuseries in which he recounted how he had bashed his face and injured his eye when Dobrik swung him in the air from an excavator machine above water. "This was where I made a mistake," Mr. Wittek commented. "I forgot that the biggest fucking idiot I know was driving it [the excavator]."[11]

Like other influencers who enjoy living on the edge and follow a muse in the tradition of Jeffrey Tremaine (producer/director of the infamous *Jackass* franchise), Mr. Dobrik has developed a fan base that targets younger male viewers. He appeared as a competitor on *Kids Choice Sports* and as a guest judge on various Nickelodeon contest programs. How many kids have been inspired to attempt ill-advised feats based on Mr. Dobrik's cultish influence? Although his scandals and reputation led to being shunned by some subscribers and followers, distancing by his sponsors (including the Dollar Shave Club), and a three-month YouTube cancellation, he is back in the game as of this writing with all-new attention-seeking videos: gorging on fast food with friends in a hot tub; pranking friends and family members by having them sit in a tub of ice disguised as a seat; cruising in police high-speed cars in Dubai . . . you get the picture.[12]

Whereas Mr. Paul and Mr. Dobrik straddle the fence between fringe fun and incivility for the sake of follower development and allegiance, there are those on the other side of the spectrum, where the behavior does a dark dive. They utilize social media to lure innocent victims with the intent of committing heinous crimes under the guise of offering love and/or spiritual enlightenment.

THE SINISTER SIDE OF SOCIAL MEDIA

In May 2021, Bangladesh police arrested TikTok influencer Ridoy Babo and five others for assault on a local woman. (Mr. Babo and one of his compadres were shot by police and injured while attempting to escape.) Further investigations unearthed that Mr. Babo and his followers had been targeting young women all over India and the Middle East with the clandestine intent of kidnapping them for sex trafficking. They had even established a Facebook group that organized a pool party with some eight hundred attendees—many of whom were intended victims.

The group's recruiting methods bore remarkable similarity to cults of the past, targeting young women who were estranged from their families, as well as runaways, high school and college introverts, and lonely housewives. They were lured in by glamorous promises of appearing in TikTok videos and/or being hired for jobs in hair salons or mall stores before Mr. Babo and his syndicate funneled them to hotel rooms. From there, they were drugged, photographed/videoed nude, raped, and/or sold into the sex trade.[13]

Dr. Rajan summed it up this way to me: "Babo had eighty thousand followers, which may not seem like a lot—but can fill up a sports stadium. He was basically leading women into slavery and human trafficking, which shows the power of social media for evil."

What makes this especially surprising is that, as of this writing, Ridoy Babo's TikTok account remains up. In his videos, he seems to be a harmless singing and dancing playboy who charms adoring women. One would never suspect any wrongdoing from his influencer feed, validating Dr. Brems's prudent advice: perception of an influencer's image doesn't always equal reality.

No matter where you live, be vigilant and on the alert: anytime a social media influencer invites you or your child to a gathering or meetup can be a potential trip wire and must be considered with caution. If you feel lonely or isolated, please be aware that these feelings might make you susceptible to cultish influences. To quote William Penn, "Only trust thyself, and another shall not betray thee."[14]

CULTISH FORCES . . . FOR GOOD?

I recognize that the above heading sounds like a paradox: How can a cult be considered good? Isn't a cult something to be reviled, no matter what?

As you've inferred throughout this book, I like to take a balanced stance. While there are fringe social media groups led by influencers that dip into cult collectives—namely, outspoken ideology and unconditional inclusion of people—their intent seems authentic and their practices responsible. They may assert dogmatic opinions, but they aren't corralling, manipulating, or abusing people. In fact, they may not have any ulterior intentions whatsoever.

As Dr. Shah pointed out to me, some social media influencers provide a genuine sense of belonging and security for those who don't have a community. As he described, "I grew up in a town where I was the only person named Muneeb Shah—and the only person who had a name that even sounded like that. I was inherently different from my peers. I didn't have a community around me that could understand my culture."

For individuals who are ostracized and/or bullied because of their sexual preferences, for example, social media groups—led by the well-intentioned influencers—can provide a place of needed comfort, commonality, support, and even catharsis. They can act like themselves without fear of being on the receiving end of taunts, threats, and other forms of prejudice. Dr. Shah stated that he has "LGBTQ friends who didn't come out for a long time because they didn't have a supportive community around them." He also told me about a video of someone he followed who came out on TikTok and "received so much support and positive comments. He couldn't tell his family, but at least he has this global community of people."

In other words, somewhere out there in the social media universe, there is an influencer for anyone and everyone—which is a potent upside to counter the bad actors and hatemongers. No matter what cause you happen to be interested in—sustainability, feeding the homeless, assistance to veterans, election fairness, cures for illnesses, and so forth—it likely exists in some form on social media. Social media crowdsourcing via influencers can serve as a powerful tool to increase awareness about an issue and possibly raise money for deserving charitable causes.

The upshot is this: Influencers have a special talent for communicating to their followers. They can choose to inculcate users into believing misinformation and possibly even incite them to harm others and/or themselves. Or they can become a reliable, authentic source for information, instruction, encouragement, and/or entertainment. Unfortunately, it's low-hanging ego fruit for creators with controversial, extremist ideas to develop a God complex and lead people astray for money, power, control, plain kicks—or just bragging rights about a viral video that went supernova.

Now that you know all about clicks and cults, you are ready to advance to the next level and discover how to become a positive influencer yourself. As wise Master Yoda said, "To be Jedi is to face the truth, and choose. Give off light, or darkness, Padawan. Be a candle, or the night."[15]

11

So, You Want to Be an Influencer

How to Be a Responsible, Successful Influencer and Lead a Balanced Life

Life is about balance.

—Snoopy *(Peanuts cartoon character)*[1]

The time is right to take you on a necessary detour. I liken our time together thus far to a culinary journey: a chef telling you all about your favorite dish. We've identified the recipe components, where the ingredients come from, and how each one provides valuable nutrients for your body (or harms it, as the case may be). Wouldn't you now love to take a sneak peek in the kitchen and view firsthand how the chef prepares your special entrée? This is that chapter: how influencers are created.

Before we probe *how* to be an influencer, it's important to first identify *why* some desire to be an influencer in the first place—a *purpose* or *why,* if you will—so then goals can be established. It seems every influencer enters the playing field for different reasons. Some fall into it by happenstance—as a result of one well-timed video post gone viral—whereas others (such as myself) are more strategic. No matter what draws people into doing it, it's prudent to have at least one (if not a few) *why(s)* and feel so passionate about it (or them) that it (they) will help get the aspirer through the emotionally charged, g-force roller-coaster ride (which we'll cover in this chapter).

While we don't have room to address every single potential *why*, I've categorized the main ones into the following buckets:

- *To create:* Dr. Fayez Ajib described his *why* in the following manner: "I think the simple answer is that I just *enjoy it*. I like using it as a creative outlet." I would home in on the words *creative outlet*. Although it may not seem obvious to the casual social media user, being a content creator can satisfy the creative itch for many influencers. Like writing, painting, quilting, and other creative endeavors, the process of content creation can be intensely gratifying, especially when one considers the immediate reactions from followers and viewers versus that of other creative mediums.

- *To inspire:* Dr. Tommy Martin said to me that he loves to "inspire as many people as I can while spreading love and positivity." Sounds like something a flower power hippie musician said during the summer of love in 1967, right? In this case, Dr. Martin is referring to content that either touches the emotions in some powerful way or galvanizes people into taking action. For example, some people become inspired to enter a profession (such as becoming a physician) because of an influencer's posts. Others might be inspired to try their hand at becoming influencers themselves.

- *To entertain:* Every social media influencer wants to entertain people to at least some degree and, in fact, is charged with needing to do so if they want sustained success. If a post doesn't contain something to captivate a viewer—something humorous, unexpected, touching, and so forth—the viewer won't become engaged. Even influencers who are physicians might have at least a splash of desire to entertain, as Dr. Muneeb Shah related to me: "If your content is too serious all the time, you won't be relatable. If you're not relatable, you seem less trustworthy. And, if you're less trustworthy, then people will trust someone else's word over yours. So, it's actually very important for physicians to be entertaining."

- *To educate*: This area—educating people—happens to be my specialty as an influencer. Medical professionals who are influencers are often driven by a desire to inform—to share knowledge, insights, and research—particularly with regard to health information that is in the zeitgeist ("the spirit of the time; the taste and outlook characteristic of a period or generation").[2] This includes creating factual awareness and correcting misinformation and disinformation (such as medical-related topics).

- *To help*: This *why* is shared by influencers in a variety of areas and is especially true of medical professionals. It's why we entered the field in the first place: to treat, to heal, to make lives better. Of course, physicians are not the only group of influencers whose *why* is rooted in helping people. There are scores of influencers—notably Beth Kanter (author of *Beth's Blog*) and Matt Flannery (cofounder of Kiva.org and Branch.co, which helps low-income entrepreneurs)—who devote their platforms to raising awareness and fundraising for their causes.

Note that none of the above is about making money or becoming famous. There is nothing wrong with either of these, but they shouldn't serve as your primary *why*. Consider fortune and fame as nice add-on bonuses or surprise perks. If you storm out of the barn seeking riches and superstardom, people will see right through it and determine that you lack authenticity, as we explored in previous chapters.

HOW TO GET STARTED AND SEEM LIKE A PROFESSIONAL

I'm hoping by now you've realized that becoming an influencer isn't as simple as hitting Record on your phone, posting it, and waking up in the morning to find you've been anointed an influencer. Like anything else worth doing well, it takes time, effort, practice, research, experience, and learning from mistakes with generous helpings of humble pie.

Shooting a Profile Picture

Let's begin with the basics: your profile picture (abbreviated to *pfp*). Some think you need to hire a Hollywood headshot photographer. You don't. Your pfp represents who you are. Studies show people like smiling faces versus nonsmiling *punims* (Yiddish for faces). So, it's best to smile, unless you don't often smile in your content. If you never wear a suit, why would you post a pfp of yourself decked out for the prom? All you need is a smartphone and good lighting. Some people have their faces and upper bodies in the pfp, whereas others prefer to appear like an animated character. You have multitudes of creative directions, but let it reflect *you*. You can also change your pfp, but I wouldn't recommend doing this too often because your pfp will become part of your brand recognition for your account, videos, and even the comments you make, since your pfp is right next to anything you post.

Developing Your Influencer Brand

At this stage, decide on your influencer brand. Who are you? What do you stand for or against? What is your passion? What is your expertise? Do you have a certain look?

Whatever influencer brand you develop, for it to be effective, you would like it to be recognized by other people as being authentic *to you*. You may happen to admire a certain influencer and hope to copy and paste that person's brand to yours, but trust me: this never works. It is perfectly okay, however, to be inspired by another influencer and take it to the next level. How did I become known as the cap doctor on social media? I made a video about my origins story. Like a superhero, I characteristically landed on one knee (and hurt my back in the process!) while wearing my signature blue cap. I looked up at the camera and asked, "How did I become the cap doctor?" I went on to explain that Dr. Youn was my inspiration, since I had seen him use the word *cap* and looked up the meaning. I then took a blue cap and emblazoned the front with the white letters *CAP*. I subsequently developed my own style of videos using the blue "cap" hat. Some people have copied it, but it doesn't seem to work for them. The moral of the story: a certain amount of homage is okay, but copying is not recommended.

Not all influencers have a consistent look, but, for my videos, I almost always don my blue surgeon's cap, blue scrubs, and surgical mask (worn down, cradling my neck). It's my signature "attire logo"—perhaps like the Nike swoosh—so, when people see me, they instantly recognize who I am before I even utter a word.

Creating Posts

Next comes the real work, creating at least two quality videos per week (such as for Instagram and TikTok; once a week for YouTube), cleverly written tweets (such as for Twitter), or photographs (all platforms) that will resonate with people and force them to stop scrolling and watch your video or post. It's fine to jump on some trends—and at least know whether your topic is in the zeitgeist—but you don't want to rely on trends, as Dr. Rajan warned against.

Please do not be fooled into thinking this will be quick and easy and that you'll get it right the first time. It can often be time consuming, arduous, and high pressure to consistently come up with fresh and relevant ideas, write good content, shoot it, and edit/produce videos without amateurish mistakes. Platforms seem to be moving to hyper-short transitions for dialogue video edits with excised dead audio space. I now edit out all pauses between most of my spoken lines. The same information gets across just a little bit faster, which can make a difference in terms of user reception and rewatching the video—a key metric for many algorithms. (I have no proof that doing so flips the algorithm viral switch on a video, but it's my observation that videos edited in this manner have a greater tendency to go viral.)

Be patient. Make your video, message, or photograph as good as possible ("good enough" can be better than perfect from a time management view); sometimes a twenty-second post can take hours and numerous takes to complete. If you have any doubt whatsoever, don't post it. Once it's live, it's out there for anyone and everyone to see. (In reality, you can always make a video private or delete it.)

Getting Verified

You may wish to become verified as an influencer. The verification process is a bit opaque, like chalk. You can apply for this status on Instagram, Twitter, and Facebook, but not on TikTok, where you need them to bestow the verification badge upon you. (As it happens, I'm verified on TikTok, Twitter, and Facebook. I've applied several times to Instagram and have been denied each time. Why? Your guess is literally as good as mine.) Verification proves you are who you say you are.[3] Some people believe that when Instagram and other social networks verify an influencer, it's a sign of prestige indicating that you are important enough for someone to emulate (create a fake account in your name). Dr. Shah downplayed the importance of verification to me: "When I was verified on Instagram, it was a new thing, and I was excited about it. But then it wore off. I thought, *My life is actually no different than it was prior to verification.*"

Your Post Is Live . . . Now What?

Don't get too comfortable—your work is hardly done. Your soufflé is now in the oven and you need to stand by and see whether it rises. Some influencers babysit their phones and feverishly refresh over and over to see whether the views blow north and responses start to roll in; others step away for a bit to focus on something else and clear their heads. Dr. Brems tends to wait for the first few comments to pop up and respond to them. "After ten minutes of doing that, I'll just walk away," she reported to me.

Sometimes the reactions drip in, which can feel like you are watching paint dry. *Relax. Breathe. Don't panic.* It could still turn out all right!

This is a good time to engage with people who write comments over the next twenty-four to forty-eight hours. You can type responses or just simply click "Like" on a favorable reaction, but you could also post a thumbs-up, smiling face, or other emoji in response to a person's comments. This demonstrates that you care about your viewers, since you took the time to read what they wrote and respond to them. You could write something along the lines of "Excellent point!" or "Thx" or answer a question posed in the comment, which can make a follower feel pretty good. It's acceptable to answer simple, noncontroversial questions, as long as you are 100 percent confident your answer is correct. Responding to trolls requires finesse. Exercise caution when adding more than just a few words, as you risk slipping into a rabbit hole with the troll and end up defending yourself and/or bickering back and forth with other people piling on against you. We'll discuss more about handling trolls in a few pages.

How many times should feeds should be checked? Often—but it depends on how obsessed influencers are with their platforms and how much available time they have to spare. (You may refer to chapter 9 for a reminder on how many hours interviewee influencers spend on their feeds.) In any case, you'll want to interact with your followers as much as is reasonable per your schedule while maintaining balance in your life.

After a post, there will be a time when views and comments begin to atrophy, which is an indication to start planning your next post. It's best to not let too much time pass by—certainly no more than five days—as people tend to forget what they've seen from one day to the next. If you have a flop, that short-term memory is your friend, and you'll want to get right back in the saddle and prepare a new post ASAP. Some influencers have many completed posts locked and loaded, ready to send them live from the drafts section (which is what I do). If you have a hit, it's pretty much the same thing: work to get a fresh follow-up out there to capitalize on your success and keep the momentum going!

HOW TO MONETIZE BEING AN INFLUENCER
As I conveyed earlier in this chapter, there's not really any reason you should feel guilty about monetizing your platform with the caveat that you approach it ethically and authentically.

Getting a Talent Manager

Once they've reached a certain level of success, some influencers recruit a talent manager (or vice versa). You might have read that and scratched your head: *A talent manager? What do I need that for? I'm not an actress or model.*

Over the last few years, a new wave of talent management agencies has emerged specializing in representing social media content creators. Many traditional talent agencies accustomed to handling theatrical, television, film, and voice-over actors and models have added talent managers to represent social media influencers. Some, such as Central Entertainment Group, INF Influencer Agency, and Shade,[4] have teams solely devoted to this purpose.

I don't mean to burst anyone's bubble, but appointing a social media manager to guide your influencer career isn't as simple as an email query (or cold call). Talent managers generally need proof of a substantial existing *engaged* following before being able to consider adding you to their stable of clientele. For example, a Los Angeles social media talent manager I spoke with explained he's "not really that interested in anybody who doesn't have less than sort of a million followers on YouTube or a half million to a million followers on Instagram." He's partial to those two specific platforms, as he isn't "really looking at TikTok for talent at the moment," and, more often than not, seeks out the talent rather than the other way around.

Another reality check is that most talent managers aren't necessarily looking to parlay your content creation success into Hollywood superstardom. Not that this doesn't occur—especially in terms of landing television roles for those influencers who demonstrate some acting talent—but the focus is more on connecting influencers with brands. Talent managers and agencies know how to match up certain products and services with the right influencers to drive exposure and sales for the businesses and earn payouts for the influencers.

While talent managers and agencies receive a commission of earnings (usually in the neighborhood of 10 to 15 percent), it may be worth the price if you are being approached for sponsored post opportunities with companies and don't know how to handle them or where to find appropriate new ones. It can be helpful to have someone else be on the lookout for you and navigate the foreign waters on your behalf, so you can focus exclusively on responsibilities related to content creation.

THE CHANGING POWER DYNAMIC

Ironically, social media has the potential to emancipate talent from the traditional power dynamic of agents. In an episode of the Netflix reality show *My Unorthodox Life*, Julia Haart—CEO of Elite World Group, a modeling talent company—discusses how she is working to empower models and use social media to disrupt the modeling industry: "It used to be the casting agents and the creative directors, so if they didn't like your look or thought you were too fat or too this or too that, [you're] finished. If we can help our talent [models] create their own brands [through social media], meaning not bikini shots but *who* they are, what they're passionate about what makes them unique and individual. So that the day they turn thirty-five and can no longer walk a runway, they have ten million [social media] followers and a sunscreen line, then it's the casting agents and creative directors who are *chasing after them*."[1]

Ms. Haart's insights reflect the thirty-thousand-foot view of how social media is disrupting the landscape of traditional power dynamics. Professor Mark Anthony Neal from Duke University insightfully explained, "Historically, power has been obscure. You know what it is. You know how it works. You don't necessarily have access to the people who really hold on to it. One of the things that's happened particularly in the context of social media in the last ten years is that people now can speak back to power and close the gaps in terms of where individual people see themselves in relationship to power."[2]

NOTES

1. *My Unorthodox Life*, season 1, episode 2: "Becoming a Haart," https://www.netflix.com/title/81175724.

2. "The Pros and Cons of America's (Extreme) Individualism," *Freakonomics*, podcast episode #470, https://freakonomics.com/podcast/american-culture-2/.

Raising the Bar

As someone who has diligently studied how social media algorithms work, I can say that the influencers who create sound strategies, consistently stick to them, and continuously learn and improve tend to end up meeting with the greatest long-term success. It all comes down to one principle: discipline. Be committed to posting on a regular basis and resist the temptation to replace hard work with shortcuts like relying on any trending bandwagon. Stay the course to remain true to your brand.

It's fine to pepper your original content with occasional trends. You can be creative within the scope of your expertise to keep your content fresh and relevant or to experiment. Perhaps due to my own insecurities, there are times when I mix my video styles too much to avoid the risk of seeming monotonous. Admittedly, on the occasions I've tried to be overtly playful (or silly, depending on your point of view), the results more often than not met with lesser success than my tried-and-true "cap game" videos, which people have come to expect from me. That said, don't let anything stop you from taking calculated creative risks every now and then. Nothing ventured, nothing gained.

Studying the Metrics

If you are going to be in the influencer game in any capacity, it's recommended that you review your metrics on a regular basis. All platforms have varying degrees of deep dive metrics. Whether the data is good, bad, or ugly, you want to be aware of how you are faring. If you struggle with technology and/or numbers—or just don't have time to figure out your engagement rates and how they compare to others—there are legitimate sites (such as Analisa.io for Instagram and TikTok) that conveniently serve up many engagement metrics to help verify whether an influencer has strong follower engagement. For example, I analyzed one TikTok account with several million followers that had an engagement rate from Analisa.io of 29.98 percent, whereas Addison Rae—a MLI—had an engagement rate of 10.31 percent. Sometimes smaller accounts have higher engagement rates than those with larger followings.

These are the data points to analyze and understand:

1. *Followers' growth:* Examples include from day to day and month to month.
2. *Viewing percentage:* TikTok specifically provides the percentage of viewers who watched the full video. Aim for more than 50 percent to increase chances of your video going viral (although sometimes it can happen with under 50 percent).
3. *Number of views and comments received for posts over time:* More comments denote greater engagement for a video launching viral.
4. *Likes received:* The ratio of likes to views doesn't seem to be as important as it once was.
5. *Shares as the year progresses:* Videos with high share rates may signify large rewatch rates. (See below for more detail on this topic.)
6. *Revenue generation over time:* This helps you track your financial success.

The key metric missing from all platforms' analytics is the percentage of viewers who watched the video more than once. As mentioned earlier, I have a theory (one I can't prove) that this is the key metric internal algorithms use to determine which videos are promoted and get more views. I deduced this noticing that the videos with a substantial number of views were the ones I watched several times; I imagined others did the same. For example, Dr. Shah's videos often go ultraviral, as he duets dermatology *fascinoma* (fascinating dermatology excisions or conditions) videos with stimulating commentary that naturally entice people to watch them over and over and surely exclaim, "*Whoa!*"

Essentially, you are looking for patterns and trends to help you assess what is working and what is not. If you spot a downtrend in your metrics, it's probably best not to do anything radical, such as calling in the Coast Guard. There could be a number of reasons why your posts aren't catching on the way you had anticipated. The objective is to drill into the data and figure out whether there are common themes to the pattern, such as the percentage of viewers who watch your video to completion. On one occasion, I searched for why one of my videos had tanked, which was like doing a high dive into an empty swimming pool. I checked to see how many people had seen the video to completion. You can hit that big Pause button on whatever you're doing right now; the view-to-completion metric was 14 percent.

Reading Your Video's Comments

If only one person makes a specific unfavorable comment, you may be able to simply shrug it off. If one out of every five comments say a similar thing—or if a negative comment receives a high number of likes—then treat it seriously and consider responding with a comment and rectifying the issue the next time around.

Perhaps this is the most important advice I have to offer: strongly consider paying attention to the metrics, but do not allow them to consume you and burn you out. As I've mentioned a few times throughout this book, I've been there, done that—as have quite a few of the other influencers I interviewed. Ms. Barbosa phrased it to me in this way: "After posting a video, I look at the metrics. They affect my emotions so much. If I don't get ten thousand views in the first ten minutes, I start to panic. But I stop and think, *Why are those numbers making me panic?* and realize it's not life or death, so I calm down."

Try to fight the urge to refresh your page every five minutes, especially if your video is doing well. It's a time waster that will distract you from being more productive as an influencer; contributing to your daytime responsibilities, such as schoolwork or a job (if it's separate from your social media platform); and enjoying your social life. We'll address this subject in greater detail in the "Handling the Ups and Downs" section later in the chapter.

I also recommend against trying to compare your video's views against those of other influencers. There could be myriad reasons why their metrics surpass yours or vice versa—including luck and things you are unaware of or can't control—so it's not worth any emotional angst. Instead, consider following the lead of Dr. Shah: "I'm constantly asking myself, *How can I get better?* I use my metrics as a way to compete against myself."

Show Me the Money

Now for the nitty-gritty: how to make money as an influencer. While I can't make any promises that you'll be able to afford a yacht the size of fashion designer Giorgio Armani's (213 feet)[5] or that you will even make a comfortable living full-time, I am able to offer coveted insights from the influencers I interviewed and my own experiences that can hopefully compensate you for your labor. Even if you happen to have a steady cash flow from other sources of income, I know how good it feels to earn income from time spent being a content creator. (It also gives you the opportunity to say, "Ha, I told you!" to anyone who thumbed their nose at your dreams of achieving influencer success.) Frank Sinatra once said, "The best revenge is massive success."[6]

In no particular order, these are just a few creative ways you can generate revenue:

- *Direct social media traffic for your services and promoting your business.* If you happen to be an author, you will want to use your platform to encourage book sales with links to online retailers (such as Amazon.com).
  - *Examples:* Dr. Youn told me he experienced an increase in the number of patients as a result of his social media efforts. Dr. Sarah Rav has parlayed her platform into expanding membership in her Lifestyle and Productivity Masterclass.
- *Spin off a podcast with sponsorship opportunities.*
  - *Example:* Based on my playful and informative role on TikTok, I created what's now become a popular podcast—*No Cap Health Show*—which is on all podcast platforms. Typically, each week I address a TikTok video as being cap or not cap and unpack that topic—sometimes with guests.
- *Create your own branded merch (merchandise) on platforms (such as Instagram, Facebook, and TikTok) that list it.*
  - *Examples:* Illusionist Zach King sells T-shirts, tanks, custom card decks, Christmas sweaters, and more. (I have merch—my signature blue CAP hats.)[7]
- *Create brand-sponsored videos or posts.*
  - *Examples:* Food commentator Kelz Wright partnered with Chipotle on TikTok for its new Quesabrisket. Bodybuilder Noel Deyzel collaborates with Ryse exercise supplements and recently launched his own pre-workout product with them. Lifestyle influencer and comedian Tinx works with a variety of brands for sponsored posts, such as Mr. Coffee.[8]
- *Generate income from making custom fan collaboration videos.*
  - *Example:* One site, PearPop.com, hooks TikTok or Instagram influencers up with fans to create duetted or stitched videos that fans pay for. This can be an effective way to build followers fast.[9] Model

Leah Svoboda added 120,000 followers after a PearPop duet with megainfluencer Anna Shumate.[10]

- *Get paid for custom videos and for DMs.*
  - *Example:* I answer a range of health-related questions on Cameo .com.[11]
- *Join platforms that offer various paid subscription models.*
  - *Example:* OnlyFans.com, where fans can join monthly or pay per video view.
- *All main platforms typically offer some compensation for successful content creators based on the performance of their videos.*

DR. BRIAN'S TOP FOURTEEN INFLUENCER DON'TS

While there are probably several dozens of *don'ts* for an influencer to avoid, I've narrowed them down to the prevalent ones and those that might cause the most damage to oneself or others, as follows:

1. *Don't intentionally or unintentionally spread misinformation. Ever.* Always conduct meticulous research and fact-check your information.

2. *Don't cancel out another creator, even if that individual has spread misinformation.* Dr. Rav conveyed to me that she encourages taking the high road: "Some influencers have it in their minds that you are done if you make one mistake. A person should have ample opportunity to apologize, pull back on a mistake and say, 'Yes, that was wrong of me. I didn't realize that I was spreading misinformation at that time.' I don't think anyone should be canceled completely."

3. *Don't be discouraged if some of your videos fail to catch on and you lose followers.* It happens to everyone. Dr. Ricky Brown shared with me these reassuring words: "I don't define myself by my followers. My biggest change in social media over the past year has been getting to the point if a post bombs I can say to myself, *Was that a real post? Did it teach something? Did it entertain the way I felt it should?* If the answer is yes, I don't care how well the post does."

4. *Don't be combative.* You are entitled to state your supported facts and have an opinion, but don't get caught up in vitriol if you disagree with someone—whether it's a post or a comment. It's not worth the emotional angst for you or the other party, so "stand down." Try not to take the comments personally.

5. *Don't alienate or insult people.* This rule is an extension of item 4. You never want to post any content that disparages a person or group. Racist and sexist slurs and language are never acceptable. Be aware that sensitivities often run high on social issues, so what you think may be an innocent observation may potentially offend others. We all sometimes accidentally steamroll over the daisies— especially when it comes to word choices and how groups are referenced or characterized—which means you need to double- and triple-check to be certain you aren't coming across as condescending or derogatory. Dr. Brems has seen some physicians "talk down to or make fun of their patients" without realizing it, something you want to avoid. In the world of social media opinion, ignorance and "oops" won't cut it.

6. *Don't copy another influencer's post without attribution.* As we've established, influencers spend a lot of time and effort creating their content. Baldly copying and pasting the fruits of someone else's blood, sweat, and missed meals without citing due credit is a form of plagiarism. For some influencers it's "uncool," whereas for others it treads on encroaching on poor ethical behavior. Mr. Otusanya described to me, "I've had a lot of people just take and rip and repurpose my content without tagging me as the creator. One time, they put their whole logo all over it to grow their platform. For some reason, that video on their page got four million views. I was so mad." So, it's good form to give credit, unless there is an indication that the creator doesn't want to receive it. Let's look at an example in which a creator turns off buttons allowing a duet and/ or stitch. If you were to duet or stitch the video—there are workarounds, such as screen recording their video, uploading it to your

account, posting it as "private," duetting/stitching it, and then posting on your account—I don't think you need to cite the user. *Why, you might ask, would I do that if the user didn't allow anyone duet/ stitch it?* My reason is that posting misinformation does not shield someone from setting the record straight.

7. *Don't include too much content in one post.* No one really wants to consume information the size of a French novel in a social media post or video that goes on too long. The point is . . . get right to the point. There can be justified exceptions. Every social media site has different criteria for maximum characters and video length in a post, so certainly be aware of these parameters before going too far down the road. Dr. Saleh shared the following with me: "Nobody will even look at lots of text. Posts should be short and simple and good quality."

8. *Don't follow people who make you feel like bad about yourself.* These wise words were provided to me by Dr. Rav. She also added, "Follow people who make you happy." Influencers often spend a lot of time looking at posts from their peers, which isn't a bad thing in terms of knowing what else is out there and picking up tips and inspirations. However, if you are in communication—whether in comments or a chat—with someone who demeans you, it's time to cut the cord. Your time is far too precious to be involved with someone like that.

9. *Don't do extreme self-deprecating and/or dangerous acts just to garner attention.* Your reputation and brand mean everything, and your mission is to keep them that way. It may feel good to vent about some bad luck you've experienced, but, as Dr. Youn said to me, "You don't want people to follow you because you're a train wreck. You want them to follow you because you're going to create positive change for them."

10. *Don't take negative comments personally or cause them to change who you are.* As I've previously explained, no matter how good you might be as a content creator, you are going to receive negative

comments at some point. Growing thick skin will serve you well when you throw yourself out there in the social media spotlight; some people will love you, while others will loathe you (sometimes stemming from jealousy). Move on. As Ms. Barbosa reminded me, "Let's say someone points out a flaw in you. Then you start changing because you are second-guessing yourself or develop insecurities you never had to begin with." If you see that someone has posted something negative about you, don't perseverate on it. Stop chewing the cud and move on.

11. *Don't promote anything that could potentially cause harm or be ineffective.* There are more than a few irresponsible people in the social media universe. This becomes especially problematic when it impacts children. Recommendations for a product or activity that don't function lead to user disappointment.

12. *Don't sell out.* In this instance, I am referring to the meaning of "sell out" in terms of advertising and marketing products that you don't believe in for money. Ms. Mayers informed me that she was once approached by a company that produced an "anxiety pen." The user would inhale it, presumably soaking up a host of vitamins and nutrients that lessen anxiety. She turned down the opportunity because "I'm not going to tell my audience that inhaling something in their lungs is good for them when inhaling *anything* is bad. I've built trust between me and my audience and I'm not going to do something to break it."

13. *Don't buy followers.* This action is unethical, and people and platforms can see through it. If you were to go from ten thousand followers in one week to one hundred thousand, it's liable to look suspect. Those who are accused of doing this risk being outed and shamed, which can cause loss of authenticity and, potentially—a *reduced* following (or stagnancy). People in the know—especially a talent manager—might sniff this out and consider you unauthentic and not worth their time. For example, an account with many thousands of followers that has paltry engagement on the videos is

a suspicious sign that they have been purchased. Worse, some platform algorithms are savvy enough to now detect "follower farms" (groups of people or fake accounts that are bought to serve as followers) and when a significant part of an influencer's base of users originates from companies that sell bogus followers. This can lead to permanent account suppression by algorithms, as the apps have zero tolerance for fraudulent followers. The same goes for buying views, likes, and comments.

14. *Avoid saying and/or doing offensive things in your life.* There are instances when an influencer's actions outside of social media have caused a storm of controversy. In June 2019, Swedish Instagrammer Natalie Schlater posted a photograph of herself in Bali dressed in a bikini while overlooking a rice field, accompanied by the caption: "Thinking about how different my life is from the man picking in the rice field every morning." The post did not sit well with the press, and Ms. Schlater was branded as "narcissistic."[12]

Confession 101

If you are guilty of committing any of the above sins, as long as no one (including the influencer) has been injured and you've done a proper apology and reversal of approach, you'll likely have plenty of time to learn from your mistake, pick up the pieces, and work toward restoring trust with the social media community and hopefully resuming your account's growth.

HANDLING THE UPS AND DOWNS

"Social media is far more consuming than I ever realized," Dr. Rajan said to me. "And the bigger you get, the more responsibility and obligation you have to entertain people and keep posting good stuff."

The pressure to post quality content can weigh heavily on an influencer—even when the demands are self-imposed. It can feel like a ten-ton burden on one's back to produce original videos twice a week over a several-year period. The dopamine floodgates repeatedly flipping open and closed from viral hits ignite spikes in the body's chemistry and cause severe stress for some influencers, potentially leading to burnout. This situation becomes worse if a successful post is followed by a marathon of flops, which dries up the dopamine well and can result in a dark and empty feeling.

Suppose you have a post that results in more than two million views. What's next? You have to gear up for the follow-up. But what if the next video only receives ten thousand views or fewer? Ditto for a number of subsequent videos. This becomes a conundrum in which you feel like you've lost control of the bus and think, *What did I do wrong? Does it mean I'm a has-been?* It's a thought that crosses the mind of nearly every influencer at some point in time.

Burnout is a serious condition experienced by many influencers. Dr. Rav was candid with me about how she faced a three-month downward slide, which she likened to an existential crisis: "TikTok was not providing me with any satisfaction. All my videos were doing terribly, probably because I wasn't in the right headspace. I wasn't creating good content. I felt like I'd posted about everything and had run out of ideas. The comments were really getting to me. I asked myself, *Why am I doing this? This brings me no joy.*"

Dr. Rav came to the realization that she was exhausted and suffering from burnout. She had to hop off the treadmill and allow herself time to replenish. She took an extended three-month break and then gradually resumed work "semi-posting" until she reclaimed her groove. Once she was back on track, she found that her passion for content generation had returned and, along with it, renewed creativity energy.

Influencers can't afford to allow social media to consume their lives. Personally, I've had to make my own adjustments and a concerted effort to shut down electronics when needed, so I could focus exclusively on my family and medical practice. Dr. Printz does something similar: "I only do work in my office. Once I am out of that office, I'm done. I don't answer questions or comments, I don't answer DMs, and I don't scroll through social media while I'm with the kids."

Coping with Trolls and Negativity

Imagine having hundreds of thousands of people attacking and insulting you at the same time. It might concern gibes about your appearance, your point of view, your insensitivity, your ignorance, or a host of other derogatory statements. Sometimes the piling is more intense than a rugby scrum. It can become so nasty and overwhelming that they cause one's self-confidence to plummet, in addition to triggering anxiety, irritability, sleeplessness, and, possibly, depression.

Dr. Shah has been disparaged by some male viewers as looking "too feminine." His reaction to these comments: "I usually don't bother to block those people because I want everyone to see that. I want people to feel comfortable with the way they look and act."

Sometimes users demean influencers to put them back down on the runway after having met with some measure of success. Other times, they are "messing around on TikTok," as Mr. Otusanya referred to it in our conversation. Dr. Printz elaborated to me, "When you get to a certain level, or a certain number of followers, people feel the need to comment about the most random things and say hurtful and mean things." The apps would be performing a vital service to require all users to have their real names in their handles or bios to cut down on faceless trolls.

Trolls have the potential to be dangerous, as their venom can spread to other people. In many cases, they are anonymous—without a profile picture or a real name—so they feel safe to say anything they want without any real repercussion. Ms. Barbosa reflected to me, "It's so easy to make fun of other people when you're just sitting behind a computer screen typing. I know that no one would ever say those things to my face."

Filtering comments or simply ignoring them entirely can be helpful to young influencers starting out who haven't grown accustomed to the merciless stings but can be used by seasoned influencers as well. Personally, I choose not to respond to trolls. Dr. Saleh told me about a different approach he tried: "One person used to say COVID was being sprayed to kill Christians. I had a chat with him, where I politely asked him to check his source. He became kind of a friend at that point and continued to follow me."

Dealing with Community Guidelines Violations

A community guidelines violation sounds much worse than it is. Typically, the platform's artificial intelligence (AI) program identifies posts that it believes have crossed the line and often removes it. Certain sexual content, for example, might raise a red flag. I imagine that AI does call out many posts that are true violations and represent a potential threat that could potentially harm or offend someone. At the same time, from an influencer perspective, it often seems random and subjective, falling into gray area a machine couldn't possibly interpret. There are also instances, such as on Instagram, when the violation is sent in error.[13] The glitch will eventually be resolved, but it doesn't necessarily recoup what has been lost due to the delay or do much to heal the open wound. You have the option to appeal a community guidelines violation, in which case a real person (presumably) will review it and decide the fate of your video. (As I mentioned earlier in this book, I have received infringement violations myself that left me puzzled. Some appeals have gone to no avail.)

Ms. Mayers shared a different concern with me about having received a violation: "I was worried and scared because I know that if a certain amount of videos get taken down, your account could be flagged. They could ban you for a couple days and maybe cut off your livestream. So, I've been very, very careful."

The main thing to know is that if you are a serious influencer, your general objective is to entertain, educate, or inform. If that means pushing the envelope every so often within the boundaries of social norms, without offending or harming anyone, let it fly! Be creative and authentic, going where your creative energy and intuition lead you. Without risk, there is no reward. Besides, after posting dozens (if not hundreds) of videos, I would be stunned if you didn't receive a violation or two for *something.* I'd say wear it as a badge of honor, but the violation is kept confidential by the platform; your followers will not know. Some may notice that the video disappeared, which may appear to the onlooker that you decided to make it private.

Do you now feel armed and ready to start your journey as an influencer? Don't worry, you don't have any obligation to do so. If you happen to be interested, you can choose to go "all in" like the influencers cited in this book, or you could get the sample platter and see what happens with it as a side endeavor. In either case, don't add unnecessary pressure on yourself and set an unrealistic bar of attracting one hundred thousand-plus followers in the first month. If you can make an impact on one hundred people—or just one—you will have accomplished something to be proud of.

One thing is for certain: since you have been reading this book, you are no doubt a social media user in at least some capacity. With that in mind, I have deliberately chosen to save the universal chapter "Living with Social Media" for last. I promise, it will prove to have been worth your wait.

12

Living with Social Media

How Can Users, Influencers, Platforms, and Businesses Safely Coexist?

It is better to light one candle than to curse the darkness.

—*Chinese proverb*[1]

Social media is like fire: you can use it for illumination, or it can badly burn you.

As with everything else that escalates into a craze, social media apps started off innocently before they flourished and veered off in myriad uncharted, surprising directions. A lot of good has come from social media influence that shouldn't be taken for granted, especially in terms of instilling knowledge, correcting misinformation, serving up entertainment, showcasing talent, introducing creative ideas, and providing extended communities for people with shared interests around the world that otherwise would never have been possible. Along with these plentiful user benefits, equally impactful downsides have emerged, many of which have been self-inflicted and, to some extent, avoidable.

Here's the reality check: social media influence is here to stay, which means we have no choice but to accept and deal with it as best as we can according to our individual needs and desires—even if we intend to steer clear of it—while also doing so as responsibly as possible for ourselves and society. As Dr. Tony Youn said to me, "Like anything that's this huge, either you jump on the bus or you are going to get run over by it." Naturally, social media will continue to evolve with technological improvements—presenting all-new, exciting opportunities, as well as unforeseen threats—which means users, influencers, platforms, and businesses hope for the best, plan for the worst, and work together to create an environment that encourages freethinking; equally welcomes, accepts, and respects all parties; eschews any kind of harm (emotional, physical, and spiritual) to others and their property (including intellectual); and continues to mine limitless, untapped potential.

With that in mind, here is the million-bitcoin question for you: *How do we safely coexist with social media?* Dr. Ricky Brown believes that it's no different from what I stated in the previous chapter regarding influencers: it's all about an individual's purpose. "First, you have to identify *why* you are personally on the platform," he explains. These are some of the many options on the user side of the equation:

- Are you there to consume content and learn?
- Are you there to be entertained?
- Are you there to engage with others for stimulation?
- Are you there to develop a hobby?
- Are you there to connect with a community and perhaps fill a need for social interaction?
- Are you there to share your knowledge or skills—even if you aren't an influencer?
- Are you there to stay in the loop with friends and family?
- Are you there to celebrate your family's accomplishments?
- Are you there to build or widen your network, personal brand, or business?
- Are you there to prove how smart and right you are?
- Are you there to be a comic and create mischief?
- Are you there to spread your political and social views, as well as other opinions?

Once the purpose is identified, Dr. Brown recommends that you "set boundaries for yourself." From my perspective, this originates with your mindset. If your mood is being negatively dictated by how people engage with you in your accounts, ask yourself these two questions: *Is there anything happening to me on social media that is a genuine matter of life and death? Can I shut down tomorrow and continue my life as a happy human being?*

If the answer to either of the above questions is no, it likely means you haven't established satisfactory boundaries between your personal life and your social media activities. As Dr. Brown emphasized to me, "You can't get caught up, like we all do, in the likes and the followers. If your TikTok, Instagram, or Twitter accounts were to disappear tomorrow, would it change who you are and what you represent? No, it wouldn't. You can't ever get to the point where it has the potential to ruin your life."

Throughout this chapter, I am going to provide some invaluable tips and techniques to help you establish those user boundaries for your family and yourself.

READING THE FINE PRINT

Think back to years ago when Facebook was brand new, and you couldn't wait to sign on and rekindle old friendships and track down long-lost relatives. In your mad rush to join in on the fun and excitement, did you blindly populate the onboarding fields with your personal information and click "Approve" on the boxes requiring your sign-off? Did you pause to review the platform's terms of service? Have you *ever* reviewed them?

If you raced through this process and didn't read the fine print, don't beat yourself up. Few people do. I readily admit that I didn't all those years ago. The squint-inducing font, the long-winded legalese, and the vague implications all seem like way too much time and effort. Some terms of service seem as if they would benefit from our hiring an outside attorney to perform a legal review.

Living with social media means that you understand—at least on a basic level—what happens to your content once it goes live. This goes for all users—from children up through seniors—as well as influencers, advertisers, and marketers. Prepare to be surprised by what you've likely consented to.

Let's focus on Facebook's current terms of service as our example, since this social media network has the most users and has been in the public eye the longest.[2] (We don't have room to cover every single social media app, but you'll get the idea. If you need specifics for other platforms, see their respective terms of service, which do vary from one to the next.) The site—which prides itself on being able to curate information it thinks you will be interested in based on your groups, preferences, posts, likes, searches, and more—makes the following clear in its current terms of service: "We don't sell your personal data to advertisers, and we don't share information that directly identifies you (such as your name, email address or other contact information) with advertisers unless you give us specific permission."[3] What this statement *doesn't* state is that third-party apps and websites you signed on to may already have your data and are sharing it with Facebook and other sites to direct content to you based on your profile information, feed content, and search history. It also doesn't preclude Facebook from using your data—including the behaviors you exhibit—for *any* and *every* internal purpose Facebook desires.[4]

Aside from shutting down your apps entirely and not using search engines such as Google that collect, track, and share your data—something few of us are willing and able to do—there are some simple ways you can protect your personal information. Facebook now has a tool that allows you to view which third parties can access your data and have been sharing it with the site. You can see the third-party sites that have been studying your Facebook feed and data. You can vaporize them by clicking "Clear History." Unfortunately, this act can't rescind the data previously collected by these third parties.

The first thing you want to do is shield your data from other users or crawling widgets by deleting your background (e.g., political party affiliation) from your profile. Or, if you want the information to be visible to some people but not others, click on your Settings tab and select "Privacy." In this space, you can pick and choose the people you will allow to see your personal information and posts. Additionally, avoid taking those fun quizzes that pop up in your social media feeds. I know, it's tempting to find out which "Disney princess" or "dog breed" you are, but by clicking on the games, you are often inviting them to snag, catalog, and share your personal information.[5]

Again, this is only for Facebook; other social media sites may have variations on how to go about keeping your information *more* private. There is no true privacy because the apps analyze everything you do. If you are on TikTok, Instagram, LinkedIn, and the like, check their respective terms of service policies and Settings tabs to determine how to go about adjusting your privacy settings.

BIG SISTER

Not to make you paranoid—but be aware that virtually all your apps on your devices might be listening in on your conversations and serving up bowls of content or ads based on what they've picked up from eavesdropping. If the apps are open on your phone, for example, they are collecting bits of information about you to help direct content that the algorithms think you will be interested in seeing in your feed. Years ago, a friend proved this to me in real time. She prompted me to talk about picture frames—something I never do—and, just a few minutes later, voilà! Ads for picture frames appeared on Facebook. Flashback: *The Social Dilemma.* The easy way to prevent this is to close your apps (often running in the background) by swiping up on them in the multi-screen window when they aren't being used. They will disappear in that window, which shuts them down. Or you can just turn off your phone when not needed.

Even Amazon's Alexa and Echo are *listening* to what you are saying. However, they only *record* audio if you state one of their two names or "computer." When the Record button is figuratively pressed, your conversations with Alexa become transcribed in Amazon's cloud and added to the algorithm on Amazon.com, so they can tailor your product searches better for you (which means you might want to change your privacy settings on that site as well).

Contrary to the above, you may have heard certain tall tales about Amazon—or even Jeff Bezos himself when he isn't shooting off into space—having listened in on conversations and sent messages to people on their behalf without their knowledge. Situations like this one have occurred (not involving Bezos), but they were unintentional. As mentioned, if Alexa hears her name (or "computer")—even if said by accident—she will listen to, obey, and record the subsequent oral commands. If your television is turned on and located near Alexa, and a character happens to say her name, the device might be activated and respond to what is said by the TV character or someone who is present in the room. If you are concerned about this situation occurring, just pull the plug on (or turn off) Big Sister Alexa when her services are not needed.

BALANCING ACT

Don't worry, I'm not going to pound out memos like Beethoven on the piano telling adults to bury their smartphones in the ground to reduce the negative—and sometimes addictive—issues related to social media overexposure. It's entirely possible to prevent user problems before they bubble to the surface while still enjoying the positives of social media and maintaining a healthy dopamine behavior balance (DBB).

If you lie awake all hours of the night reviewing influencer feeds, your dopamine levels may be more imbalanced than tires coming from an auto shop run by Gru's Minions. Staying up late causes reduced availability of dopamine receptors in the morning.[6] Evidence suggests that sleep deprivation downregulates dopamine in the ventral striatum in the human brain. Further, the blue light of smartphones interferes with sleep patterns by messing with your melatonin level. This effect can be ameliorated by using "night shift" mode on phones to reduce screen blue light. (Also, reducing screen brightness lowers blue light.)[7]

Here are some signs indicating that you may need to neuter your social media usage:

- You check social media accounts at red lights and stop signs.
- You are unable to have one meal without checking your social media feeds.
- You aren't progressing with your career and personal goals.
- You are falling behind at work in terms of production and/or quality.
- You neglect and put off household chores.
- You feel lonely and/or disconnected from friends and family.
- You spend more than two hours per day on social media.
- You have been exercising less than usual and feel out of shape.
- You don't know where your lost time has been going.
- You feel nervous, irritable, and depressed.
- You feel lazy and lethargic.

If you answered yes to any of the above questions, here are three comforting facts: (1) research has shown that habits don't form automatically and can take three weeks to develop, sometimes longer; (2) you are not alone; and (3) the impact of screen addiction is not irreversible. A few simple changes to your lifestyle and habits can be a game changer. For example, thirty minutes per day of exercise can increase dopamine while replacing inactive time spent on the phone and other devices. Individual and team sports of any kind provide an important counterbalance to the instant gratification of social media. Dopamine is also released while doing yoga and meditation.[8]

Dr. Siya Saleh maintains that it's not just about physical health. "Mental health is very important as well. I always advocate to people that they take breaks. I've taken few weeks here and there and come back feeling way better."

Other simple ways to naturally increase dopamine and feel healthier in mind, body, and spirit:

- Listening to music
- Exposing yourself to outdoor sunlight to receive vitamin D from UV rays
- Consuming foods high in:
  - Amino acids, such as nuts
  - Iron and folate, such as spinach
  - Vegetarian proteins, such as legumes and beans
  - Niacin, such as chicken
  - Vitamin B6, such as salmon
  - Magnesium, such as avocados
- Reducing (if not eliminating) intake of processed foods, sugar, fructose, and sucrose
- Experimenting with essential oils, such as bergamot, lavender, and lemon
- Experiencing positive emotions, such as humor and gratitude[9]

As is the case with any addictive-type behaviors, the first thing to do when one has been identified is to acknowledge the problem. According to Josh Otusanya, the next step is to see whether you can "add a little bit of structure to your social media activities. It doesn't have to be *super* structured. Maybe you say to yourself, *Hey, during these general periods of time, I'm not going to access social media, scroll through my Instagram feed, or binge-watch videos all day. I'm going to spend time with my friends or family or just have time periods where I'm not accessing.* It's really good to unplug from time to time."

Cutting back is not always as elementary as reading and implementing the solutions. We *are* battling Death Star tractor-beam-level dopamine forces responsible for drug, gambling, sex, and other addictions, which means you need some strong armament to defend yourself. To combat my own social media temptation, I restructured my digital space on my devices. I create content on a separate iPad dedicated to social media activities. When I'm at home and it's not in use, I leave it in the kitchen. I removed *all* social media apps from my mobile phone, making it impossible for me to check the status of my posts throughout the day or even first thing in the morning when I wake up. Dr. Karan Rajan recommends the same method: "Don't check your phone first thing in the morning or as the last thing before you go to bed. Stop checking your phone whenever you're bored or watching TV. Instead, prioritize the things you would normally do first: go to the gym, walk your dog, make dinner, et cetera. Focus on your life first and social media second."

In the following sections, I've provided a few more valuable tips and tricks to help limit screen time and balance your life.

Set Forced Limited Screen Time

On your device, you can click on Settings and select "Screen Time" to set the amount of time you wish to spend on your apps. Once your allowance has been met, the app shuts down automatically. (Note: There is an override feature, but you can add a screen time passcode that prevents you—or your kids—from overriding the limit.) If you wish to block yourself from overriding the limit, set a screen time passcode you won't know. Close your eyes and wipe your fingers back and forth across the numbers, so you have no idea of what the password you created might be. You will then save it, sight unseen. This makes it impossible to enter a password and exceed your time limit.

Turn Off Notifications

The incessant buzzing, ringing, and other audible notifications of social media alerts throughout the day can feel like a perpetual poison ivy itch calling for your attention. Dr. Fayez Ajib put it this way to me: "If you are spending a lot of time on these apps, it means you are also spending a lot of time checking notifications and replying to people. Something that I've recently done is to completely turn off all social media apps for a while. It's like the saying 'out of sight, out of mind.'"

If you want to stop being constantly pestered by notifications, you can either turn them (and vibrations) off entirely in Settings or at least switch to silent mode. If you're still in the social media sinkhole, there are apps (Offtime, Freedom, Flipd, and Moment) that track usage and analytics, and others (StayFree, StayFocusd, QualityTime, and AppDetox) that can regulate (or block) social media apps according to your designated times. (If you use the above screen time tip involving an unknown password, it should be impossible for you to go past the time you allotted to yourself.)

Get a Pet

Another great way to force regular breaks from social media is to get a pet. (Sorry, goldfish don't count.) The responsibilities involved in pet ownership can distract you from social media fixation. In the case of a dog, you are generally obligated to head outside with it for periodic walks and fresh air, which will do a world of good for your mental (as well as physical) health and be appreciated by your pooch. Dr. Rajan explained to me the effectiveness of dog adoption for him as a diversion, in addition to all the other benefits of canine ownership.

Enlist Friends

At times you may be unable to self-regulate and need a little help from your friends to prod you into a social life. Spencer Barbosa admitted to me that "sometimes they'll kind of force me out of the door. Afterwards, I'm grateful that they did it because I need a life outside of my job. My friends are the most supportive people ever."

When involved in face-to-face social settings, make a concerted effort to be present. No one wants to hang out with someone who is constantly checking their phone. There are some people who will scroll through their phones while conversing, attending business meetings, dining at a restaurant, or sitting in a theater with the phone light flickering when they are otherwise supposed to be looking at the big screen. Not only are all these behaviors disrespectful, but important information might also get lost because of the distraction—and the fun and joy of human interaction with flesh-and-blood people along with it.

LIMITING SCREEN TIME AND IMPROVING THEIR SOCIAL MEDIA LITERACY

Despite their reservations and fears, most parents have accepted that there is little they can do to prevent their kids from falling into the social media black hole. Even if a parent or legal guardian were to permanently rescind the phone—to protect or to punish—resourceful children born in the age of technology will find some other way to sneak onto social media through another device.[10] As history has proven time and time again in dealing with younger generations: the stricter the restrictions, the more rebellious and daring kids will likely become.

WHAT IS THE RIGHT AGE FOR A CHILD TO START ON SOCIAL MEDIA?

As time goes by, parents are gifting mobile phones to their kids at younger ages. One survey indicates that the largest percentage of children (25.7 percent) receive their first phone between eleven and twelve.[1] However, an astonishing *40 percent* of children are receiving phones between the combined age range groups of one/ two and ten. No matter how old they may be, if kids have phones and can press buttons, they are being inquisitive and checking out social media.

I get it. There is reasonable justification for parents to purchase phones for their young children; it provides peace of mind. They can reach their kids anytime through texting, phone calls, and emails and exchange important information about schedules, pickups, and family events. With phone tracking apps, parents also know where their kids are throughout the day and ensure that they are safe.

What do the experts think is the most suitable age for kids to be join social media? Psychologist Dr. Lisa Stroman and digital authority Dr. Kristy Goodwin believe that, while there is no "one size fits all" because every child is unique and matures at a different pace, thirteen is generally an acceptable rule of thumb.[2] Dr. Jess Andrade informed me that she generally concurs, with the caveat that parental supervision must also be involved at that age.

NOTES

1. S. O'Dea, "What Age Are Kids When Parents First Buy/Give Them Their Own Cell Phone?" Statista, October 19, 2021, https://www.statista.com/statistics/1058938/cell-phone-owhnership-among-children-in-the-us-by-age/.

2. William Worrall, "What Age Should Children Have Social Media Accounts?" Hacked, July 10, 2020, https://hacked.com/what-age-should-children-have-social-media-accounts/.

Earlier we discussed how you can use screen time in Settings to create limits. What about the opposite approach—just yanking the phone out of their hands? Even if children are addicted to social media, forcing them to quit cold turkey is a perilous idea. Research has shown that kids and teens may face withdrawals like that of a drug addict with increases in anxiety and other mood changes. They might also be cut off from their friend communities, which could cause them to feel left out and isolated.[11]

Knowing that most kids and teens don't have the interest in or power to self-manage or prepare themselves to fend off the potential collateral damage of social media, what are parents to do? Should you toss the cards in the air and look the other away? No—because, thankfully, there are effective ways to help you manage their screen time while simultaneously broadening their social media literacy. In the following sections, I've provided four areas to consider exploring with your children.

Get Involved

Download and join Instagram, TikTok, Twitter, and YouTube yourself, as these are Gen Z's most frequented apps. (Chances are you already familiar with Facebook and your kids couldn't care less about it, so we don't need to go there.) The thought of being a part of these platforms may make your forehead appear like it's time to exit the sauna, but trust me, it will be well worth it in the long run. As Ms. Barbosa said to me, "Some parents don't even know that their kids are on social media at all. They have no idea what kind of creepy people are trying to talk to your kid or what she or he is consuming for hours and hours of the day. It's the parents' responsibility."

The idea is to keep up with the new trending apps as well as the latest developments on existing ones. I would assert, based on my own parenting experiences, that you stand a chance monitoring and protecting your kids *if* you know and understand what is going on in their digital playground from the onset. Krysten Mayers struck a bulls-eye when she said to me, "In the beginning, I think it's a good idea for parents to be a part of it because social media can be a dangerous place."

As several studies have revealed, being knowledgeable, informed, and active with your child on social media helps avert hazards.[12] You can view influencers together and point out which ones are marketers in disguise and profiting from their followers. In doing so, you are conveying the message that not all influencers are as pure and authentic as they may seem. On the flip side, passive parenting—such as ignoring or being uninvolved with what one's kids are doing on social media—has been shown to have a negative impact, tending to make children more vulnerable to advertising ploys.

To summarize: the pros of getting involved with your child on social media far outweigh the cons (e.g., your investment of time and being accused of cramping their style). You will have improved the PI of your kids, as well as yourself, and made their lives safer all around.

Have the Crucial Conversation

Every parent needs to have the important life lesson talks about certain tough subjects, such as sex, drugs, and money. In today's environment, quality time also needs to be devoted to discussing social media apps. According to their book *Crucial Conversations*, authors Kerry Patterson and Joseph Grenny define the title of their work as follows: "A discussion between two or more people where (1) stakes are high, (2) opinions vary, and (3) emotions run strong."[13] This definition unequivocally applies to social media. The stakes are indeed high when it comes to knowing which influencers your kids follow, what they are posting, and where/how they are spending money.

The more you listen to your kids *without passing judgment*, the more you'll know and understand and be prepared for anything that may go sideways. If you have faith in them and loosen a little rope, they might be trusting enough to share details with you, should their DBB turn tsunamic and threaten to wash away the important things in their lives.

Establish Ground Rules

While you shouldn't enact limitations and rules your kids will deem medieval, you still need to establish some practical safeguards and boundaries. You are the parent in the room and the ultimate gatekeeper of social media influence for your family, although at times it may not seem that way.

A major issue parents face that is worth reiteration from prior chapters is the 24/7 nature of the internet and social media. Their kids could be up all hours of the night scrolling through influencer feeds. Sleep deprivation and exhaustion can lead to poor physical and mental health, which will most certainly impact their performance at school. They could also be saying they are doing their homework and/or studying when they are engaging with platforms instead. Even the most assiduous student can be tempted to toggle back and forth between schoolwork and social media feeds.

Dr. Jess Andrade informed me that she has been seeing a pervasive amount of this activity among teens: "Teens have been telling me, 'I spend so much time on social media. Every day I wake up, I turn on my iPhone and watch TikTok for hours and hours. My mood during the day keeps going down.' By the end of the day, they have no motivation to do anything."

Setting time parameters and enforcing them are important steps (as discussed above, re: screen time). You might also consider instituting a "no phone homework rule"—separating the device from the child—until all homework has been sufficiently completed, enough study time put in, and some physical activity (exercise and/or chores) performed.

Another useful tactic can involve tracking the amount of time each family member spends on social media while at home and displaying the information out in the open. If your screen time app doesn't already do that, an oversized dry-erase calendar might work, as everyone can visually see the results on a regular basis. Family members can fill in the number of hours they spent on each influencer site (based on screen time usage in Settings); add them up at the end of each day, week, and month; and then compare the results. If anyone is involved in influencer-related activities at home for more than seven hours a week total, it may suggest a problem. At that stage, you can identify more productive things this person could be doing during those time slots.

Turn Off Phones during Meals

Schoolwork is far from the only prize to protect. Parents have had to contend with kids who spend entire mealtimes at home and/or in restaurants on their phones. (I've even seen kids seated at the same table interact with each other on social media and not utter a single verbal word to each other.) This kind of behavior can become habitual and difficult to control if not nipped in the bud. Realistically, for your children to have a chance of following this recommendation, it would be wise for you to set the example. If your kids refuse to shut down during mealtimes, you can follow the lead of the mother depicted in *The Social Dilemma* who locks the family's phones in a container before everyone sits down together.[14]

Protecting the Babes in the Woods

This statement cannot be emphasized enough: *Your child's safety always comes first.* Throughout this book I've outlined some of the many threats out there—trolls, predators, bullying, dangerous pranks, shaming, cults, sex trafficking, scams—along with the mental and emotional damage that might occur if left on autopilot. This might include social media–related issues such as low self-esteem, mood swings, stress, anxiety, loneliness, eating orders, and even depression. Ms. Barbosa recounted to me some of what she has witnessed among young girls on her accounts: "It's so sad when I see little girls duetting with another girl who looks absolutely perfect. The young girls start crying, and I have to assure them that they are just as perfect."

Preteens are by no means the only ones susceptible to threats and challenges on social media. Teenagers can be vulnerable and have their egos crushed too, especially when it comes to navigating peer relationships. Dr. Tony Youn, who happens to have a son in high school, phrased it this way to me: "You just need one post or message to a teenager, and it can make a huge impact on her or his self-esteem."

The social media space may seem harmless and trivial on the surface, but parents should be aware that it can sometimes be brutal. If you have kids, stay in frequent communication with them and be as attuned as possible to identify any shift in mood, attitude, or behavior. Be on the alert for even the most subtle signs, which inevitably seem obvious after the fact. If a child who is generally outgoing seems down and out without specific reason, probe further to see whether you can detect an underlying cause. If social media is at the root of it, it's time for the child to scale back or take a temporary social media break. The self-esteem of thousands of kids plummets at some point each year because not enough friends liked their posts, people ganged up on their seemingly innocuous comments, or they were unfollowed for reasons they can't comprehend.

Regarding misinformation and disinformation, at least one reliable entity—a nonprofit known as the News Literacy Project—is striking back. The organization publishes *The Sift*, a newsletter that turns conspiracy theories and viral rumors into lessons for educators. They also created Checkology, a program that helps kids between grades 6 and 12 verify whether a news story is fact or fiction.[15]

I've saved the most important recommendation for last: *Never, ever allow your child to meet with a stranger met through social media.* There are far too many cases of children attacked or gone missing because an adult predator adopted an alias, manipulated them to gain trust, cyberstalked them, and then set up an in-person introduction. No matter how intelligent or precocious your child might be, they can still be duped into doing something dangerous by deviants, con artists, and cult recruiters. (Recall that their teen prefrontal cortexes have a long way to go in terms of development.) If you ever suspect anything is amiss, immediately dial 911 and connect to victim services to determine the best course of action to handle the situation.

THINK CRITICALLY!

The good news is that you've always had the power within yourself to reveal the best that social media influence has to offer you while discarding—if not warding off—its dark arts. I am referring to your critical thinking function—the ability to help your brain distinguish fantasy from reality, falsehood from truth—which I refer to as PI. Once you've honed this skill, you become more equipped to discern the facts and make better decisions.

In November 2021, nine people were tragically crushed and trampled to death and hundreds of others injured amid surging crowds during rapper Travis Scott's performance at the Astroworld Festival in Houston, Texas. The catastrophic event resulted in lawsuits with fingers pointing all around as to where the blame should be placed. It didn't take long for conspiracy theories to propagate.[16] The most prominent fallacy involved the claim that the event had been Mr. Scott's preplanned demonic ritual involving Satan himself. The subject "Astroworld Sacrifice" went ballistic on Facebook, and all social media sites became inundated with a rise in chatter-filled conspiracy theories involving Satan. At that point, someone said, "Why not?" to tossing Hillary Clinton's name into the conspiracy theory.[17]

Absurd as it may seem, thousands of people were seduced by this bizarre explanation of the event's outcome without questioning it. Maybe, just maybe, the clues were precisely as they seemed: props and logos intended to create a freaky stage atmosphere for the artist. Hadn't musical acts such as the Rolling Stones, Judas Priest, and Black Sabbath been using satanic imagery in their songs and stage acts for decades?

When first encountering a sensationalized video about this news story, a person with high PI would most likely not buy in and just move on. If this individual were to be challenged about their interpretation of what had transpired, the response would probably be along the lines of "Okay, show me the evidence." Despite all the videos, photos, and articles thrown at the person with strong critical thinking skills, they would remain unmoved—unless some genuine proof were to surface.

What about the hordes who accepted the satanic version of the story? Why did they fall for it? Was it due to lack of intelligence or excessive gullibility? I don't think so. Rather, they were predominately following the herd (as explored in chapters 2 and 6) and experiencing low PI (like the flat-earthers). If an abundance of people share the conspiracy-infused videos and articles and accept such content as fact, the individual with low PI may believe it is true based on face value. The same might be said for cases in which influencers lead the charge and decide to spread misinformation. They coddle the trust of millions of followers, which means any post involving a conspiracy theory might proliferate, with throngs hopping aboard.

How do you raise your PI and defend against omnipresent false information? To power on your critical thinking skills, lay out the proposed fact and objectively—while checking your emotions at the door—critique its plausibility. Is there any internal reason you might *want* the flight of fancy to be true? (This is self-diagnosing to determine whether you have an internal bias.) Are you accepting it as fact because so many others already do (following the herd)? Are you longing to fit in and be associated with a certain crowd (emotional desire to belong)?

These next three steps can be beneficial:

1. *Challenge the theory:* Is it logical? How else might it be explained?
2. *Ask questions:* Why might people believe—or want to believe—this story? What incontrovertible evidence exists proving it, other than someone's assertion?
3. *Determine who or what is the initial source:* Is it trustworthy? Is there anything credible that backs up the claim?

If the above steps fail to provide answers, consider any downsides of what might happen if you were to walk away from supporting and spreading the story. What might be lost or gained? If you are dismissing a fantasy, nothing whatsoever would happen; the sky wouldn't fall, universes wouldn't collide, and baristas would keep baristing. However, accepting and passing along disinformation or misinformation as fact—such a conspiracy theories surrounding COVID vaccines—can cause a lot of undue harm to innocent people—namely, people getting sick and requiring hospital care.

Social media should inform, educate, instruct, create communities, and provide joy. Anyone who does otherwise may be jeopardizing the integrity of the social media fabric and lessening the experience for everyone else—if not indirectly or directly encouraging problems to manifest.

We now come full circle back to the question that opened this, our final chapter: *How can users, influencers, platforms, and businesses safely coexist?* We work together to create a limitless, fact-based, balanced, healthy, open-minded, intellectually curious sandbox in which there is plenty of room for everyone to play, connect, share, discover, comment, and grow as a burgeoning, harmonious community.

And that, I assure you, is *not cap.*

Conclusion

The Future of
Social Media Influence

You must not let anyone define your limits because of where you come from. Your only limit is your soul.

—*Chef Gusteau, from the animated feature* Ratatouille[1]

I could say that I'm going to look in my crystal ball and boldly lay out everything else that is going to happen regarding social media influence with 100 percent accuracy. That would make me a character in the Harry Potter books and films. No one can truly predict the future in our protean digital universe that echoes our volatile real world.

We can, however, speculate from the patterns and signals what *might* occur, though even these areas will probably look different from what we might currently visualize. I'm grateful to have had several peer influencers help me out on this front and weigh in with their insights.

Certain social media celebrities will become bigger than traditional celebrities.
Dr. Fayez Ajib: "You have these social media celebrities, such as Charli D'Amelio, who are already bigger than TV stars we watched when we were growing up. I think you're going to see a lot more of that, especially since we continue to become more consumed with social media and every kid now has an iPad. The growth is only just starting."

The impact of social media influencers will continue to expand.
Krysten Mayers: "I think those content creators are going to have an increasing impact on society. Some will solve a big problem, while others will invent something new."

More influencer feeds will go live versus prerecorded.
Dr. Fayez Ajib: "Part of me feels like the future is going to be about going live. People want to see you live. They don't want to see prerehearsed stuff, and they want to see a live vlog of your daily life as a doctor."

Social media will become safer as we curb anonymity and trolling.
Dr. Karan Rajan: "If we can get rid of people who hide between things—the fake accounts—it will resolve a lot of the problems in social media. We need to see a name and a face."

People in the future will have a much greater sense of what it was like to live in our era than previous generations.
Krysten Mayers: "We often wonder what it was like living in the 1940s and 1950s. Now we have current videos capturing everyday people living during our time."

People will turn to social media more for their searches than to the internet.
Krysten Mayers: "Social media is becoming more of a search engine. I can see people looking for a lasagna recipe on TikTok instead of Google."
Dr. Dana Brems: "Whenever I have a question about anything, I'll just go on YouTube, not the internet. For example, if I have a question about taxes, I'll check out a YouTube channel, not the government's website."

Education will widen on social media platforms even more than entertainment.

Dr. Jess Andrade: "Education is going to take a larger role. YouTube is starting an educational platform, just like TikTok. Instagram is also looking into different video creation education platforms and maybe a news-type platform."

Spencer Barbosa: "I get a lot of messages from teachers who they say they've shown my TikTok videos to their classes. I thought that was amazing and insane. I felt like I made it. These teachers approve of what I'm saying and think my content is relatable."

Krysten Mayers: "Social media is going to be a part of everything. In my school, we have these independent projects we have to do to graduate."

Lastly . . . holograms.

Dr. Siya Saleh: "Holograms will be the future."

Dr. Tony Youn: "One hundred years from now, we're going to be watching holograms."

Dr. Brian Boxer Wachler: "I expect that we will see the rise of the AI (artificial intelligence) influencers."

Separate from everything referenced in this chapter, I know what I *hope* to see in social media's future. It dovetails with my personal philosophy and the reason why I became a physician. I would like to see everyone try to do good. It's not just my purpose; I believe it's really everyone's reason for being on this planet. Why post any content on social media—as an influencer, businessperson, or user—if your intent isn't to help someone, in some way? As my beloved mother-in-law, Regina Boxer, says, "It is just by the way the cards have been dealt that you are helping and not being helped."

NEW SOCIAL MEDIA WORLDS AND CIVILIZATIONS THAT LOOK A BIT LIKE OURS

There is one more area for us to explore in social media's future: the *metaverse*. Before we go there, we must first address the subject in relation to its counterpart—the *multiverse*. How do we distinguish these two intersecting and often confusing words?

One similarity is that both are virtual worlds that exist in different galaxies in a way. The metaverse virtual world—often appearing in computers and video games—is separate from reality but may be entered by "real" people, as depicted in the 2018 film *Ready Player One*.

Meanwhile, the multiverse, which has existed for years in science fiction/fantasy, commonly refers to when one set of fictional characters—through magic, wizardry, or some other cosmic, powerful force—meets up with a separate set of their doppelganger selves (plus their nemeses and others) who had existed along a separate timeline in a different reality or virtual world. The original *Star Trek* television series, for example, dabbled in the multiverse theory in the "Mirror Universe" episode (in which Captain Kirk meets up with a bearded, evil Mr. Spock). More recently, the 2018 *Spider-Man: Into the Spider-Verse* animated feature presented multitudes of Peter Parkers/Spider-Men (including a pig named Peter Porker whose alter ego is Spider-Ham) from different realities, along with their rivals. The 2021 film *Spider-Man: No Way Home* totally geeked out fans (in a good way) by seamlessly reintroducing characters (and the actors portraying them) from several prior unrelated film series.

The multiverse concept raises the creative bar of in terms of what could potentially happen in the worlds of science fiction and comic book characters for entertainment value. Whether the multiverse exists in *our* reality has been debated for some time by scientists; as of today, there is no tangible proof—nor a way to get there. Could social media turn out to be our transporter?

GOING META

In October 2021, Facebook renamed itself under a new umbrella brand: Meta. According to company CEO Mark Zuckerberg, "Meta's focus will be to bring the metaverse to life and help people connect, find communities, and grow businesses."[2]

One wonders whether the timing of the branding change was part of a megaplan to get a head start on future trends and encapsulate all the possible entities residing in the company's forward-thinking strategy, or to shift focus away from some of Facebook's very public issues (including its concealment of internal research on how Instagram was impacting the body image of teen girls and its inability to snuff out widespread misinformation about COVID vaccines on its platform).[3] Whatever the underlying reason for the change, I believe Facebook—I mean, Meta—may be excavating something special here.

How do we define the word *meta* when it has so many different meanings? As usual, when in doubt, we turn to the ancient Greeks. During their time, *meta* translated to *after*. Since then, it has come to imply our world plus other realms beyond it.[4] Anything tacked on to the end of *meta* takes on an otherworldly next level to it, such as *metaphysical*, which refers to what cannot be perceived by human senses or perhaps something supernatural.

With respect to our current digital universe, *meta* plus *verse* refers to a world in which humans beings engage with apps, software, and each other to simulate an entirely new perceived reality. The first official appearance of the term is believed to be in Neal Stephenson's 1992 science fiction novel *Snow Crash*. Sounds mind blowing, right? Well, perhaps not as much for those who earned their stripes through all-nighters, food deprivation, and suppressed bathroom urges from virtual gaming, which utilizes augmented reality (AR) to enhance the experience via heightened visuals and sounds. The ultimate sensation for gamers is when they become immersed in other worlds and universes (e.g., doing battle against other gamers, hideous creatures, aliens, etc.) through simulation technology (e.g., goggles).[5]

In our current world of pandemics and social distancing, advances in metaverse technology offer us a twofold benefit: (1) we have engaging activities to occupy our time; and (2) we are given forums to imagine and experience being together in the same place at the same time on another level. Videoconferencing (such as Zoom) enables us to see and hear each other in real time to conduct business or even see friends when in-person gatherings aren't possible. We interact with other on our screens, see into each other's living spaces (offices, kitchens, etc.) or whatever manipulated backgrounds and emojis we choose to display.

Imagine our future when all of this goes *meta*, thanks to AR, 3D technology, and other advancements. Imagine joining a business conference and engaging with others as if we are sitting in the chair next to the company's CEO. Similarly, we could be made to *feel* as if we are in the front row of a live concert from our living room couches or on the mound with a major-league pitcher during a live baseball game.

Buckle up your five-point harness for what the social media metaverse might mean for us.

A CONFLUENCE OF INFLUENCE AND META

"Metaverse's power is in the relationships that people develop with each other," Daniel Liebeskind, the CEO of Topia—a cutting-edge site where social experiences are created in the metaverse for real-time connection and play—explained to me.[6]

At the risk of throwing more in jargon while we are midway through the conclusion (is that considered breaking the fourth wall?), the internet is *asynchronous* (two or more things that do not occur at the same time). Mr. Liebeskind offered the following example: "You send an email, then wait for reply."

By contrast, the metaverse is *synchronous*, meaning things happen simultaneously. Those who engage people in this manner have the potential to raise the bar on digital human interaction by enabling their users to see, hear, and commingle with others at the same time.

What does it look like to establish genuine friendships online in the social media metaverse? As Mr. Liebeskind described to me, the metaverse will "create a space for real relationships, real community. In this way, it's easier to be part of a community, regardless of economics and irrespective of location based on synchronous experiences and connections."

I speculate that, in the foreseeable future, influencers in the synchronous social media metaverse will be known as *confluencers*.[7] By its standard definition, *confluence* means when two things come together or meet at the same time (such as a pair of rivers).[8] When we merge *confluence* with social media *influencer*, we aren't just referring to an individual with a large community of engaged followers. A confluencer has the potential to take their community to a new dimension of connectivity because engagements will feature live, face-to-face video—while also monetizing it (if that happens to be the confluencer's goal).

Within the metaverse, people take on avatar bodies (think Wii video games) that explore worlds created by the users. "When an avatar exploring around gets close to another avatar in a virtual world, a digital video chat pops up, simulating walking down the street, stopping, and then striking up a conversation," Mr. Liebeskind informed me. "The two people, via live video, can begin talking. Video chats are usually limited to a certain max number of people—ten persons on Topia, as more wouldn't be practical and productivity drops off with a live video, like in real life." (To his point, it can be challenging to have a conversation involving fifty people.)

In the metaverse, live events of all varieties—concerts, sports events, speaking engagements, parties, and so forth—can be exclusive or non-exclusive. Promoters can sell tickets to these gatherings, or they might be offered for free. Marketers and salespeople who bring in attendees may be incentivized by commission or offered something else of value in exchange, such as advertising or a free video or written report on a topic (e.g., lead generation).

It's entirely possible that, when Facebook changed its corporate name to Meta, it had noted the successes of rapper Travis Scott's "Astronomical" show in April 2020 and/or Ariana Grande's "Rift" performance on August 6, 2021—both of which were sponsored by Fortnite and each drew more than one million participants. The latter metaverse event combined music, gaming, psychedelic graphics, and storytelling (with alien creatures), while granting attendees the ability to engage with—and compete against—each other at the same time for a unique immersive experience.[9]

Ms. Grande, for example, didn't appear as a singer on a stage for her performance, but rather as an avatar with glowing eyes. Attendees could "get in the skin of her avatar" for 2,000 V-bucks—virtual currency—or purchase the "V-bucks bundle" for 2,800 V-bucks ($19.99) with 800 in V-buck change to spare.[10] A wide range of other options were available to enhance the experience. The sponsor's cosmetic products were also offered for additional V-bucks.

Mr. Liebeskind suggested that the possibilities are endless in the metaverse: "Worlds are customizable—virtually any content can be hosted, including prior content produced on social media—such as Instagram, YouTube, and TikTok videos—or articles, PowerPoint presentations, Zoom presentations, et cetera."

Like any group in the real world, people may come and go and never return. Mr. Liebeskind observed, "Groups that seem to have the highest retention of users are metaverse worlds with special interests, such as those about health, global warming, and politics and hobbies, like pets, sports, and cooking."

Major players are rapidly moving to have a presence in this space because it affords users the best of several worlds in synchronous fashion: a chance to get a glimpse of an influencer (for up-close learning or entertainment), an opportunity to know what it feels like to be in the influencer's shoes, and a way to engage with and/or compete against people with similar interests all around the world at any time.

For those who try to resist the inevitable expanded evolution of social media to the metaverse, I refer to the words of Dr. Tony Youn in the last chapter: "Like anything that's this huge, you either jump on the bus or you are going to get run over by it."

My advice? Get your bus ticket ready.

Epilogue

When the whole world is silent, even one voice becomes powerful.

—*Malala Yousafzai, activist*[1]

As we draw to a close, I thought it might be useful to list some of the most liked posts of all time up through the present across several platforms:

Tweet (from the family of Chadwick Boseman): *It is with immeasurable grief that we confirm the passing of Chadwick Boseman. It was the honor of his life to bring King T'Challa to life in* Black Panther. (7.2 million+ likes)[2]

Facebook (from Nick Vujicic): A photograph of Nick Vujicic (*New York Times* best-selling author, world-renowned speaker, coach, and entrepreneur who happens to be limbless) with his family on the beach. (15 million+ likes)

YouTube: A video of the song "Despacito," by Luis Fonsi, featuring Daddy Yankee (47+ million likes)[3]

TikTok: A video of Bella Poarch bopping to "M to the B" (54 million+ likes)[4]

Instagram (from world_record_egg): A photograph of an egg (55 million+ likes)[5]

There is a lot that may be distilled from these posts, but I am most interested in answering the following question: *Do they have a common thread?* These popular posts feature a celebrity epitaph, a snapshot of a family, an original music video, a clip of an entertainer grooving to music, and a photo of an object. The commonality is they all *moved* people, albeit in different ways: sadness, warmth, uplift, excitement, and humor. A successful post deeply touches people. The reportage of Mr. Boseman's tragic passing from his family, for example, triggered a deep emotional reserve of a great many people and enabled collective catharsis on a scale that never would have been possible before social media. This says it all about the power of social media influence.

Another top-line observation is that these megaposts were diverse, international, and from people who were both extremes: well known and relatively obscure. (The solitary egg photo is the sole post from world_record_egg's account with no bio, simply "Eugene.") Note that not a single most-liked post had a negative tone or was political. Good triumphs over bad and ugly; human beings just tend to focus more on the latter two. Call me naïve, but I wholeheartedly believe we are better than we think we are when it comes to upright citizenry and to good graces on social media and general kindness in life. These posts represent the intersection of authenticity and human connection in a dopamine-heightened environment. "Eugene" is the pinnacle of the impact influencers strive for while having none of the actual influence or motivation to influence. Why? What is it about humans + social media that = magic? Deep down, we all have the psychological need to be connected to something authentic that's bigger than who we individually are.

MY FINAL MESSAGE
Silence Dogood—a pen name for none other than Benjamin Franklin—once wrote, "Without freedom of thought there can be no such

thing as wisdom; and no such thing as public liberty, without freedom of speech."[6]

If Mr. Dogood were alive today, he would likely observe through bifocals the fly heading straight into the social media ointment. Amid the staggering amount of invaluable public education and self-expression to be found across the social media spectrum, some platforms are gradually silencing opposing viewpoints through—dare I use the word—*censorship*. In an ironic twist, many university and college campuses once considered safe havens for free speech are baldly excluding opposing opinions from open debate and discussions. It is up to all of us—platform executives, influencers, users, and sponsors—to insist on freedom of speech on social media, even if we don't share a particular view. This goes for everyone from someone with three followers to a MLI. As British philosopher John Stuart Mill astutely wrote, "The peculiar evil of silencing the expression of an opinion is, that it is robbing the human race; posterity as well as the existing generation; those who dissent from the opinion, still more than those who hold it. If the opinion is right, they are deprived of the opportunity of exchanging error for truth: if wrong, they lose, what is almost as great a benefit, the clearer perception and livelier impression of truth, produced by its collision with error."[7]

I've emphasized throughout the preceding pages that the platforms have a responsibility to protect the public from imminent dangers and threats, especially when it comes to preventing exposure to children and teens. Instead of censoring safe posts that merely represent contrary points of view, we have a secret weapon to battle misinformation, disinformation, and anything else that might be harmful to democratic thought: our critical thinking skills, which may be tapped through Perceptual Intelligence. Our PI helps us distinguish fact from fiction; educate ourselves; know when and how to question things; and, ultimately, make the right decisions for ourselves and society—no matter what we see or hear on influencer or user feeds. Being proficient with critical thinking empowers us to self-regulate social media content while also supporting freedom of speech—a right that people in democratic countries consider sacred.

Social media has replaced all other outlets as the world's most colossal forum for combined self-expression, information, opinions, and news. We the people can help ensure that our freedoms remain bright by insisting that all platforms allow a variety of ideas to marinate—not in the shadows, but openly in the light, where they can be evaluated by all.

I leave you with this parting message that just might go viral:

Let free speech reign supreme

Appendix A
Glossary

This glossary is by no means intended to serve as a definitive diction-ary of terms pertaining to social media influence, but rather as a tool to follow the terminology referenced in this book. It includes concise definitions of some technical and scientific jargon, as well as words I confess to having created myself or borrowed from someone else. The latter instances are denoted by an asterisk *.

abnormal red reflex: when a black, white, or yellow reflection appears in the pupil of one or both eyes in a photo used with a flash. (Red reflec-tion is the normal color.)

ACC: See *anterior cingulate cortex.*

account(s): in social media, a place where users join and participate in a platform.

AI: See *artificial intelligence.*

analytics: the data used to evaluate social media performance.

anterior cingulate cortex (ACC): a part of the brain believed to be in-volved in impulse control, emotion, decision-making, and error detec-tion; the anterior is specifically in the front.

app: a shortened version of the word *application* that generally refers to a software that can run on a variety of devices, including computers and smartphones; some social media platforms (such as Instagram and TikTok) are created as apps for smartphones.

AR: See *augmented reality.*

artificial intelligence (AI): a system, robot, or other technology that controls tasks otherwise run by humans.

asynchronous: when one occurrence takes place at a different time from another.

atrophy: the act of shrinking or being diminished in size or capacity.

augmented reality (AR): when a user's physical world is enhanced as a result of computer technology.

authentic: when a person on social media behaves in a way that is considered true to themselves. See also *authenticity.*

authenticity: when one is true to one's own personality, values, and spirit, regardless of the pressure to act otherwise. When an individual is honest with themselves and with others, that person is taking responsibility for mistakes, and therefore their values, ideals, and actions align.[1]

avatar: a figure or icon representing a person in the digital world (such as in a video game).

baby boomer: anyone born between the years 1946 and 1964.

balance: when one can equally manage work, social life, and free time without undue stress.

bank: in social media (rather than concerning the institution), this may be used as a verb meaning "to generate" ("she *banked* lots of money on that ad") or as a noun ("he earned major *bank* from the ad").

baristing*: the act of being a barista—one who prepares and serves coffee in a store.

block: the act of prohibiting one or more people from seeing your social media profile and/or posts. Apps may block users, if indicated.

blog: a recurring online journal in which a person or entity informs viewers about thoughts, beliefs, activities, information, or certain skills.

blogger: a person who creates a blog.

blow up: See *viral.*

boundaries: an influencer or user's ability to separate social media life from work and personal life.

brand: the representation of a person, company, or product that is presented to the public. See also *influencer brand.*

brand-sponsored video: a video posted by an influencer that is paid for by an organization or business, typically intended to increase brand awareness for that entity or one of its products and often with goal to generate sales.

burnout: when a person is exhausted and overwrought from devoting too much time to any one activity, usually work related and can be experienced by influencers.

cancel: the act of silencing someone and perhaps even causing others to shun that person. See also *cancel culture.*

cancel culture: when large groups of people target an individual or corporation on social media with the intent of ostracizing them out of their circle. Damaged reputation of the entity is among the potential losses.

cap: in social media, this refers to a falsehood.

capademic*: when falsehoods run amok like a widespread disease. See also *cap.*

carrotted*: incentivized.

celebrity DBI: an index created by the company the Marketing Arm that quantifies and qualifies consumer perceptions of celebrities.

censorship (censor): when a person or entity blocks or suppresses content or messaging from reaching the public.

cerebral cortex: See *frontal lobe.*

chat: a side discussion within a social media feed or other type of electronic communication; the conversation may be private between two or more people or made visible to a wider group.

click: when a computer mouse is tapped to select an option on an electronic screen; in social media, this often refers to each time users select a specific post.

clinkage: in the context of this book, this is a noun that refers to the sound of two glasses clinking in celebration. The term was first coined by rowing coach Pat Hayes. When a rower won medals for multiple races in a single day, the sound of the medals around the rower's neck made this jangling sound.

clip: a brief segment of video appearing in a feed.

comment: any kind of writing (or visual) entered into a feed from a user; it may also involve influencer responses to those posts.

community: a group of people who follow a specific influencer and generally share similar interests.

community guidelines: the rules specific to a platform.

community guidelines violation: when one of the platform rules is broken by either a user or an influencer. Depending on the site's guidelines, the platform may issue a warning; force removal of the post; or turn off the user's account (temporarily or permanently), which is more likely if there is a perpetual pattern of violations.

confluence: when two things come together or meet at the same time (such as a pair of rivers). In social media, this refers to an influencer engaging with users in real-time metaverse.[2] See also *confluencer* and *metaverse*.

confluencer: an influencer who takes their community to a new dimension of connectivity by engaging with participants via live, face-to-face video and created assets within the metaverse. See also *confluence* and *metaverse*.

conspiracy theory: the concept that an act has taken place by a sinister or powerful group and is intentionally being concealed. In reality, there are often more likely explanations based on supportive evidence.

content: any material that is posted online, including but not limited to a few written words in a feed, a blog, a photograph or other graphic, or a video.

content creator: in social media, any individual or entity that produces content for posting, including users, influencers, bloggers, vloggers, experts, and even animals/inanimate objects/babies/toddlers/memes. See also *content*.

content generation: the production of content for posting in social media. See also *content*.

copycat behavior: when a group of people mimic the actions of another person; in the case of social media posts, this can be damaging when the subject matter involves suicide or other forms of self-harm.

cornea: the clear outer lens of the eye that helps focus light rays for vision.

creative drive: what motivates an individual to produce any kind of resulting work; in the case of social media, this refers to content.

creator: See *content creator*.

credibility: the extent to which an influencer is believable, especially in terms of posted content matching their brand image. See also *trust*.

critical thinking: one's ability to distinguish fantasy versus reality and falsehood from truth. See also *Perceptual Intelligence*.

crowdsource: when a large group of people contribute to the formulation of an idea, help with a decision, or offer solicited opinions on content. Influencers, users, individuals, and businesses can use this method to gain insights, help cocreate (content or a product), and/or engage with a specific intended group.

crucial conversation: "a discussion between two or more people where (1) stakes are high, (2) opinions vary, and (3) emotions run strong."[3]

cult (cultish): in social media, a small group that typically seeks to persuade members and nonmembers to adopt certain thoughts and/or behaviors.

cyberbullying: online attacks (insults and/or threats) against an individual or group, usually with the intent of humiliation and often resulting in hurt feelings and low self-esteem.

cyberstalking: the act of harassing or stalking another individual or entity online. This may manifest in the form of taunts, false accusations, defamation, slander, libel, threats, blackmail, and/or lead to identity theft or physical harm (such as unwanted sexual advances).

dark arts: magic spells used for evil; the term originated in the Harry Potter novels.

dark (darker) halo effect: when a celebrity or public figure's negative or harmful actions inspire others to perform the same or similar dangerous, potentially deadly, acts.

DBB: See *dopamine behavior balance.*

deepfake: sophisticated 3D AI technology that enables a person to create a video of oneself as someone else, often a celebrity. The problem arises when the imitations are so convincing that many people believe them to be real.

digital-first: the concept that everything produced by an individual or company should have a primary technological (usually online) component to it.

digital footprint: a quantification of a person's online history; for example, a simple evaluation may be conducted with a Google search of a person or entity.

digital presence: a measurement of a person or company's visibility online.

direct message: See *DM.*

disclosure: in social media, this is when influencers or users reveal a detail that contributes to their authenticity. This often refers to when an influencer denotes advertising and/or sponsorship by including #ad and/or #[brandname]partner in the post.

disinformation: the intentional doctoring of facts and/or visuals (such as photographs) to suit an agenda, vendetta, or whim. This may cause emotional, physical, and perhaps reputational harm to others.

distraction: in social media, when devices (and the apps on them) cause an individual to switch focus away from something else.

DM: a private direct message; typically, a form of shorthand communication used in social media.

DNA: scientifically known as deoxyribonucleic acid, this consists of the self-replicating genetic material that is passed down from one generation to the next.

doctored images: photographs that are manipulated to make a person, place, or thing appear more attractive or to mislead others into believing the appearance is more complimentary than the reality.

doomscrolling: the act of spending an inordinate amount of time on apps and sites that usurp one's time, often focus on negative news, and can be misleading and sometimes even dangerous.

dopamine: a tiny yet powerful neurotransmitter or chemical messenger that plays a large role in feeling pleasure. See also *dopamine behavior balance.*

dopamine behavior balance (DBB)*: the balance of dopamine stimulation manifested within individuals seeking out activities that satisfy dopamine release and its pleasure effects.

dope: slang for excellent or awesome; synonym for "sick" or "fire."

doxxing: the act of making someone else's private information (such as a home address) public with the intent to cause harm to that person.

drafts section: a private place where material for a potential future post is kept until a user or influencer adds it live to a feed.

duet: on TikTok, a post involving one video adjacent to another video.

dwarfism: when a person is short of stature as a result of a genetic or medical condition.

emoji: a small image or graphic that represents a person's emotional reaction to something or current state of mind.

empathy: the ability to relate to, understand, or perhaps feel another person's emotions.

engage: the act of users interacting with a content creator's posted content. See also *engagement.*

engagement: the interactions between users and a creator's content; the expression of this occurs in the form of views, likes, comments, shares, profile views, saves, replies, website taps, email taps, and so forth. Metrics can differ from platform to platform. See also *engage* and *engagement rate.*

engagement rate: the metrics of users' interactions with a creator's content; the expression of this occurs based on numbers of views, likes, comments, shares, profile views, saves, replies, website taps, email taps, and so forth. Some of the data points to analyze may include growth day to day, week to week, month to month; number of views, likes, comments, and shares; and user time spent watching a video and percentage of users who watched a video to completion. Some companies have proprietary algorithms to determine overall aggregate engagement rates for influencers. See also *metrics*.

erectile dysfunction (ED): when a man suffers from an inability to generate and/or maintain an erection for satisfying sexual activity; porn addiction can contribute to this condition.

fact: a verifiable, true statement.

fake account: a social media imposter profile for an influencer, celebrity, individual, or entity.

fake news: false or misleading information that knowingly or unknowingly spreads misinformation and/or disinformation.

fan: a follower who is fully devoted to and engaged with an influencer.

fap: slang verb meaning to masturbate. See also *NoFap*.

fapping: slang noun referring to the act of masturbation. See also *NoFap*.

fapstronaut: a male who is antimasturbation and antipornography.[4] See also *NoFap*.

fascinoma: a fascinating medical nodule, growth, or mass. If there were an Urban Dictionary in the field of medicine, this term would be in it.

fat shaming: the act of shaming an individual based on weight or body shape. See also *shaming*.

feed: a social media app's widget that aggregates themed content, such as searching a word, or word preceded by # or @, depending on the platform. This word many also refer to a user's content posted on their account.

femstronaut: a female who is antimasturbation and antipornography.[5] See also *NoFap*.

flat-earther: a present-day proponent of the concept that the earth is flat and not round.

flexy*: adjective of flex; internet slang for showing off.

fMRI: magnetic resonance imaging generally used to check blood flow changes in the brain. See also *MRI*.

follower: a user who opts in on a creator's account and sees the account's content, such as on TikTok, Instagram, and Twitter.

follower efficiency ratio*: the number of total video likes for an account divided by the number of new followers for a given time period.

followers (following): a group of people who see content on a creator's account.

following the herd: going along with the thinking of a mass of people rather than breaking away based on your own individual thought process.

FOMO: the fear of missing out.

frontal lobe: the front part of the brain's cerebral cortex responsible for higher-level functions.

FYP: See *TikTok FYP*.

Gen alpha: individuals born from 2013 to 2025.

Gen X: individuals born between the years 1965 and 1980.

Gen Z: individuals born between the years 1997 and 2012.

gray (or grey) matter: parts of the brain that enable humans to control memory and movement and a number of other critical functions, including regulation of emotion.

ground rules: in social media, an organizational system used by an individual (or family) to monitor and limit excessive time spent on social media.

growth hormone deficiency (GHD): See *dwarfism*.

gua sha: an ancient Chinese stone usually made of quartz or jade. Some influencers mislead users into believing the stone has special properties that improve one's jawline. Studies have shown that it can improve muscle soreness.

habit: an activity done repeatedly to such extent that it becomes second nature and/or hard to give up.

hack: an attack of a person or entity's technology—email, computer, social media feeds, user profiles, and the like—for malicious purposes.

halo effect: how a celebrity's positive public image can influence others in terms of thought and/or behavior.

hashtag: the symbol # (pound sign) used before a word or phrase in a post to help widen its reach.

high PI: having the ability to use critical thinking skills to separate reality from fantasy through the pursuit and analysis of available logical facts. See also *low PI* and *Perceptual Intelligence*.

Holcomb C3-R' cross-linking: a noninvasive procedure for keratoconus to stabilize further vision loss by strengthening the weakened cornea fibers. Patients typically return to full daily function the next day with no side effects. See also *keratoconus*.

hologram: a photographic or video image that is recorded using 3D technology and accurately presented in virtual form.

hopeium*: noun for "wishful thinking," coined by my longtime friend Ari Galper; the term is a play on the drug opium.

influence: in social media, the ability to engage viewers on a regular basis with content that elicits specific thoughts and/or actions from them. See also *influenced, influencee,* and *influencer.*

influenced: in social media, the state when an influencee is moved in thought and/or action by an influencer. See also *influence, influencee,* and *influencer.*

influencee*: a user who is moved in thought and/or action by an influencer.

influencer: anyone with a strong presence on social media who produces content, has an online community, engages with a multitude of followers, and posts ideas and recommendations with the intent of eliciting emotional responses and behaviors from viewers. See also *influence, influenced,* and *influencee.*

influencer brand: the physical or perceived representation of an influencer and what they represent or are known for.

influencer marketing: a type of social media marketing that involves soliciting and contacting influencers for paid brand, product, or service endorsements.

internet (the): a seemingly unlimited amalgam of interconnected networks on which users can consume and post information, communicate with each other, and share content via innumerable websites and apps.

internet porn (pornography): sites and apps that feature explicit sexual content, including photographs and videos. See also *porn addiction.*

intuition: an ability to understand things without conscious reasoning.

keratoconus: a condition in which the cornea bulges outward, causing a range of visual distortions. See also *cornea* and *Holcomb C3-R° crosslinking.*

kidfluencer: a child who is an influencer. See also *influence, influenced, influencee,* and *influencer.*

left frontal lobe: See *frontal lobe.*

left nucleus accumbens: See *nucleus accumbens.*

LGBTQIA+: an acronym for lesbian, gay, bisexual, transgender, queer, intersex, asexual, and more sexual identities.

lifecaster: a person with a special talent, such as an entrepreneur, model, actor, celebrity, athlete, or politician.

Like: in social media, a button users can click on to express appreciation for someone's post.

lol: acronym for laugh out loud.

low PI: weak critical thinking skills when it comes to distinguishing fantasy from reality and failing to pursue and analyze available logical facts. See also *high PI* and *Perceptual Intelligence.*

magnetoreception: a sense that enables an organism to detect a magnetic field's direction and other characteristics.

magnetic resonance imaging: See *MRI.*

malinformation: when private information about an individual or organization is intentionally made public. This might involve a leak from a whistleblower, sabotage by someone in the victim's inner circle, or hacking from an outside source.

merch: for social media purposes, products (which may or may not be branded) sold by influencers that are usually offered for sale on their accounts or through links.

mesocortical pathway: one of four dopamine pathways into the brain. This system regulates motivation, emotional response, and other functions. See also *dopamine.*

mesolimbic pathway: one of four dopamine pathways into the brain. This system is often thought of as the "rewards" pathway and regulates learning and reinforcement. See also *dopamine.*

meta: a reference to our world plus other realms beyond it; also, Meta (capital *M*) is the umbrella corporate name for Facebook and other associated entities.[6]

metaverse: in the digital space, a world in which humans beings as avatars engage with apps and software and interact within virtual worlds, including with other avatars, to simulate an entirely new perceived reality.

metrics: the data points content creators may use to identify their level of interactivity with followers. See also *engagement rate.*

millennial: individuals born between 1981 and 1996.

misinformation: pieces of information that are unintentionally incorrect. They might include things such as spellings, translations, dates, and statistics.

MLI*: a macro-level influencer who has a following the size of a large country's population. Pronounced "m'lee."

monetization: the act of generating revenue from established activities, such as social media success as an influencer (via channels such as sponsorship, advertising, or a subscription model).

MRI: magnetic resonance imaging used to measure structures in the body. The difference between an fMRI and MRI is that the latter scans show anatomical structure, whereas fMRI displays blood flow resulting from brain activity. See also *fMRI.*

mukbang: an amalgam of the Korean words *mukja* ("let's eat") and *bang song* ("broadcast"), this is a trend that originated in South Korea and involves people binge-eating large amounts of food while others watch on social media.[7]

multiverse: when one set of fictional characters—through magic, wizardry, or some other cosmic, powerful force—meets up with a separate set of their doppelganger selves (plus their nemeses and others) who exist along a separate timeline in a different reality or virtual world.

neuronal: the adjective form of neuron.

neurons: nerve cells that transmit impulses.

neurotransmitter: a chemical messenger that sends signals throughout the nervous system of the human body.

nigrostriatal pathway: one of four dopamine pathways into the brain. This system influences voluntary movement. See also *dopamine*.

NoFap: a modern-day antimasturbation movement.[8] See also *fap*.

not cap: in social media, a true statement.

notification: an alert on a device—such as a buzzing, ringing, vibrating, or music—that reminds the users of an event or informs them that something has occurred in a feed or elsewhere.

nucleus accumbens: a part of the brain involved in motivation and taking action (motor function) as related to processing and weighing rewards, which may have a role in addiction.

oversharent: when a parent discloses too many personal, sensitive details about their child on social media. See also *sharent*.

parasocial relationship (PSR): in social media, a situation that arises when a follower is so connected to an influencer that they interpret the emotional connection as indicating a sense of a real-life relationship.[9]

perception: the ability to use the senses (see, hear, touch, feel, or taste) to be aware of something.

Perceptual Intelligence (PI): a person's ability to distinguish reality from fantasy using critical thinking skills by the pursuit and analysis of available logical facts. See also *critical thinking*.

pfp: the profile picture users select for their accounts.

PI: See *Perceptual Intelligence*.

pile on: in social media, when a substantial number of users post negative comments in response to a post (or a comment), often with the intent of insulting, shunning, embarrassing, trolling, or canceling someone.

platform: a social media app intended to foster engagement of users; the term may also be used to refer to the entire breadth of an influencer or user's account, including marketing or publicity reach with a following.

porn addiction: when an individual is emotionally dependent on viewing sexual adult content while concurrently performing sexual acts to the point that it adversely impacts daily life, the ability to function, and relationships.

post: as a noun in the world of social media, this refers to any content (such as a text, a photograph, a video, or an image) that has been added to a user's feed. In verb form, "to post" means the act of making the content available on the feed.

ppl: abbreviation for *people.*

precuneus: part of the brain involved in memory and perception, among other functions.

privacy: in social media, this signifies a user's right to keep personal information (such as profile details) hidden from some or all other users; posts may also be considered private and made available to only select people. Every social media platform has different rules regarding what data points they may share with third parties (such as marketers). See also *terms of service.*

profile: information on a user's account that typically includes personal facts. Users determine what information they are willing to share.

PSA: acronym for public service announcement.

PSR: See *parasocial relationship.*

punim: a Yiddish word for a person's face. The word is most often used in an affectionate way, such as from a grandparent to a young child (e.g., "You have such a beautiful *punim!*").

purpose: a strong motivating factor—sometimes referred to as a person's *why*—behind choosing to do or create something.

reaction video: a video follow-up duetted or stitched to an original post prior to reposting.

real time: in the virtual world, this refers to an event or action that can be viewed live by others.

relatability: an influencer's ability to understand and connect with users and be capable of demonstrating empathy. See also *authenticity*.

reshare: when a user or influencer reposts content on their account.

right frontal lobe: See *frontal lobe*.

screen time: the number of minutes or hours a person spends on devices.

scroll: in social media, this is a verb referring to the act of moving the cursor up or down to view posts in the feed of a user or influencer.

selfie: a photograph taken of oneself, typically with a smartphone and intended for posting in social media.

sex addiction: when an individual cannot control sexual urges that leads to compulsively performing sexual acts, despite negative consequences.

sexuality doula: a term coined by Ev'Yan Whitney meaning to "educate, facilitate, support, and hold space for women and nonbinary folks [to] help them reclaim their unique sexual expressions, reconnect to their sensual bodies, and define themselves in these areas on their own terms."[10]

sexually transmitted illness: See *STI*.

sexverse*: the inordinate spectrum of online sexual content.

sex worker: a person who—on a regular or occasional basis—provides the exchange of sexual services, performance, or products for material compensation.

shaming: to make someone feel ashamed or inadequate. See also *fat shaming* and *slut shaming*.

share (sharing): the act of sending content from an influencer or another user.

sharent: the act of disclosing information about one's child publicly on social media. See also *oversharent.*

sirens: in ancient Greek mythology, these were the beautiful maidens who would sit half naked on rocks near the shore and sing to lure in sailors. The hypnotic effect would cause the navigators to direct the ships into shallow, rocky water and often lead them to crash. Odysseus encountered the Sirens in Homer's epic poem *The Odyssey.* A modern equivalent would be *thirst trap.*

slut shaming: the act of shaming an individual based on perceived or real sexual activity. See also *shaming.*

social media: interactive technologies that facilitate the creation and sharing of information, ideas, interests, and other forms of expression through asynchronous virtual communities and networks. See also *asynchronous* and *synchronous.*

social media addiction: when an individual is emotionally dependent on social media to the point that it adversely impacts daily life, the ability to function, and/or relationships.

social media engagement: See *engagement.*

social media handle: a person or entity's username. Certain platforms, such as TikTok and Instagram, require the @ symbol before the name.

spam: digital junk mail that may appear via email, on user social media feeds, and in DMs.

sponsor (sponsorship): a company or individual that purchases advertising, endorsements, and/or use of a product and/or service from an influencer. See also *brand.*

STI: a sexually transmitted infection, such as herpes. The name reverted from *sexually transmitted disease* (STD) because not all diseases begin as illnesses (though many do). Another reason for change was due to the stigma associated with sexually transmitted disease, as with venereal disease.

stitch: when a user or influencer adds a reaction video to a video from another user or influencer.

subscriber: a user who opts in to be a follower of a specific content creator's account on certain platforms like YouTube, where subscriber is synonymous with follower.

subscription model: a social media strategy in which an influencer charges followers to receive exclusive content. Charges typically recur at a regular interval and followers can opt out.

supernova*: in the context of this book, a viral video that reaches an astronomically high number of video views.

synchronous: when two or more events are occurring at the same time.

tachophobia: the fear of speed.

tag: the act of identifying another person or entity in a post by typing their social media handle. The tagged party will often receive a notification of having been mentioned.

talent manager: in social media, a professional who helps influencers monetize their platforms, often by soliciting sponsorships with brands.

terms of service: the legal agreement a person must sign to join a platform. The terms often cite their privacy practices, as well as modes of conduct while on the app.

text neck: repetitive stress injury in the cervical area caused by having the head down and looking on one's phone for prolonged periods of time.

thirst trap: a sexually themed social media post intended to entice viewers.

thread: in social media, a string of messages from different users that make up a conversation in response to a post. They are all connected and can be viewed.

TikTok addiction*: when an individual is emotionally dependent on TikTok to the point that it adversely impacts daily life, ability to function, and/or relationships. This person would be a TikTokaholic. See also *TikTokaholic*.

TikTokaholic*: an individual who is emotionally dependent on TikTok to the point that it adversely impacts daily life, the ability to function, and/or relationships.

TikTok famous: denotes a user who has amassed a large number of followers on TikTok.

TikTok FYP: the "For You page" on this platform.

traffic: in social media, the volume of users and visitors visiting an account at a given time.

troll: a person who posts inflammatory comments on a feed; typically, this individual hides behind anonymity.

trust (trustworthy): when a follower believes that an influencer is honest, authentic, and not concealing a hidden agenda.

tuberoinfundibular pathway: one of four dopamine pathways into the brain. This system regulates prolactin secretion (responsible for lactation and breast development among women) by the pituitary gland. See also *dopamine.*

user: a person or entity with a social media account.

username: a user's account name or social media handle.

verification: a check mark, typically blue, next to a user's name to denote an authentic account from an influencer, public figure, celebrity, or brand. See also *verified.*

verified: when a social media platform confirms that the account authentically represents the influencer, public figure, celebrity, or brand as identified by a check mark (often blue) next to the username. Some people see this as a sign of prestige indicating that the influencer is important enough to attract people who might fake the influencer's account.

view(s): used as a noun in the context of social media, this is each time a user opens a post.

viral: adjective to describe when a video becomes highly popular and accumulates a large number of views.

virtual: computer software that is created to simulate the real world, though often in creative fashion.

visual cortex: the primary part of the brain responsible for receiving, processing, and interpreting visual information from the eyes.

vlog: a combination of the words *video* and *blog* (or *log*); a recurring series of videos in which a person or entity informs users about thoughts, beliefs, activities, information, or certain skills.

vlogger: a person who produces a vlog and may monetize such content.

white matter: the collection of extensions of nerve cells found in the brain and spinal cord; its primary responsibility is to transfer information.

woke: when a person has a heightened awareness of social injustice.

zeitgeist (zeitgeisty*): the spirit or mood of a particular period in time; "the taste and outlook characteristic of a period or generation."[11]

Appendix B

Hidden Meanings of Commonly Used Social Media Emojis

G-RATED[1]

billed cap: something is cap, meaning false. (I admit to being a bit partial to this one.)

chair: funny or lol (laugh out loud) while creating confusion on TikTok for ppl (people) not in the know.

clown face: mocking or making fun of a user.

coffin: same meaning as *skull and crossbones* but less commonly used.

crown: high compliment saying someone is like GOAT (acronym for "greatest of all time").

folded hands: "thank you" or gratitude.

lips between eyes: watching a post that was shocking or unexpected.

lips between eyes with droplets: feeling sad.

moai: when something isn't funny; a deadpan face, such as when a joke bombs.

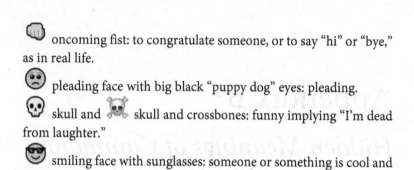 oncoming fist: to congratulate someone, or to say "hi" or "bye," as in real life.

pleading face with big black "puppy dog" eyes: pleading.

skull and skull and crossbones: funny implying "I'm dead from laughter."

smiling face with sunglasses: someone or something is cool and badass, like an achievement.

two fingers together: the user is shy or commenting in shy way; sometimes accompanied by for emphasis.

woman or man with a white cane: a person is not seeing something or is ignoring it.

[word] : a word between two sparkles, which add emphasis.

writing hand: something was useful and being mentally noted.

NOT SO G-RATED

brain: oral sex ("giving head").

cat face: a woman's vagina.

cherries: a woman's breasts.

eggplant: a man's penis.

peach: a person's butt/buttocks.

peanuts: to ejaculate; most often used regarding males.

right-facing fist with cut of meat: masturbation ("beating meat").

sweat droplets: an orgasm or sexual fluids.

Notes

EPIGRAPH

1. https://www.wow4u.com/influence-quotes/.

2. https://brandongaille.com/44-breathtaking-robert-b-cialdini-quotes/.

3. https://quotefancy.com/quote/848920/Kim-Kardashian-I-m-not-trying-to-influence-anyone-else-I-m-not-saying-Do-what-I-do-I.

PROLOGUE

1. https://www.azquotes.com/quote/624677.

2. https://www.azquotes.com/quote/789404.

INTRODUCTION

1. Adam D. I. Kramer, "The Spread of Emotion via Facebook," ACM Digital Library, May 5, 2012, https://dl.acm.org/doi/abs/10.1145/2207676.2207787.

2. Influencer Marketing Hub, *Influencer Marketing Benchmark Report 2022*, 2022, https://influencermarketinghub.com/influencer-marketing-benchmark-report/.

3. https://www.instagram.com/coco_pinkprincess/.

4. Kelly McSweeney, "This Is Your Brain on Instagram: Effects of Social Media on the Brain," Now, March 17, 2019, https://now.northropgrumman.com/this-is-your-brain-on-instagram-effects-of-social-media-on-the-brain/.

5. Lauren E. Sherman, Patricia M. Greenfield, Leanna M. Hernandez, and Mirella Dapretto, "Peer Influence via Instagram: Effects on Brain and Behavior in Adolescence and Young Adulthood," *Child Development* 89, no. 1 (January 2018), https://pubmed.ncbi.nlm.nih.gov/28612930/.

6. https://pubmed.ncbi.nlm.nih.gov/26893270/.

7. https://www.instagram.com/waltergoodboy/?hl=en.

8. https://danschawbel.com/quotes/.

CHAPTER 1

1. https://quotefancy.com/quote/957439/Salvador-Dal-I-want-to-perceive-and-understand-the-hidden-powers-and-laws-of-things-in.

2. "Everything We Know So Far about YouTube Star James Charles' Feud with Tati Westbrook," *Us* magazine, June 30, 2020, https://www.usmagazine.com/celebrity-news/pictures/james-charles-tati-westbrook-feud-everything-we-know/.

3. Werner Geyser, "What Is TikTok?—The Fastest Growing Social Media App Uncovered," Influencer Marketing Hub, June 11, 2021, https://influencermarketinghub.com/what-is-tiktok/.

4. Pat LaDouceur, "What We Fear More Than Death," *MentalHelp* (blog), n.d., https://www.mentalhelp.net/blogs/what-we-fear-more-than-death/.

5. https://www.tiktok.com/@nnatalieaguilar?lang=en.

6. Harish B., "Brand Update: Colgate Slimsoft Charcoal Toothbrush Will Make You Say WhattheBlack!" *Marketing Practice* (blog), November 6, 2014, http://marketingpractice.blogspot.com/2014/11/brand-update-colgate-slimsoft-charcoal.html.

7. Jason Falls, *Winfluence* (Irvine, CA: Entrepreneur, 2021).

CHAPTER 2

1. https://www.oxfordreference.com/view/10.1093/
acref/9780191826719.001.0001/q-oro-ed4-00003457#:~:text=Charles%20
Darwin%201809%E2%80%9382&text=Ignorance%20more%20frequently%20
begets%20confidence,never%20be%20solved%20by%20science.

2. Robert Cialdini, *Influence: The Psychology of Persuasion*, new and expanded (New York: Harper Business, 2021).

3. Aimee Ortiz, "Peloton Ad Is Criticized as Sexist and Dystopian," *New York Times*, December 3, 2019, https://www.nytimes.com/2019/12/03/business/peloton-bike-ad-stock.html.

4. Longjam Dineshwori, "Gua Sha Cannot Give You a Sharper Jawline: Common Misconceptions Debunked," The Health Site, June 11, 2021, https://www.thehealthsite.com/beauty/skin-care/gua-sha-cannot-give-you-a-sharper-jawline-dr-rashmi-shettyra-debunks-misconceptions-about-this-beauty-tool-819246/.

5. Peter Suciu, "Social Media and the Need to Believe," *Forbes*, November 11, 2019, https://www.forbes.com/sites/petersuciu/2019/11/11/social-media-and-the-need-to-believe/?sh=739bd1d37bf3.

6. "Mott Poll: Nearly Two-Thirds of Mothers 'Shamed' by Others about Their Parenting Skills," June 19, 2017, https://www.mottchildren.org/news/archive/201706/mott-poll-nearly-two-thirds-mothers-%E2%80%9Cshamed%E2%80%9D-others-about.

7. J. D. Simkins, "Air Force Vet Hoarded 17,700 Bottles of Hand Sanitizer, Then Had No Place to Sell Them—Sad!" *Air Force Times*, March 17, 2020, https://www.airforcetimes.com/off-duty/military-culture/2020/03/17/air-force-vet-stuck-with-17700-bottles-of-hand-sanitizer-with-no-place-to-sell-them-sad/.

8. Richard Roeper, "*15 Minutes of Shame*: Sobering HBO Max Doc Profiles People Chastised on the Internet," *Chicago Sun-Times*, October 6, 2021, https://chicago.suntimes.com/movies-and-tv/2021/10/6/22710729/15-minutes-of-shame-review-hbo-max-movie-monica-lewinsky-documentary-matt-colvin-emmanuel-cafferty.

9. Caroline Miller, "Does Social Media Use Cause Depression?" Child Mind Institute, n.d., https://childmind.org/article/is-social-media-use-causing-depression/.

10. Remy Blumenfeld, "Gen Z at Work—8 Reasons to Be Afraid," *Forbes*, October 15, 2019, https://www.forbes.com/sites/remyblumenfeld/2019/10/15/gen-z-at-work8-reasons-to-be-afraid/?sh=18b33bf533a9.

11. Saumya Agrawal, "This Video Has Convinced Men That Women Peel Their Skin Off after Periods," Times Now News, May 13, 2021, https://www.timesnownews.com/the-buzz/article/this-video-has-convinced-men-that-women-peel-their-skin-off-after-periods-watch/756411.

12. Ashley Moser, "Park City Family Reunited with Stolen Dog Thanks to Social Media," KSL TV, April 22, 2021, https://ksltv.com/460476/park-city-family-reunited-with-stolen-dog-thanks-to-social-media/.

13. https://www.youtube.com/watch?v=Ed_Kxyqgp1c.

14. Rhea Arora, "Your Social Media Posts Can Reveal Your Health Condition. Here's How," Qrius, June 23, 2019, https://qrius.com/your-social-media-posts-can-be-reveal-your-health-condition-heres-how/.

15. Andrew G. Reece and Christopher M. Danforth, "Instagram Photos Reveal Predictive Markers of Depression," Research Gate, August 2016, https://www.researchgate.net/publication/306186650_Instagram_photos_reveal_predictive_markers_of_depression.

16. Reena Mukamai, "Photos Can Help Diagnose Children's Eye Problems and Save Sight," American Academy of Ophthalmology, February 25, 2021, https://www.aao.org/eye-health/tips-prevention/diagnosing-children-from-photographs.

CHAPTER 3

1. Natalie Muller, "Animals Getting High: 10 Common Drunks," *Australian Geographic*, October 14, 2011, https://www.australiangeographic.com.au/topics/wildlife/2011/10/animals-getting-high-10-common-drunks/.

2. Bec Crew, "Bennett's Wallabies Get High on Poppy Seeds," *Australian Geographic*, February 27, 2015, https://www.australiangeographic.com.au/blogs/creatura-blog/2015/02/bennetts-wallabies-get-high/.

3. Kristy Hamilton, "Jaguar Tastes the Hallucinogenic Effects of Yage," IFL Science, October 29, 2014, https://www.iflscience.com/plants-and-animals/jaguar-tastes-hallucinogenic-effects-yage/.

4. Heidi Fay-Thompson, "What Is Catnip & What Does It Do to My Cat?" Animal Emergency & Referral Center of Minnesota, n.d., https://aercmn.com/what-is-catnip-what-does-it-do-to-my-cat/.

5. Ed Yong, "Why a Little Mammal Has So Much Sex That It Disintegrates," *National Geographic*, October 7, 2013, https://www.nationalgeographic.com/science/article/why-a-little-mammal-has-so-much-sex-that-it-disintegrates.

6. "Americans Choose Smartphones over Sex," Sachs Media, April 12 (no year), https://sachsmedia.com/poll-americans-choose-smartphones-over-sex/.

7. https://www.azquotes.com/quote/1136094.

8. Jean M. Twenge, "Have Smartphones Destroyed a Generation?" *Atlantic*, September 2017, https://www.theatlantic.com/magazine/archive/2017/09/has-the-smartphone-destroyed-a-generation/534198.

9. https://www.cdc.gov/teenpregnancy/about/index.htm.

10. "This Is the Teenage Brain on Social Media," Neuroscience News, May 31, 2016, https://neurosciencenews.com/nucleus-accumbens-social-media-4348/.

11. Lauren E. Sherman, Ashley A. Payton, Leanna M. Hernandez, Patricia M. Greenfield, and Mirella Dapretto, "The Power of the Like in Adolescence," *Psychological Science* 27, no. 7 (July 2016), https://www.ncbi.nlm.nih.gov/pmc/articles/PMC5387999.

12. Kep Kee Loh and Ryota Kanai, "Higher Media Multi-tasking Activity Is Associated with Smaller Gray-Matter Density in the Anterior Cingulate Cortex," *PLOS One* 9, no. 9 (September 24, 2014), https://journals.plos.org/plosone/article?id=10.1371/journal.pone.0106698.

13. Mona Moisala, Viljami Salmela, Emma Salo, Synnöve Carlson, Virve Vuontela, Oili Salonen, and Kimmo Alho, "Brain Activity during Divided and Selective Attention to Auditory and Visual Sentence Comprehension Tasks," *Frontiers in Human Neuroscience* 9 (February 19, 2015), https://www.frontiersin.org/articles/10.3389/fnhum.2015.00086/full.

14. R. Douglas Fields, "Does TV Rot Your Brain?" *Scientific American*, January 1, 2016, https://www.scientificamerican.com/article/does-tv-rot-your-brain/.

15. Hae Yeon Lee, Jeremy Jamieson, Harry Reis, Christopher G. Beevers, Robert A. Josephs, Michael C. Mullarkey, Joseph Michael O'Brien, and David S. Yeager, "Getting Fewer 'Likes' Than Others on Social Media Elicits Emotional Distress among Victimized Adolescents," *Child Development* 91, no. 6 (September 2020), https://www.researchgate.net/publication/344195460_Getting_Fewer_Likes_Than_Others_on_Social_Media_Elicits_Emotional_Distress_Among_Victimized_Adolescents.

16. Abby Heverin, "For Teens, More Screen Time Equals Less Happiness," International Coaching Federation, February 7, 2018, https://coachingfederation.org/blog/teens-screen-time-equals-less-happiness.

17. Anthony L. Fisher, "Social Media Is a Parasite, It Bleeds You to Live," Business Insider, September 6, 2020, https://www.businessinsider.com/delete-social-media-phone-parasite-mental-health-instagram-twitter-facebook-2020-9.

18. Amy Blaschka, "This Is Why You Need to Turn Off Social Media Notifications," *Forbes*, September 21, 2020, https://www.forbes.com/sites/amyblaschka/2020/09/21/this-is-why-you-need-to-turn-off-social-media-notifications/?sh=3ac9b506690a.

CHAPTER 4

1. https://www.reddit.com/r/quotes/comments/hgceeb/it_is_morally_as_bad_not_to_care_whether_a_thing/.

2. Erin Spencer, "The Real Power of the Pistol Shrimp," *Ocean Currents* (blog), September 10, 2020, https://oceanconservancy.org/blog/2020/09/10/pistol-shrimp/.

3. Henry H. Wilmer, William H. Hampton, Thomas M. Olino, Ingrid R. Olson, and Jason M. Chein, "Wired to Be Connected? Links between Mobile Technology Engagement, Intertemporal Preference and Frontostriatal White Matter Connectivity," *Social Cognitive and Affective Neuroscience* 14, no. 4 (April 2019), https://academic.oup.com/scan/article/14/4/367/5479340.

4. Ethan S. Bromberg-Martin and Okihide Hikosaka, "Midbrain Dopamine Neurons Signal Preference for Advance Information about Upcoming Rewards," *Neuron* 63, no. 1 (July 16, 2009), https://www.ncbi.nlm.nih.gov/pmc/articles/PMC2723053/.

5. Sarah Spinks, "Adolescent Brains Are Works in Progress," *Frontline*, PBS, March 9, 2000, https://www.pbs.org/wgbh/pages/frontline/shows/teenbrain/work/adolescent.html.

6. John Bargh, *Before You Know It* (New York: Atria, 2018).

7. Russell D. Romeo, "The Teenage Brain: The Stress Response and the Adolescent Brain," *Current Directions in Psychological Science* 22, no. 2 (April 2013), https://www.ncbi.nlm.nih.gov/pmc/articles/PMC4274618/.

8. Blake Te'Neil Lloyd, "A Conceptual Framework for Examining Adolescent Identity, Media Influence, and Social Development," *Review of General Psychology* 6, no. 1 (2002), https://journals.sagepub.com/doi/10.1037/1089-2680.6.1.73; Cynthia Hoffner and Martha Buchanan, "Young Adults' Wishful Identification with Television Characters: The Role of Perceived Similarity and Character Attributes," *Media Psychology* 7, no. 4 (2005), https://www.tandfonline.com/doi/abs/10.1207/S1532785XMEP0704_2.

9. Carolina Martinez and Tobias Olsson, "Making Sense of YouTubers: How Swedish Children Construct and Negotiate the YouTuber Misslisibell as a Girl Celebrity," *Journal of Children and Media* 13, no. 1 (2019), https://www.tandfonline.com/doi/full/10.1080/17482798.2018.1517656.

10. Marijke De Veirman, Liselot Hudders, and Michelle R. Nelson, "What Is Influencer Marketing and How Does It Target Children? A Review and Direction for Future Research," *Frontiers in Psychology*, December 3, 2019, https://www.frontiersin.org/articles/10.3389/fpsyg.2019.02685/full.

11. https://www.misterrogers.org/about-fred-rogers/.

12. "9-Year-Old Boy Is Named Highest-Earning YouTube Star of 2020," NPR, December 24, 2020, https://www.npr.org/2020/12/24/949926198/9-year -old-boy-is-named-highest-earning-youtube-star-of-2020.

13. "Ryan ToysReview Targets Preschoolers in Violation of FTC Law," Truth in Advertising, August 29, 2019, https://truthinadvertising.org/articles/ryan -toysreview-targets-preschoolers-in-violation-of-ftc-law/.

14. Marijke De Veirman, Steffi De Jans, Elisabeth Van den Abeele, and Liselot Hudders, "Unravelling the Power of Social Media Influencers: A Qualitative Study on Teenage Influencers as Commercial Content Creators on Social Media," in *The Regulation of Social Media Influencers*, ed. Catalina Goanta and Sofia Ranchordás (Cheltenham, UK: Edward Elgar, 2020), 126–66, https://www.researchgate.net/publication/342025696_Unravelling _the_power_of_social_media_influencers_a_qualitative_study_on_teenage _influencers_as_commercial_content_creators_on_social_media.

15. Karuna Sharma, "No Kidding: How Kids Influencers in the Age Group of 6–12 Are Wooing Brands," Business Insider, January 24, 2020, https:// www.businessinsider.in/advertising/ad-tech/article/no-kidding-how-kids -influencers-in-the-age-group-of-6-12-are-wooing-brands/articleshow/ 73560858.cms.

16. Marian Friestad and Peter Wright, "The Persuasion Knowledge Model: How People Cope with Persuasion Attempts," *Journal of Consumer Research* 21, no. 1 (June 1, 1994), https://academic.oup.com/jcr/article/21/1/1/1853712.

17. Liselot Hudders, Pieter De Pauw, Veroline Cauberghe, Katarina Panic, Brahim Zarauali, and Esther Rozendaal, "Shedding New Light on How Advertising Literacy Can Affect Children's Processing of Embedded Advertising Formats: A Future Research Agenda," *Journal of Advertising* 46, no. 2 (December 2016), https://www.researchgate.net/publication/311310928_ Shedding_New_Light_on_How_Advertising_Literacy_Can_Affect_Children's _Processing_of_Embedded_Advertising_Formats_A_Future_Research_ Agenda.

18. Influencer Marketing Hub, *Influencer Marketing Benchmark Report 2022*, 2022, https://influencermarketinghub.com/influencer-marketing-benchmark- report/.

19. Taylor Mooney, "Companies Make Millions Off Kid Influencers, and the Law Hasn't Kept Up," CBS News, August 26, 2019, https://www.cbsnews .com/news/kid-influencers-companies-make-millions-law-hasnt-kept-up -cbsn-originals/.

20. Larry Magid, "Study: 92% of U.S. Two-Year-Olds Have Online Record," CNET, 2010, https://www.cnet.com/tech/services-and-software/study-92-of -u-s-2-year-olds-have-online-record/.

21. Hanneke Hendriks, Danii Wilmsen, Wim van Dalen, and Winifred A. Gebhardt, "Picture Me Drinking: Alcohol-Related Posts by Instagram Influencers Popular among Adolescents and Young Adults," *Frontiers in Psychology*, January 1, 2019, https://europepmc.org/article/med/32038379.

22. Femke Geusens, Cabral A. Bigman-Galimore, and Kathleen Beullens, "A Cross-Cultural Comparison of the Processes Underlying the Associations between Sharing of and Exposure to Alcohol References and Drinking Intentions," *New Media & Society* 22, no. 1 (2020), https://journals.sagepub .com/doi/full/10.1177/1461444819860057.

23. Centers for Disease Control and Prevention, *National Diabetes Statistics Report 2020*, p. 4, https://www.cdc.gov/diabetes/pdfs/data/statistics/national -diabetes-statistics-report.pdf.

24. "Childhood Overweight & Obesity," Centers for Disease Control and Prevention, n.d., page last reviewed August 30, 2021, https://www.cdc .gov/obesity/childhood/index.html#:~:text=1%20in%205%20children%20 and,than%20what%20is%20considered%20healthy.

25. Anna E. Coates, Charlotte A. Hardman, Jason C. G. Halford, Paul Christiansen, and Emma J. Boyland, "Social Media Influencer Marketing and Children's Food Intake: A Randomized Trial," *Pediatrics* 143, no. 4 (April 1, 2019), https://publications.aap.org/pediatrics/article/143/4/e20182554/37177/ Social-Media-Influencer-Marketing-and-Children-s.

CHAPTER 5

1. E. M. Butler, *The Myth of the Magus* (Cambridge: Cambridge University Press, 1993).

2. https://www.quotetab.com/quote/by-harry-houdini/what-the-eyes-see -and-the-ears-hear-the-mind-believes.

3. https://www.tiktok.com/@footdocdana/video/7010890753870155013.

4. Matt Binder, "Inside the Shady World of Influencers Promoting Cryptocurrency," Mashable, June 25, 2021, https://mashable.com/article/ influencers-altcoin-scams.

5. John Bargh, *Before You Know It* (New York: Atria, 2018), 146.

6. University of Buffalo, "Science Shows Attractiveness Pays Off at Work— but There's a Trick to Level the Playing Field," SciTechDaily, August 27, 2021, https://scitechdaily.com/science-shows-attractiveness-pays-off-at-work-but -theres-a-trick-to-level-the-playing-field/.

7. Omri Wallach, "The World's Top 50 Influencers across Social Media Platform," Visual Capitalist, May 14, 2021, https://www.visualcapitalist.com/ worlds-top-50-influencers-across-social-media-platforms/.

8. Ashley Butcher, "15 Male Stars Who've Been Body Shamed, from Leonardo DiCaprio to Jonah Hill," The Wrap, October 15, 2021, https://www .thewrap.com/male-stars-actors-body-shamed-vin-diesel-leonardo-dicaprio -photos/.

9. "Dropping Lizzo on Iran," https://knowyourmeme.com/memes/dropping -lizzo-on-iran.

10. Billy Perrigo, "Instagram Makes Teen Girls Hate Themselves. Is That a Bug or a Feature?" *Time*, September 16, 2021, https://time.com/6098771/ instagram-body-image-teen-girls/.

11. Marina Pitofsky, "Facebook Officials Knew Instagram Can Have Negative Mental Health Impacts for Teens, Report Claims," *USA Today*, September 14, 2021, https://www.usatoday.com/story/tech/2021/09/14/facebook-knew -instagram-could-bad-teens-mental-health/8340578002/.

12. Allyson Chiu, "Why Norway's Experts Say a Retouched Photo Won't Help Fight Body Image Issues," *Washington Post*, July 8, 2021, https://www.washingtonpost.com/lifestyle/wellness/photo-edit-social-media -norway/2021/07/08/f30d59ca-df2c-11eb-ae31-6b7c5c34f0d6_story.html.

13. https://www.tiktok.com/@brianboxerwachlermd/video/692147903541128 7302?lang=en&is_copy_url=1&is_from_webapp=v1.

14. Cait Munro, "Meet the New Social Media Stars Making a Hobby of Dismantling Influencer Culture," Refinery29, August 13, 2020, https://www .refinery29.com/en-us/2020/08/9961712/social-media-accounts-ending -influencer-culture.

15. https://www.merriam-webster.com/dictionary/fact.

16. Alessandro Boglia, "Influencer Marketing and FTC Regulations," *Forbes*, December 2, 2020, https://www.forbes.com/sites/forbesagencycouncil/2020/ 12/02/influencer-marketing-and-ftc-regulations/?sh=4c647d51566e and https://www.forbes.com/sites/davidkroll/2015/08/11/fda-spanks-drug-maker -over-kim-kardashian-instagram-endorsement/?sh=668d7b39587b.

17. Hayden Field, "'Influencer Fraud' Costs Companies Millions of Dollars. An AI-Powered Tool Can Now Show Who Paid to Boost Their Engagement," Entrepreneur, April 4, 2019, https://www.entrepreneur.com/article/331719.

18. Anna Elizabeth Coates, Charlotte Alice Hardman, Jason Christian Grovenor Halford, Paul Christiansen, and Emma Jane Boyland, "The Effect of Influencer Marketing of Food and a 'Protective' Advertising Disclosure on Children's Food Intake," *Pediatric Obesity* 14, no. 10 (October 2019), https:// onlinelibrary.wiley.com/doi/abs/10.1111/ijpo.12540.

19. Federal Trade Commission, *Disclosures 101 for Social Media Users*, November 2019, https://www.ftc.gov/system/files/documents/plain-language/ 1001a-influencer-guide-508_1.pdf.

20. Taylor Lorenz, "Rising Instagram Stars Are Posting Fake Sponsored Content," *Atlantic*, September 18, 2018, https://www.theatlantic.com/ technology/archive/2018/12/influencers-are-faking-brand-deals/578401/.

CHAPTER 6

1. https://clip.cafe/the-little-mermaid-1989/ive-never-seen-a-human-close-before/.

2. Jesslyn Shields, "Lemmings Jumping Off Cliffs En Masse Is a Myth," HowStuffWorks, July 20, 2020, https://animals.howstuffworks.com/mammals/lemmings.htm.

3. Dalton Cooper, "Petition to Ban Content Creator and Twitch Streamer Onlyjayus from TikTok Is Blowing Up," Game Rant, June 17, 2021, https://gamerant.com/onlyjayus-petition-tiktok-ban/.

4. No author, "Ban OnlyJayus from TikTok," Change.org, January 2022, https://www.change.org/p/tiktok-social-media-ban-onlyjayus-from-tiktok.

5. Cooper, "Petition to Ban Content Creator."

6. Quentin Fottrell, "Studies Show Suicides Increase in the Months after a Celebrity Takes Their Own Life," MarketWatch, June 10, 2018, https://www.marketwatch.com/story/there-was-a-10-rise-in-suicides-after-the-death-of-robin-williams-2018-02-08.

7. M. S. Gould, S. Wallenstein, M. H. Kleinman, P. O'Carroll, and J. Mercy, "Suicide Clusters: An Examination of Age-Specific Effects," *American Journal of Public Health* 80, no. 2 (February 1990), https://www.ncbi.nlm.nih.gov/pmc/articles/PMC1404629/.

8. Matthew S. Schwartz, "Teen Suicide Spiked after Debut of Netflix's *13 Reasons Why*, Study Says," NPR, April 30, 2019, https://www.npr.org/2019/04/30/718529255/teen-suicide-spiked-after-debut-of-netflixs-13-reasons-why-report-says.

9. Alan Mozes, "As Social Media Time Rises, So Does Teen Girls' Suicide Risk," U.S. News, February 26, 2021, https://www.usnews.com/news/health-news/articles/2021-02-16/as-social-media-time-rises-so-does-teen-girls-suicide-risk.

10. Serena Gordon, "Instagram 'Self-Harm' Posts Give Rise to Copycat Behavior," *Chicago Tribune*, June 5, 2019, https://www.chicagotribune.com/lifestyles/health/sc-hlth-instagram-self-harm-posts-0626-story.html; Aneri

Pattani, "Instagram and Self-Harm: 1 in 3 Youth Who See Cutting Images Try It Themselves, Study Suggests," *Philadelphia Inquirer*, May 28, 2019, https://www.inquirer.com/health/instagram-cutting-self-harm-social-media-mental-health-20190528.html.

11. Forrest Sanders, "'Salt and Ice Challenge' Leaves Iowa Kids with Severe Burns," KCRG, January 25, 2019, https://www.kcrg.com/content/news/Salt-and-ice-challenge-leaves-Iowans-with-severe-burns--504847271.html.

12. Arone Wondwossen Fantaye and Anne T. M. Konkle, "Social Media Representation of Female Genital Cutting: A YouTube Analysis," *Women's Health* 16 (September 22, 2020), https://journals.sagepub.com/doi/full/10.1177/1745506520949732.

13. Carrie Hunnicutt, "Five Ways Social Media Can Trigger an Eating Disorder," Clementine, March 13, 2020, https://clementineprograms.com/social-media-trigger-eating-disorder/.

14. David Cohen, "TikTok, Dove Join Forces on Body Inclusivity and Acceptance," AdWeek, May 13, 2021, https://www.adweek.com/social-marketing/tiktok-dove-join-forces-on-body-inclusivity-and-acceptance/.

15. https://vm.tiktok.com/ZMdqFJYoX/; Melissa Matthews, "These Viral 'Mukbang' Stars Get Paid to Gorge on Food—at the Expense of Their Bodies," *Men's Health*, January 18, 2019, https://www.menshealth.com/health/a25892411/youtube-mukbang-stars-binge-eat/.

16. https://www.youtube.com/user/NikocadoAvocado.

17. Sowon Yun, Hyunjoo Kang, and Hongmie Lee, "Mukbang- and Cookbang-Watching Status and Dietary Life of University Students Who Are Not Food and Nutrition Majors," *Nutrition Research and Practice* 14, no. 3 (June 2020), https://pubmed.ncbi.nlm.nih.gov/32528634/.

18. Timothy Bella, "The Viral Milk Crate Challenge Has Left People Injured. Doctors Are Begging Them to Stop," *Washington Post*, August 24, 2021, https://www.washingtonpost.com/technology/2021/08/24/milk-crate-challenge/.

19. "Vaccine Myths Debunked," PublicHealth, https://www.publichealth.org/public-awareness/understanding-vaccines/vaccine-myths-debunked.

20. Doha Modani, "Fyre Festival Organizer Billy McFarland Sentenced to Six Years on Fraud Charges," NBC News, October 11, 2018, https://www.nbcnews.com/news/us-news/fyre-festival-organizer-billy-mcfarland-sentenced-6-years-fraud-charges-n919086.

21. Claudia Rosenbaum, "IMG Models, Bella Hadid, Hailey Bieber & More to Return Fraction of $1.7M Fyre Fest Promo Fees," Billboard, August 26, 2020, https://www.billboard.com/pro/bella-hadid-hailey-bieber-icm-models-fyre-festival-settlement/.

22. Rachel Metz, "How a Deepfake Tom Cruise on TikTok Turned into a Very Real AI Company," CNN Business, August 6, 2021, https://www.cnn.com/2021/08/06/tech/tom-cruise-deepfake-tiktok-company/index.html.

23. Sara Rimer, "Q&A: LAW's Danielle Citron Warns That Deepfake Videos Could Undermine the 2020 Election," BU Today, September 11, 2019, https://www.bu.edu/articles/2019/qa-laws-danielle-citron-warns-that-deepfake-videos-could-undermine-the-2020-election/.

24. https://quotefancy.com/quote/1140010/James-C-Collins-Bad-decisions-made-with-good-intentions-are-still-bad-decisions.

CHAPTER 7

1. https://www.quotenova.net/authors/richard-pryor/qdkpap.

2. Kira Martin, "How Original Star Trek Actor George Takei Became a Social Media Sensation in His '70s," CheatSheet, June 6, 2020, https://www.cheatsheet.com/entertainment/how-original-star-trek-actor-george-takei-became-a-social-media-sensation-in-his-70s.html/.

3. Etelka Lehoczky, "George Takei Recalls Time in an American Internment Camp in 'They Called Us Enemy,'" NPR, July 17, 2019, https://www.npr.org/2019/07/17/742558996/george-takei-recalls-time-in-an-american-internment-camp-in-they-called-us-enemy.

4. Rick Marshall, "*Star Trek* Icon George Takei Talks Social Media, Diversity, and *Discovery*," Digital Trends, August 8, 2018, https://www.digital trends.com/movies/george-takei-star-trek-interview/.

5. Sophie McEvoy, "The Jaclyn Hill Makeup Line Controversy Explained," The List, April 5, 2021, https://www.thelist.com/374133/the-jaclyn-hill -makeup-line-controversy-explained/.

6. Layla Ilchi, "Jaclyn Hill's Makeup Brand Drama: Everything You Need to Know," WWD, January 2, 2019, https://wwd.com/fashion-news/fashion -scoops/jaclyn-hill-cosmetics-lipstick-controversy-everything-to-know -1203212382/.

7. Siobhan McGeechan, "A Bad Influence?" theGIST, May 29, 2020, https://the-gist.org/2020/05/a-bad-influence/; Julie Mazziotta, "Are the Kim Kardashian–Endorsed Appetite Suppressant Lollipops Safe? A Nutritionist Weighs In," *People*, May 17, 2018, https://people.com/health/kim-kardashian -endorsed-appetite-suppressing-lollipops-safe/.

8. Kourtnee Jackson, "Kim Kardashian West Says She'll Keep Her Kids' Social Media Use in Check," CheatSheet, October 9, 2019, https://www.cheat sheet.com/entertainment/kim-kardashian-west-says-shell-keep-her-kids -social-media-use-in-check.html/.

9. https://www.youtube.com/watch?v=Qe6ZQP1_TnY.

10. Fanuel Lampiao, Debby Krom, and Stefan S. du Plessis, "The In Vitro Effects of Mondia Whitei on Human Sperm Motility Parameters," *Phytotherapy Research* 22, no. 9 (September 22, 2008), https://pubmed.ncbi .nlm.nih.gov/18570264/.

11. Pierre Watcho, Marc-Aurèle Tchuenchie Gatchueng, Patrick Brice Defo Deeh, Modeste Wankeu-Nya, Esther Ngadjui, Georges Romeo Fozin Bonsou, Albert Kamanyi, and Pierre Kamtchouing, "Sexual Stimulant Effects of the Mixture of Mondia Whitei, Dracaena Arborea, and Bridelia Ferruginea in Normal and Prediabetic Male Wistar Rats," *Journal of Basic and Clinical Physiology and Pharmacology* 30, no. 4 (July 17, 2019), https:// pubmed.ncbi.nlm.nih.gov/31314740/; Pierre Watcho, Pierre Kamtchouing, Selestin D. Sokeng, Paul F. Moundipa, Justine Tantchou, Jean L. Essame, and

Noussithe Koueta, "Androgenic Effect of Mondia Whitei Roots in Male Rats," *Asian Journal of Andrology* 6, no. 3 (September 6, 2004), https://pubmed .ncbi.nlm.nih.gov/15273878/; O. Quasie, O. N. K. Martey, A. K. Nyarko, W. S. K. Gbewonyo, and L. K. N. Okine, "Modulation of Penile Erection in Rabbits by Mondia Whitei: Possible Mechanism of Action," *African Journal of Traditional, Complementary, and Alternative Medicines* 7, no. 3 (April 3, 2010), https://pubmed.ncbi.nlm.nih.gov/21461152/; P. Watcho, P. Kamtchouing, S. Sokeng, P. F. Moundipa, J. Tantchou, J. L. Essame, and N. Koueta, "Reversible Antispermatogenic and Antifertility Activities of Mondia Whitei L. in Male Albino Rat," *Phytotherapy Research* 15, no. 1 (February 15, 2001), https://pubmed.ncbi.nlm.nih.gov/11180518/.

12. Akram Ahangarpour, Ali Akbar Oroojan, Hamid Heidari, Ehsan Ghaedi, and Reza Taherkhani, "Effects of Hydro-alcoholic Extract from Arctium lappa L. (Burdock) Root on Gonadotropins, Testosterone, and Sperm Count and Viability in Male Mice with Nicotinamide/Streptozotocin-Induced Type 2 Diabetes," *Malaysian Journal of Medical Sciences* 22, no. 2 (March–April 2015), https://pubmed.ncbi.nlm.nih.gov/26023292/; Yu-Jun Tan, Yu-Shan Ren, Lei Gao, Lan-Fang Li, Li-Juan Cui, Bin Li, Xin Li, et al., "28-Day Oral Chronic Toxicity Study of Arctigenin in Rats," *Frontiers in Pharmacology* 9 (September 26, 2016), https://pubmed.ncbi.nlm.nih.gov/30319414/.

13. Mackenzie Schimpf, Thomas Ulmer, Hugh Hiller, and Alexander F. Barbuto, "Toxicity from Blue Lotus (Nymphaea caerulea) after Ingestion or Inhalation: A Case Series," *Military Medicine*, August 4, 2021, https://pubmed .ncbi.nlm.nih.gov/34345890/.

14. https://youtu.be/Qe6ZQP1_TnY.

CHAPTER 8

1. https://news.disney.com/the-best-15-frozen-quotes-according-to-you.

2. Diane Kelley, "9 Animals That Masturbate (Other Than Humans)," Gizmodo, August 12, 2015, https://gizmodo.com/9-animals-that-masturbate -other-than-humans-1723592357.

3. https://www.azquotes.com/author/38934-Ruth_Westheimer.

4. "Sex Addiction Facts and Statistics," The Recovery Village, November 10, 2021, https://www.therecoveryvillage.com/process-addiction/sex-addiction/sexual-addiction-statistics/.

5. Norine Dworkin-McDaniel, "Is Your Guy Addicted to Sex?" Everyday Health, November 15, 2017, https://www.everydayhealth.com/emotional-health/addiction/your-guy-addicted-sex/.

6. Kate MacDonnell, "Top 10 Strongest (Most Caffeinated) Coffee Brands in the World," Coffee Affection, November 16, 2021, https://coffeeaffection.com/top-strongest-coffee-brands/.

7. Beth Ashley, "How Sex Toys Became the New Celebrity Fragrance," Vice, February 16, 2021, https://www.vice.com/en/article/4ad8bp/sex-positivity-trend-influencers-sex-toys.

8. Susannah Breslin, "Porn Star 3.0: This X-Rated Social Media Influencer Makes Seven Figures a Year," Forbes, May 26, 2020, https://www.forbes.com/sites/susannahbreslin/2020/05/26/porn-star-30-this-x-rated-social-media-influencer-makes-seven-figures-a-year/?sh=2da2ca1e7966.

9. https://onlyfans.com/about.

10. Valeriya Safronova, "OnlyFans May Be a Refuge for Fine Art," New York Times, October 21, 2021, https://www.nytimes.com/2021/10/21/style/only-fans-nude-art-vienna.html.

11. Ryan Browne, "OnlyFans Says It Will No Longer Ban Porn in Stunning U-Turn after User Backlash," CNBC, August 25, 2021, https://www.cnbc.com/2021/08/25/onlyfans-says-it-will-no-longer-ban-porn-after-backlash-from-users.html.

12. Cydney Henderson, "Bella Thorne Made $2 Million on OnlyFans under a Week? What to Know about the Site," USA Today, August 20, 2020, https://www.usatoday.com/story/entertainment/celebrities/2020/08/20/whats-only-fans-cardi-b-and-bella-thorne-join-popular-site/3402066001/.

13. https://screenrant.com/netflix-sex-education-best-quotes/.

14. Helen Vlasova, "The State of Sex Education (Statistics & Facts—2021)," *Admissionsly*, December 4, 2021, https://admissionsly.com/sex-education-statistics/.

15. Robin Stevens, Stacia Gilliard-Matthews, Jamie Dunaey, Abigail Todhunter-Reid, Bridgette Brawner, and Jennifer Stewart, "Social Media Use and Sexual Risk Reduction Behavior among Minority Youth: Seeking Safe Sex Information," *Nursing Research* 66, no. 5 (September-October 2017), https://www.ncbi.nlm.nih.gov/pmc/articles/PMC5661993/.

16. https://www.evyanwhitney.com/about.

17. https://www.thegoodtrade.com/features/sex-positive-influencers-for-feminist-perspective.

18. https://pink-bits.com/pages/about.

19. Camille Noe Pagán, "Female Masturbation: 5 Things You May Not Know," WebMD, March 11, 2014, https://www.webmd.com/women/features/female-masturbation-5-things-know.

20. Sam Dean, "Where Did 'Fap' Come From?" *MEL*, 2020, https://mel magazine.com/en-us/story/where-did-fap-come-from.

21. "NoFap: Can Giving Up Masturbation Really Boost Men's Testosterone Levels? An Expert's View," The Conversation, March 29, 2021, https://the conversation.com/nofap-can-giving-up-masturbation-really-boost-mens-testosterone-levels-an-experts-view-157701.

22. Debra Halseth, "What Is Sex Addiction Treatment and Does It Work?" BetterHelp, August 27, 2020, https://www.betterhelp.com/advice/intimacy/what-is-sex-addiction-treatment-and-does-it-work/?utm_source=AdWords&utm_medium=Search_PPC_c&utm_term=_b&utm_content=104984140479&network=g&placement=&target=&matchtype=b&utm_campaign=6459244691&ad_type=text&adposition=&gclid=Cj0KCQiA-K2MBhC-ARIsAMtLKRtDepGn0hxrc51gvKHJr2guPqu93Bv9bUPAFPYveE U2neL4AWaVajAaAoCeEALw_wcB.

23. https://www.youtube.com/watch?v=XHg0oqtColk.

24. https://www.tiktok.com/@doctorsood/video/7026448915608194351.

25. https://www.tiktok.com/@doctorsood/video/7026076716384734510.

26. https://www.tiktok.com/@doctorsood/video/7026829187885616430.

CHAPTER 9

1. https://www.brainyquote.com/quotes/christian_lous_lange_335254.

2. Amy Vetter, "Want to Be More Productive? Start Thinking Like a Wild Animal," Inc., March 23, 2018, https://www.inc.com/amy-vetter/3-things -lions-tigers-bears-can-teach-you-about-productivity.html.

3. David Malakoff, "Death by Distraction," *Conservation*, March 19, 2011, https://www.conservationmagazine.org/2011/03/death-by-distraction/.

4. Dave Chaffey, "Global Social Media Statistics Research Summary 2022," Smart Insights, December 6, 2021, https://www.smartinsights.com/social -media-marketing/social-media-strategy/new-global-social-media-research/.

5. Christina Gough, "Average Amount of Time Spent on Sports, Exercise and Recreation in the U.S. from 2009 to 2020," Statista, July 9, 2021, https:// www.statista.com/statistics/189535/daily-average-time-spent-on-sports-and -exercise-in-the-us/.

6. Sarah Fielding, "How Often Couples Should Have Sex, According to Three Sex Therapists," Insider, August 11, 2020, https://www.insider.com/how -often-do-couples-have-sex.

7. Brendan Zietsch, "How Long Does Sex Normally Last?" The Conversation, April 3, 2016, https://theconversation.com/how-long-does-sex-normally-last -56432.

8. Let's run the numbers: Two hours and twenty-seven minutes (average online time) equals 147 minutes. If we were to multiply 147 by 6 (the number of days on social media but without sex), the total equals 14.7 hours (882 minutes). Let's say the seventh day marks the weekly sexual encounter— rounded up to forty-five minutes—that's about fourteen hours (837 minutes) more time spent on social media than having sex.

9. https://usustatesman.com/six-chilling-quotes-from-the-social-dilemma/.

10. Blake Droesch, "What Does Your Brain on Influencer Marketing Look Like?" eMarketer, August 26, 2019, https://www.emarketer.com/content/your-brain-on-influencers-neuroscience-study-explains-the-effects-of-influencer-marketing.

11. "Social Media and Teens," American Academy of Child and Adolescent Psychiatry, March 2018, https://www.aacap.org/AACAP/Families_and_Youth/Facts_for_Families/FFF-Guide/Social-Media-and-Teens-100.aspx#:~:text=Social%20media%20plays%20a%20big,media%20site%20at%20least%20dail.

12. Ben Davis, "How Does Social Media Distract Us from Real Life?" MVOrganizing, May 31, 2021, https://www.mvorganizing.org/how-does-social-media-distract-us-from-real-life/.

13. Nick Hazelrigg, "Survey: Nearly Half of Students Distracted by Technology," Inside Higher Ed, July 10, 2019, https://www.insidehighered.com/digital-learning/article/2019/07/10/survey-shows-nearly-half-students-distracted-technology.

14. Alan Mozes, "Study: 97% of College Students Are Distracted by Phones during Class," EAB, February 2, 2016, https://eab.com/insights/daily-briefing/academic-affairs/study-97-of-college-students-are-distracted-by-phones-during-class/.

15. Martha C. White, "These Are America's Biggest Productivity Killers," Time, June 16, 2015, https://time.com/3919680/productivity/.

16. Steve Todd, "25 Problems with Social Media in the Workplace," Open Sourced Workplace, n.d., https://opensourcedworkplace.com/news/25-problems-with-social-media-in-the-workplace-employee-and-employer-adverse-effects.

17. Taylor Lorenz, "Young Creators Are Burning Out and Breaking Down," New York Times, September 17, 2021, https://www.nytimes.com/2021/06/08/style/creator-burnout-social-media.html.

18. Rebecca Jarvis, Taylor Dunn, and Erica Scott, "The End of Social Media, as Told by Internet Star 'Fat Jewish,'" ABC News, June 30, 2016, https://

abcnews.go.com/Business/end-social-media-told-internet-star-fat-jewish/story?id=40232487.

CHAPTER 10

1. https://nosweatshakespeare.com/quotes/famous/all-that-glitters-is-not-gold/.

2. Oscar Schwartz, "My Journey into the Dark, Hypnotic World of a Millennial Guru," *Guardian*, January 9, 2020, https://www.theguardian.com/world/2020/jan/09/strange-hypnotic-world-millennial-guru-bentinho-massaro-youtube.

3. Taylor Lorenz, "Step Chickens and the Rise of TikTok 'Cults,'" *New York Times*, May 26, 2020, https://www.nytimes.com/2020/05/26/style/step-chickens-tiktok-cult-wars.html.

4. "The Death Toll of Europe's Witch Trials," Statista, October 29, 2019, https://www.statista.com/chart/19801/people-tried-and-executed-in-witch-trials-in-europe/.

5. Trevor Nace, "Only Two-Thirds of American Millennials Believe the Earth Is Round," *Forbes*, April 4, 2018, https://www.forbes.com/sites/trevornace/2018/04/04/only-two-thirds-of-american-millennials-believe-the-earth-is-round/?sh=4dcf8aaa7ec6.

6. Rachel Brazil, "Fighting Flat-Earth Theory," *Physics World*, July 14, 2020, https://physicsworld.com/a/fighting-flat-earth-theory/.

7. NBA.com staff, "Kyrie Irving on Flat-Earth Comments: 'I'm Sorry,'" NBA.com, July 14, 2020, https://www.nba.com/news/kyrie-irving-regrets-flat-earth-comments.

8. Ione Wells, "Celery Juice: The Big Problem with a Viral Instagram 'Cure,'" BBC News, September 22, 2019, https://www.bbc.com/news/blogs-trending-49763144.

9. Tarleton Gillespie, "The Logan Paul YouTube Controversy and What We Should Expect from Internet Platforms," Vox, January 12, 2018, https://www.vox.com/the-big-idea/2018/1/12/16881046/logan-paul-youtube

-controversy-internet-companies; Lennox Lewis, "The Story of Logan Paul and Maverick: Why Does the YouTube Star Call Himself 'the Maverick'?" *Sports Manor*, June 6, 2021, https://www.sportsmanor.com/the-story-of -logan-paul-and-maverick-why-does-the-youtube-star-call-himself-the -maverick/#:~:text=Logan%20Paul%20is%20also%20recognized,before%20 he%20had%20started%20Vine.

10. E. J. Dickinson, "David Dobrik Was the King of YouTube. Then He Went Too Far," *Rolling Stone*, June 23, 2021, https://www.rollingstone.com/culture/ culture-features/david-dobrik-youtube-vlog-squad-profile-1185706/.

11. Lindsay Dodgson, "Vlog Squad Member Jeff Wittek Revealed He Injured His Eye While Swinging from an Excavator David Dobrik Was Controlling," Insider, April 22, 2021, https://www.insider.com/jeff-wittek-eye-injury-david -dobrik-documentary-2021-4.

12. Aida Ylanan, "Thought David Dobrik Was Canceled after His Colleague Was Accused of Rape? He's Back," *Los Angeles Times*, June 17, 2021, https:// www.latimes.com/entertainment-arts/story/2021-06-17/david-dobrik-is -back-on-youtube-months-after-vlog-squad-rape-allegation; https://www .youtube.com/c/DavidDobrik/videos.

13. Senior correspondent, "Rape Suspect Ridoy Babo Coordinates International Trafficking Ring: Police," bbdnews24.com, May 29, 2021, https://bdnews24.com/bangladesh/2021/05/29/rape-suspect-ridoy-babo -coordinates-international-trafficking-ring-police.

14. https://www.therandomvibez.com/trust-no-one-quotes/.

15. https://www.goalcast.com/yoda-quotes-star-wars/.

CHAPTER 11

1. https://www.pinterest.com/pin/575123814913154274/.

2. https://www.yourdictionary.com/zeitgeist.

3. Werner Geyser, "How to Get Verified on Instagram—Seven Instagram Tips to Help Verification [+ Fun Tool]," Influencer Marketing Hub,

September 24, 2021, https://influencermarketinghub.com/how-to-get-verified-on-instagram/.

4. Alex Ates, "Six Talent Agencies Where Social Media Influencers Can Find Representation," Backstage, January 6, 2021, https://www.backstage.com/magazine/article/social-media-influencer-talent-agencies-70413/.

5. "The Most Iconic Celebrity Superyachts," Yachting Pages, June 10, 2020, https://yachting-pages.com/articles/the-most-iconic-celebrity-superyachts.html.

6. https://due.com/blog/the-best-revenge-is-massive-success-frank-sinatra/#:~:text=%E2%80%9CThe%20best%20revenge%20is%20massive%20success.%E2%80%9D&text=Pity%20the%20poor%20soul%20who,burn%20of%20an%20unstoppable%20opponent.

7. Jacinda Santora, "Twenty Best Influencer Merch Stores and the Products We Love Right Now," Influencer Marketing Hub, August 23, 2021, https://influencermarketinghub.com/best-influencer-merch-stores/.

8. Lisa Jennings, "Smoked Brisket Meets Hacked Spicy Queso in Chipotle's New Quesabrisket," Nation's Restaurant News, September 27, 2021, https://www.nrn.com/fast-casual/smoked-brisket-meets-hacked-spicy-queso-chipotle-s-new-quesabrisket; "RYSE's Highly-Anticipated Pre-workout Is Dropping Tonight and It's Competitively Priced," stackj3D.com, November 25, 2021, https://www.stack3d.com/2021/11/where-to-buy-ryse-noel-deyzel-signature-pre-workout.html; No author, "Mr. Coffee and ManiMe Partner to Create the Gift You Didn't Know You Needed This Holiday Season," Yahoo!, December 8, 2021, https://currently.att.yahoo.com/att/mr-coffee-manime-partner-create-101700322.html?guccounter=1&guce_referrer=aHR0cHM6Ly93d3cuZ29vZ2xlLmNvbS88&guce_referrer_sig=AQAAAEHdSDFHzmfHm1rrsnrXy2v6KIAr_mY_p0-focEihm4Q9kDMmPVRWQlUspl1B7XbEeIhpdcbpwpRZ9xIspJgaPccD0ps7tYDbCHTyaZ4IqKz2lKlv3j7f4WKC2yUjjv-QL9Clv4l57wIGRg3Pr2grn8sJuZz3YnRUnhKI9JYYLGr.

9. https://pearpop.com/.

10. K. C. Ifeanyi, "PearPop Wants to Boost Your Social Following by Connecting You to TikTok Stars for Collabs," Fast Company, April 15, 2021,

https://www.fastcompany.com/90575666/pearpop-wants-to-boost-your
-social-following-by-connecting-you-to-tiktok-stars-for-collabs.

11. https://www.cameo.com/.

12. Chloe Morgan, "Influencer Who Posed in a Bikini to Ponder How
Different Her Life Is to 'the Man Picking Rice Every Morning' in a Field
in Bali Is Branded 'Narcissistic,'" *Daily Mail*, June 14, 2019, https://www
.dailymail.co.uk/femail/article-7141965/Influencer-posed-bikini-overlooking
-rice-field-SLAMMED-humble-brag.html.

13. Lim How Wei, "Your Post Goes against Our Community Guidelines
Instagram (How to Fix)," Followchain, November 11, 2020, https://www
.followchain.org/post-goes-against-community-guidelines/.

CHAPTER 12

1. https://www.linkedin.com/pulse/its-better-light-single-candle-than-curse
-darkness-robert-zulkoski.

2. "Most Popular Social Networks Worldwide as of October 2021, Ranked
by Number of Active Users," Statista, n.d., https://www.statista.com/
statistics/272014/global-social-networks-ranked-by-number-of-users/.

3. https://www.facebook.com/terms.php.

4. Sylvester Rodriguez, "How to See Which Sites Are Sharing Your
Information with Facebook, and Make Them Stop," January 29, 2020, CNBC,
https://www.cnbc.com/2020/01/29/facebook-gets-info-about-you-from-other
-web-sites-how-to-stop-it.html.

5. Natalie Maxfield, "Quizzes and Other Identity Theft Schemes to Avoid on
Social Media," McAfee blog, December 15, 2021, https://www.mcafee.com/
blogs/consumer-cyber-awareness/quizzes-and-other-identity-theft-schemes
-to-avoid-on-social-media/.

6. Brett Milano, "Probing the Sleep-Deprived Brain," *Harvard Gazette*,
March 30, 2018, https://news.harvard.edu/gazette/story/2018/03/harvard-talk
-probes-sleep-deprived-brain/.

7. Anmol Bhatia, Jennifer R. Lenchner, and Abdolreza Saadabadi, *Biochemistry, Dopamine Receptors* (Treasure Island, FL: StatPearls, 2022), https://www.ncbi.nlm.nih.gov/books/NBK538242/; Nora D. Volkow, Dardo Tomasi, Gene-Jack Wang, Frank Telang, Joanna S. Fowler, Jean Logan, Helene Benveniste, Ron Kim, Panayotis K. Thanos, and Sergi Ferré, "Evidence That Sleep Deprivation Downregulates Dopamine D2R in Ventral Striatum in the Human Brain," *Journal of Neuroscience* 32, no. 19 (2012), https://www.ncbi.nlm.nih.gov/pmc/articles/PMC3433285/.

8. Lisi Bratcher, "Thirty Days to Forming New Habits," TeamUSA.org, May 31, 2021, https://www.teamusa.org/USA-Triathlon/News/Blogs/Multisport-Lab/2019/June/17/Form-new-habits-in-30-days#:~:text=Everyone%20is%20different%2C%20but%2030,things%20that%20work%20for; Scott Frothingham, "How Long Does It Take for a New Behavior to Become Automatic?" Healthline, October 24, 2019, https://www.healthline.com/health/how-long-does-it-take-to-form-a-habit.

9. Eric W. Dolan, "Listening to the Music You Love Will Make Your Brain Release More Dopamine, Study Finds," PsyPost, February 2, 2019, https://www.psypost.org/2019/02/listening-to-the-music-you-love-will-make-your-brain-release-more-dopamine-study-finds-53059; Toketemu Ohwovoriole, "Seven Natural Ways to Increase Your Dopamine Levels," Verywell Mind, April 25, 2021, https://www.verywellmind.com/natural-ways-to-increase-your-dopamine-levels-5120223; Sonakshi Kohli, "These Seven Dopamine-Boosting Boods Will Make You Feel Happy and Energized," Health Shots, April 3, 2020, https://www.healthshots.com/healthy-eating/superfoods/these-7-dopamine-boosting-foods-will-make-you-feel-happy-and-energized/; "Foods That Boost Your Mood," Le Creuset, January 17, 2018, https://www.lecreuset.co.za/blog/foods-boost-mood.

10. Ana Homayoun, "What Teens Wish Their Parents Knew about Social Media," *Washington Post*, January 9, 2018, https://www.washingtonpost.com/news/parenting/wp/2018/01/09/what-teens-wish-their-parents-knew-about-social-media/.

11. Karl Landsteiner, "Even Brief Abstinence from Social Media Causes Withdrawal Symptoms," Medical Xpress, November 14, 2018, https://medicalxpress.com/news/2018-11-abstinence-social-media-symptoms.html.

12. Meng-Hsien Lin1, Akshaya Vijayalakshmi, and Russell Laczniak, "Toward an Understanding of Parental Views and Actions on Social Media Influencers Targeted at Adolescents: The Roles of Parents' Social Media Use and Empowerment," *Frontiers in Psychology*, December 6, 2019, https://www.frontiersin.org/articles/10.3389/fpsyg.2019.02664/full.

13. Kerry Patterson and Joseph Grenny, *Crucial Conversations*, 2nd ed. (New York: McGraw-Hill, 2012), https://www.leadershipnow.com/Crucial ConversationsExcerpt.html.

14. Helen Blunden, "The Social Dilemma," *Activate Learning* (blog), September 18, 2020, https://activatelearning.com.au/2020/09/the-social -dilemma/.

15. Valerie Strauss, "Teaching Kids to Spot Misinformation on Social Media—and Whether Enough Is Being Done to Get Rid of It," *Washington Post*, October 20, 2020, https://www.washingtonpost.com/ education/2020/10/22/teaching-kids-spot-misinformation-social-media -whether-enough-is-being-done-get-rid-it/.

16. Ray Sanchez, Rosa Flores, and Ed Lavandera, "Deadly Astroworld Festival Spiraled Out of Control for Hours, Houston FD Logs Show," CNN, November 12, 2021, https://www.cnn.com/2021/11/12/us/travis-scott-concert -houston-friday/index.html.

17. E. J. Dickson, "TikTok Isn't Stopping Astroworld Demonic Conspiracy Theories," *Rolling Stone*, November 9, 2021, https://www.rollingstone.com/ music/music-news/tiktok-astroworld-conspiracy-theories-satanism-1255358/.

CONCLUSION

1. https://www.imdb.com/title/tt0382932/characters/nm0004951.

2. "Introducing Meta: A Social Technology Company," Meta Press Release, October 28, 2021, https://about.fb.com/news/2021/10/facebook-company-is -now-meta/.

3. Kevin Roose, "Facebook Is Weaker Than We Knew," *New York Times*, November 12, 2021, https://www.nytimes.com/2021/10/04/technology/facebook-files.html.

4. https://www.merriam-webster.com/words-at-play/meaning-of-metaverse.

5. "Explainer: What Is the 'Metaverse'?" Reuters, October 21, 2021, https://www.reuters.com/technology/what-is-metaverse-2021-10-18/.

6. https://topia.io/.

7. "[The Future of Now x Topia]: The Metaverse and the Rise of the Confluencer," Community Mural, October 13, 2021, https://community.mural.co/events/43-the-future-of-now-x-topia-the-metaverse-and-the-rise-of-the-confluencer.

8. https://www.merriam-webster.com/dictionary/confluence.

9. Daria Belous, "Fortnite x Ariana Grande Rift Tour Viewership Stats," Streams Charts, August 12, 2021, https://streamscharts.com/news/fortnite-x-ariana-grande-rift-tour-viewership-stats; Adrian Penington, "Ariana Grande's Fortnite Concert Opens Up the Metaverse," NAB Amplify, August 2021, https://amplify.nabshow.com/articles/ariana-grandes-fortnite-concert-opens-up-the-metaverse/.

10. "Fortnite V-Bucks: What They Are, How Much Do They Cost, and Can You Get Free V-Bucks?" PCGamesN, December 14, 2021, https://www.pcgamesn.com/fortnite/fortnite-free-v-bucks-win-prices-buy.

EPILOGUE

1. https://www.goodreads.com/quotes/930638-when-the-whole-world-is-silent-even-one-voice-becomes.

2. Davis Baer, "Here Is a List of the Most Liked Tweets Ever (2022 Update)," *OneUp Blog*, January 3, 2022, https://blog.oneupapp.io/here-is-a-list-of-the-most-liked-tweets-ever-2020-update/.

3. https://www.youtube.com/watch?v=kJQP7kiw5Fk.

4. https://www.popbuzz.com/internet/social-media/most-liked-video-tiktok/.

5. https://opoyi.com/world-photography-day-an-egg-with-more-than-55 -million-likes-is-most-liked-instagram-photo.

6. https://founders.archives.gov/documents/Franklin/01-01-02-0015.

7. https://www.goodreads.com/quotes/26613-the-peculiar-evil-of-silencing -the-expression-of-an-opinion.

APPENDIX A

1. "Authenticity: How to Be True to Yourself," Mind Tools, n.d., https:// www.mindtools.com/pages/article/authenticity.htm.

2. "[The Future of Now x Topia]: The Metaverse and the Rise of the Confluencer," Community Mural, October 13, 2021, https://community .mural.co/events/43-the-future-of-now-x-topia-the-metaverse-and-the-rise-of -the-confluencer; https://www.merriam-webster.com/dictionary/confluence.

3. Kerry Patterson, Joseph Grenny, Ron McMillan, and Al Switzler, *Crucial Conversations*, 2nd ed. (New York: McGraw-Hill, 2012), https://www.leader shipnow.com/CrucialConversationsExcerpt.html.

4. Sam Dean, "Where Did 'Fap' Come From?" *MEL*, 2020, https://mel magazine.com/en-us/story/where-did-fap-come-from.

5. Dean, "Where Did 'Fap' Come From?"

6. https://www.merriam-webster.com/words-at-play/meaning-of-metaverse.

7. Melissa Matthews, "These Viral 'Mukbang' Stars Get Paid to Gorge on Food—at the Expense of Their Bodies," *Men's Health*, January 18, 2019, https://www.menshealth.com/health/a25892411/youtube-mukbang-stars -binge-eat/; https://vm.tiktok.com/ZMdqFJYoX/.

8. Dean, "Where Did 'Fap' Come From?"

9. Marijke De Veirman, Liselot Hudders, and Michelle R. Nelson, "What Is Influencer Marketing and How Does It Target Children? A Review and Direction for Future Research," *Frontiers in Psychology*, December 3, 2019, https://www.frontiersin.org/articles/10.3389/fpsyg.2019.02685/full.

10. https://www.evyanwhitney.com/about.

11. https://www.yourdictionary.com/zeitgeist.

APPENDIX B

1. References for this section: https://emojipedia.org/; https://emojis.wiki/.

Selected Bibliography

Bargh, John. *Before You Know It*. New York: Atria, 2018.

Boxer Wachler, Brian. *Perceptual Intelligence*. Novato, CA: New World Library, 2017.

Butler, E. M. *The Myth of the Magus*. Cambridge: Cambridge University Press, 1993.

Cialdini, Robert B. *Influence: The Psychology of Persuasion*. New and expanded. New York: Harper Business, 2021.

Collins, Jim. *Good to Great*. New York: Harper Business, 2001.

Falls, Jason. *Winfluence*. Irvine, CA: Entrepreneur, 2021.

Gladwell, Malcolm. *Blink*. New York: Back Bay Books, 2007.

Hennessy, Brittany. *Influencer*. New York: Citadel, 2018.

Kane, Brendan. *Hook Point*. Cardiff-by-the-Sea, CA: Waterside Productions, 2020.

Kawasaki, Guy. *The Art of Social Media*. New York: Portfolio, 2014.

Keenan, Kelly. *Everyone Is an "Influencer."* Ideapress, 2021.

Kerpen, Dave. *Likeable Social Media*. 3rd ed. New York: McGraw-Hill, 2019.

Lanier, Jaron. *Ten Arguments for Deleting Your Social Media Accounts Right Now*. New York: Picador, 2019.

Miles, Jason. *Instagram Power*. 2nd ed. New York: McGraw-Hill, 2019.

Patterson, Kerry, Joseph Grenny, Ron McMillan, and Al Switzler. *Crucial Conversations*. 2nd ed. New York: McGraw-Hill, 2011.

Peace, Jeremy. *Social Media Marketing 2022*. Independently published, 2021.

Peltz, Chelsea. *What to Post*. Independently published, 2020.

Russell, Amanda. *The Influencer Code*. Long Island City, NY: Hatherleigh, 2020.

Index

About the Author

Widely known as "Dr. Brian," **Brian Boxer Wachler, MD**, is an enormously popular social media influencer, most prominently on TikTok, and is a board-certified, renowned eye surgeon.

Dr. Brian Boxer Wachler's previous book, *Perceptual Intelligence: The Brain's Secret to Seeing Past Illusion, Misperception, and Self-Deception,* shook the worlds of neuroscience and psychology, coining the acronym *PI* for Perceptual Intelligence and educating thousands of readers on how they can better understand the world around them and make better decisions in their lives.

Praised by high-profile authorities such as Dr. Phil McGraw (host of *Dr. Phil*), Dr. Travis Stork (ER physician and former host of *The Doctors*), and Robert Cialdini, PhD (author of *Influence*), the book also caught the attention of celebrities such as Montel Williams, Caitlyn Jenner, and Victoria Principal. Dr. Brian became a recognized authority on human perception, extensively promoting the work on television and radio networks.

Dr. Brian has pioneered treatments in vision correction, keratoconus, and whiter eyes. Creator of the revolutionary testosterone dry eye treatment, he has become one of the most sought-after eye surgeons in the world and is often the first surgeon physicians themselves turn to when they're in need of vision correction. He has a history of awards and accomplishments—many of which have single-handedly changed the practice of ophthalmic surgery. In 2010, Dr. Brian was presented with the Jules Stein Living Tribute Award for inventing noninvasive (epi-on) cross-linking for keratoconus (called Holcomb C3-R') after saving the vision of Olympian Steven Holcomb, who later won Olympic gold after a sixty-two-year drought for the United States in the dangerous sport of bobsled. He has published three books on keratoconus and its treatments. Dr. Brian is the medical director of the eponymous Boxer Wachler Vision Institute in Beverly Hills and a staff physician at Los Angeles's famed Cedars-Sinai Medical Center. After graduating from UCLA with a degree in psychobiology, he attended Edinburgh University on a Rotary Foundation International Scholarship and earned his medical degree from Dartmouth Medical School. On completing an internship in internal medicine at St. Mary's Hospital and Medical Center in San Francisco, Dr. Brian entered the residency program in ophthalmology at Saint Louis University Eye Institute at the renowned Saint Louis University School of Medicine. He followed that by specializing in refractive surgery and cornea during a fellowship year with Dan Durrie, MD, and at the University of Kansas School of Medicine.

Dr. Brian's productive research has opened the door to new techniques for treating a wide range of eye problems. He is a recognized leader in the treatment of vision problems such as myopia (nearsightedness), hyperopia (farsightedness), astigmatism, and presbyopia. Dr. Brian wrote the *LASIK Consumer Report*, about one of the most widely performed vision correction procedures, and read by more than one hundred thousand people. Dr. Brian's work on LASIK led to the formation of industry-wide guidelines to reduce the risk of halos and glare.

Dr. Brian participated in fifteen FDA clinical research trials evaluating new technologies for vision correction. His impactful research and esteemed professional reputation are evidenced by his 277 scientific presentations and 56 peer-reviewed published medical journal articles. He is a member of the American Academy of Ophthalmology and has held several leadership positions within this organization, earning him several awards for his accomplishments.

Dr. Brian held and continues to hold leadership positions in numerous prestigious organizations. He is a member of the medical advisory board of AllAboutVision.com and served on the editorial board of the *Journal of Refractive Surgery*. Dr. Brian has been a panel member or chair of several national committees and has cochaired international symposia.

Charismatic, passionate, brilliant, and down to earth, Dr. Brian is a tireless doctor, surgeon, medical practitioner, pioneer, researcher, media expert, and social media influencer who challenges us to question what we see, perceive, and accept as fact.

Dr. Brian lives in Los Angeles with his wife. They have twin daughters and three dogs, Tati (a black Lab), Roxy (a Great Pyrenees), and Rhubarb, nicknamed Barbie (a Boxer puppy).

His website may be found here:

www.BoxerWachler.com

Dr. Brian's main social media handles:

TikTok @brianboxerwachlermd

Instagram @drboxerwachler

YouTube @Brian Boxer Wachler

Metaverse: https://topia.io/t/profile/drbrian

Dr. Brian's *No Cap Health Show* podcast can be found on all your favorite podcast platforms.